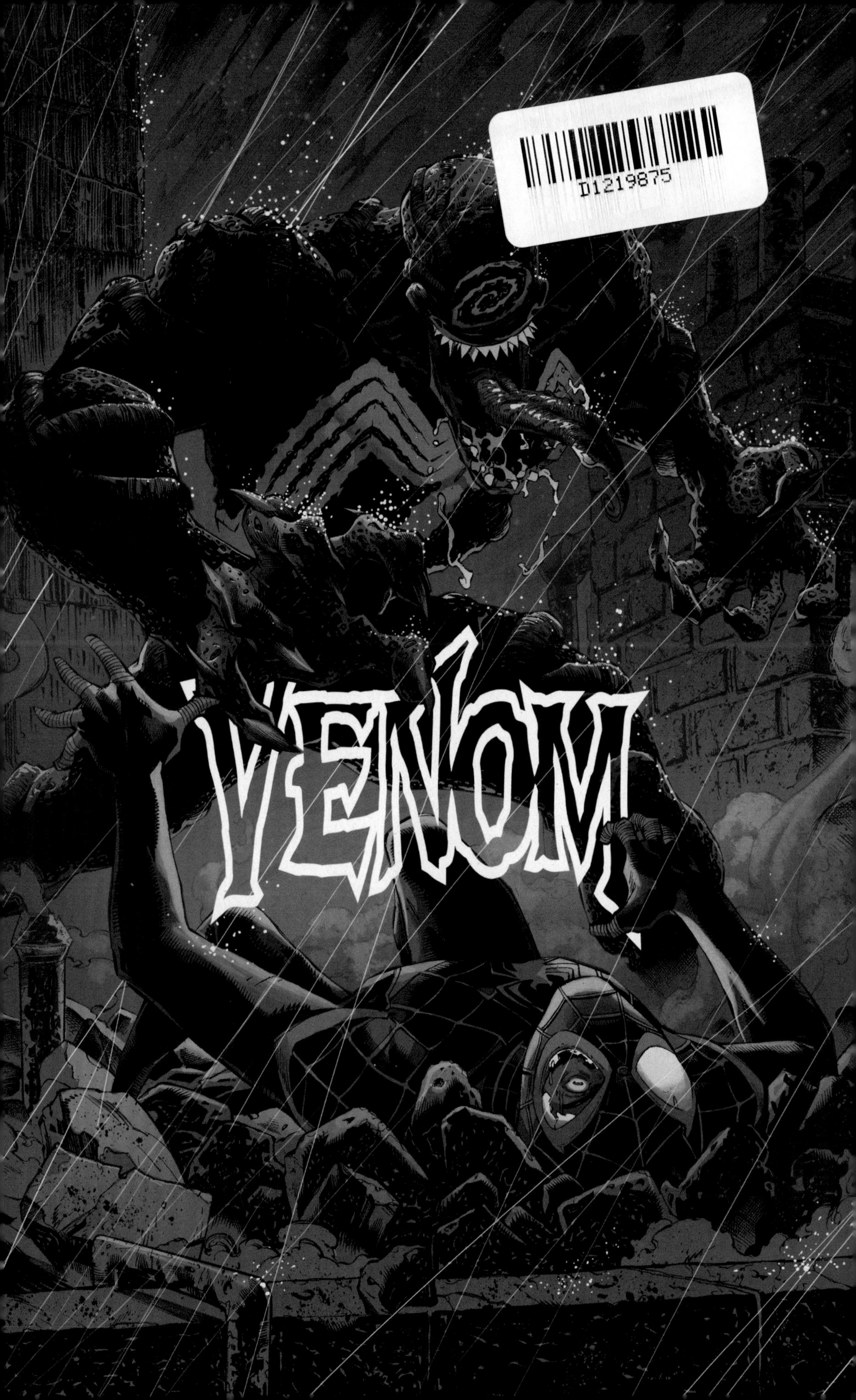
VENOM

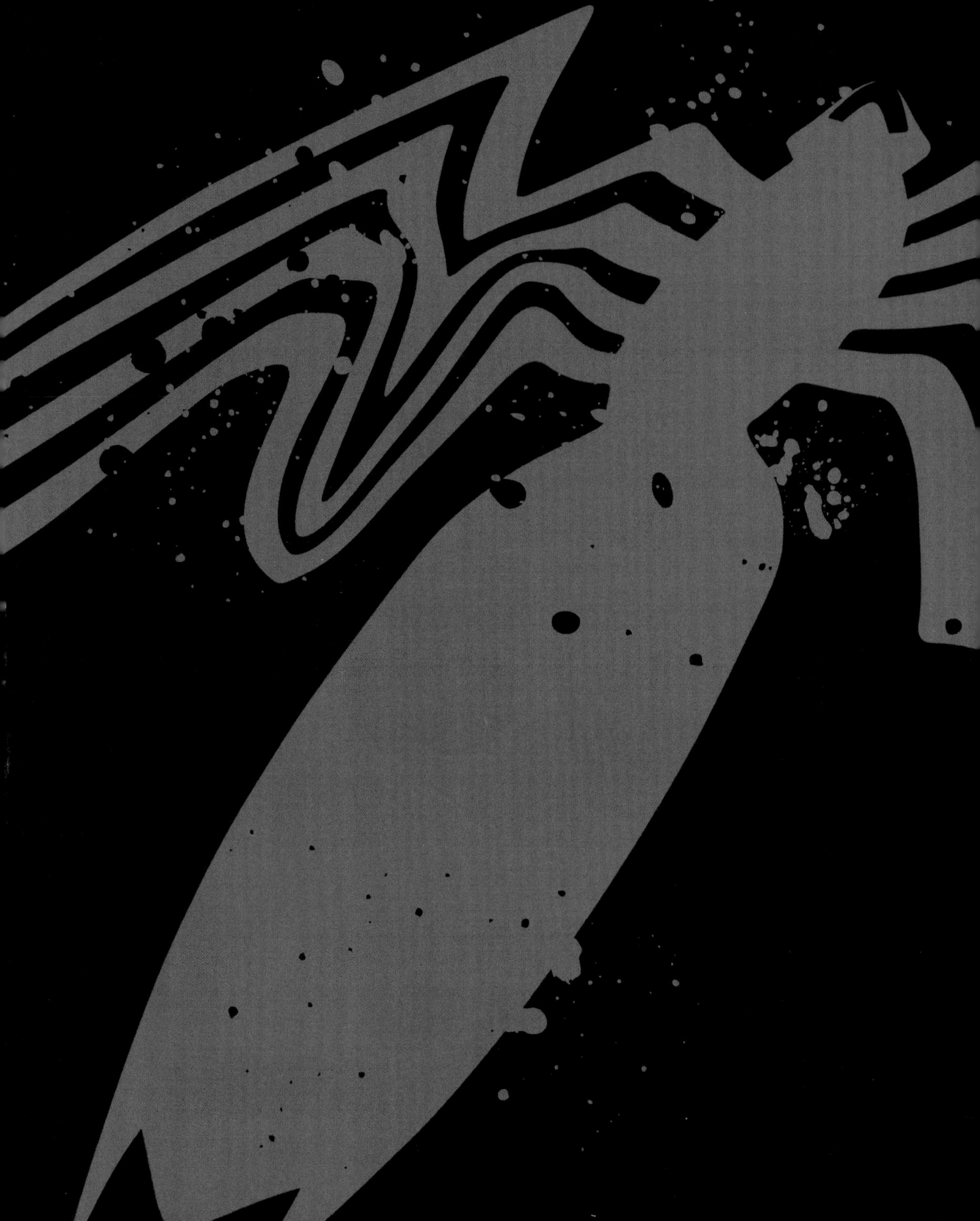

COLLECTION EDITOR MARK D. BEAZLEY
ASSISTANT EDITOR DANIEL KIRCHHOFFER
ASSISTANT MANAGING EDITOR MAIA LOY
ASSISTANT MANAGING EDITOR LISA MONTALBANO
SENIOR EDITOR, SPECIAL PROJECTS JENNIFER GRÜNWALD
VP PRODUCTION & SPECIAL PROJECTS JEFF YOUNGQUIST
BOOK DESIGNER JAY BOWEN
SVP PRINT, SALES & MARKETING DAVID GABRIEL
EDITOR IN CHIEF C.B. CEBULSKI

YEARS AGO, THE AMAZING SPIDER-MAN ACCIDENTALLY BONDED WITH A UNIQUE ALIEN ORGANISM CALLED A SYMBIOTE. AFTER REALIZING THE COSTUME WAS READING HIS MIND AND TRYING TO MAKE THEIR UNION PERMANENT, SPIDER-MAN REJECTED IT. BETRAYED AND LEFT FOR DEAD, THE SYMBIOTE FOUND A WILLING HOST IN EDDIE BROCK, A REPORTER WHOSE LIFE SPIDER-MAN HAD ALSO RUINED. BROCK WELCOMED THE SYMBIOTE AND THE TWO WERE JOINED, SWEARING VENGEANCE ON SPIDER-MAN AND BECOMING THE SINGULAR ENTITY CALLED...

VENOM

WRITER
DONNY CATES

RYAN STEGMAN

PENCILER

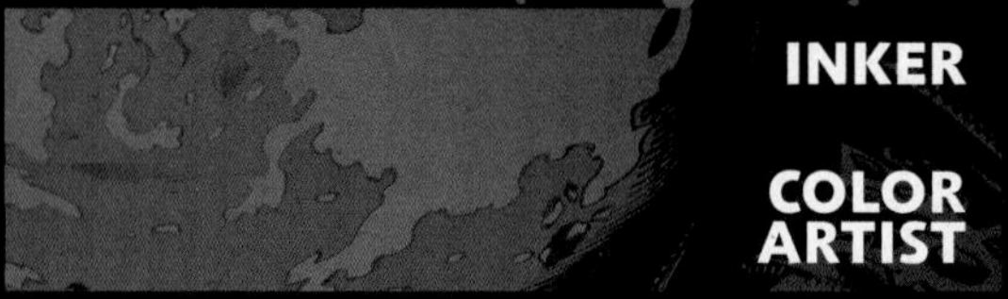

INKER
JP MAYER

COLOR ARTIST
FRANK MARTIN

LETTERER
VC'S CLAYTON COWLES

RYAN **STEGMAN** & FRANK **MARTIN** (#1-2);
RYAN **STEGMAN**, JP **MAYER**
& FRANK **MARTIN** (#3-6)

COVER ARTISTS

ASSISTANT EDITORS
LAUREN **AMARO**, TOM **GRONEMAN** & EMILY **NEWCOMEN**

EDITOR
DEVIN LEWIS

EXECUTIVE EDITOR
NICK LOWE

VENOM BY DONNY CATES VOL. 1: REX. Contains material originally published in magazine form as VENOM (2018) #1-6. Fifth printing 2021. ISBN 978-1-302-91306-9. Published by MARVEL WORLDWIDE, INC., a subsidiary of MARVEL ENTERTAINMENT, LLC. OFFICE OF PUBLICATION: 1290 Avenue of the Americas, New York, NY 10104. © 2018 MARVEL No similarity between any of the names, characters, persons, and/or institutions in this book with those of any living or dead person or institution is intended, and any such similarity which may exist is purely coincidental. **Printed in Canada.** KKEVIN FEIGE, Chief Creative Officer; DAN BUCKLEY, President, Marvel Entertainment; JOE QUESADA, EVP & Creative Director; DAVID BOGART, Associate Publisher & SVP of Talent Affairs; TOM BREVOORT, VP, Executive Editor; NICK LOWE, Executive Editor, VP of Content, Digital Publishing; DAVID GABRIEL, VP of Print & Digital Publishing; JEFF YOUNGQUIST, VP of Production & Special Projects; ALEX MORALES, Director of Publishing Operations; DAN EDINGTON, Managing Editor; RICKEY PURDIN, Director of Talent Relations; JENNIFER GRÜNWALD, Senior Editor, Special Projects; SUSAN CRESPI, Production Manager; STAN LEE, Chairman Emeritus. For information regarding advertising in Marvel Comics or on Marvel.com, please contact Vit DeBellis, Custom Solutions & Integrated Advertising Manager, at vdebellis@marvel.com. For Marvel subscription inquiries, please call 888-511-5480. **Manufactured between 8/20/2021 and 9/21/2021 by SOLISCO PRINTERS, SCOTT, QC, CANADA.**

1098765

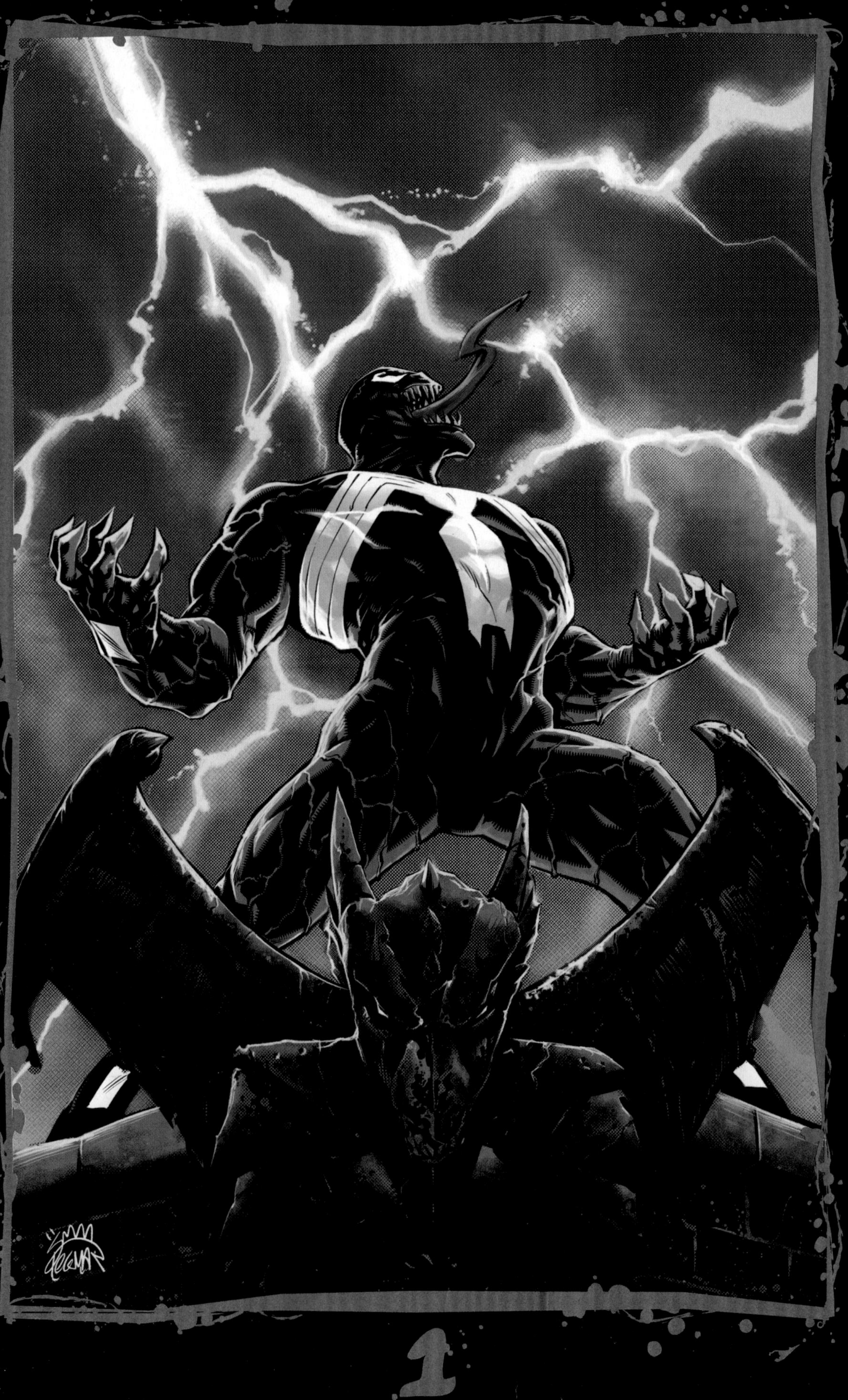
1

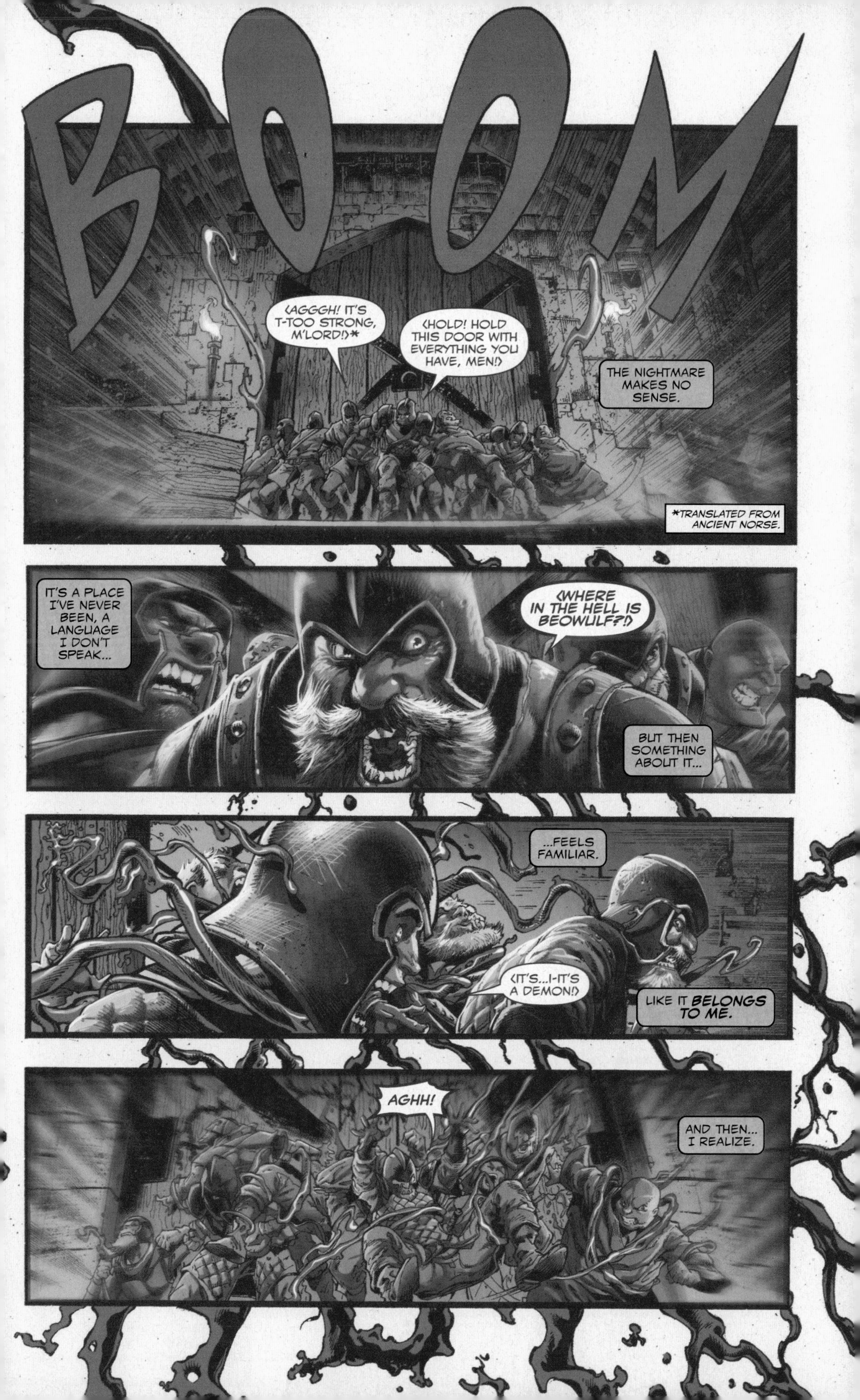
BOOM
‹AGGGH! IT'S T-TOO STRONG, M'LORD!›*
‹HOLD! HOLD THIS DOOR WITH EVERYTHING YOU HAVE, MEN!›
THE NIGHTMARE MAKES NO SENSE.
*TRANSLATED FROM ANCIENT NORSE.
IT'S A PLACE I'VE NEVER BEEN, A LANGUAGE I DON'T SPEAK...
‹WHERE IN THE HELL IS BEOWULF?!›
BUT THEN SOMETHING ABOUT IT...
...FEELS FAMILIAR.
‹IT'S...I-IT'S A DEMON!›
LIKE IT BELONGS TO ME.
AGHH!
AND THEN... I REALIZE.

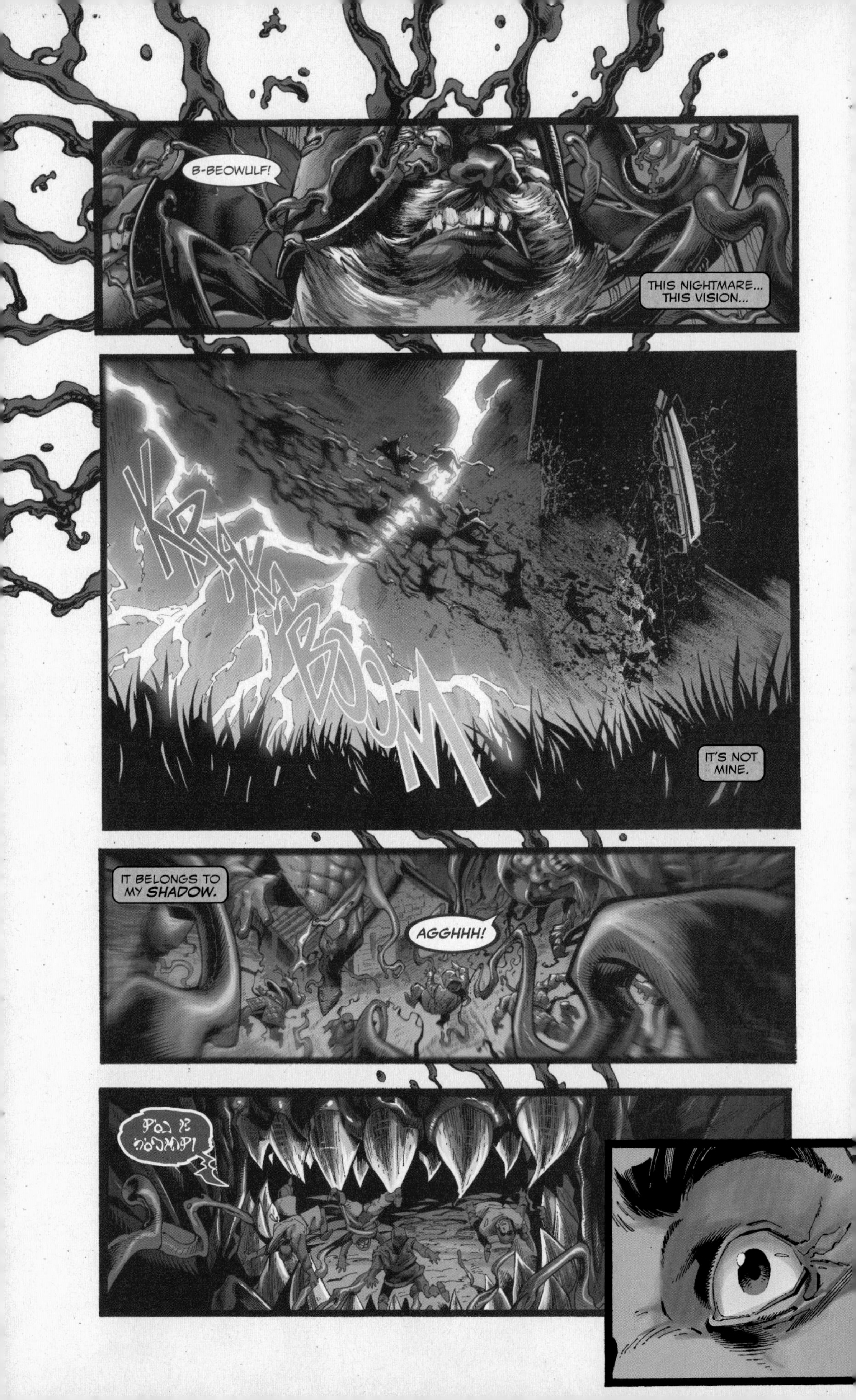
B-BEOWULF!
THIS NIGHTMARE... THIS VISION...
KRAKA BOOM
IT'S NOT MINE.
IT BELONGS TO MY SHADOW.
AGGHHH!

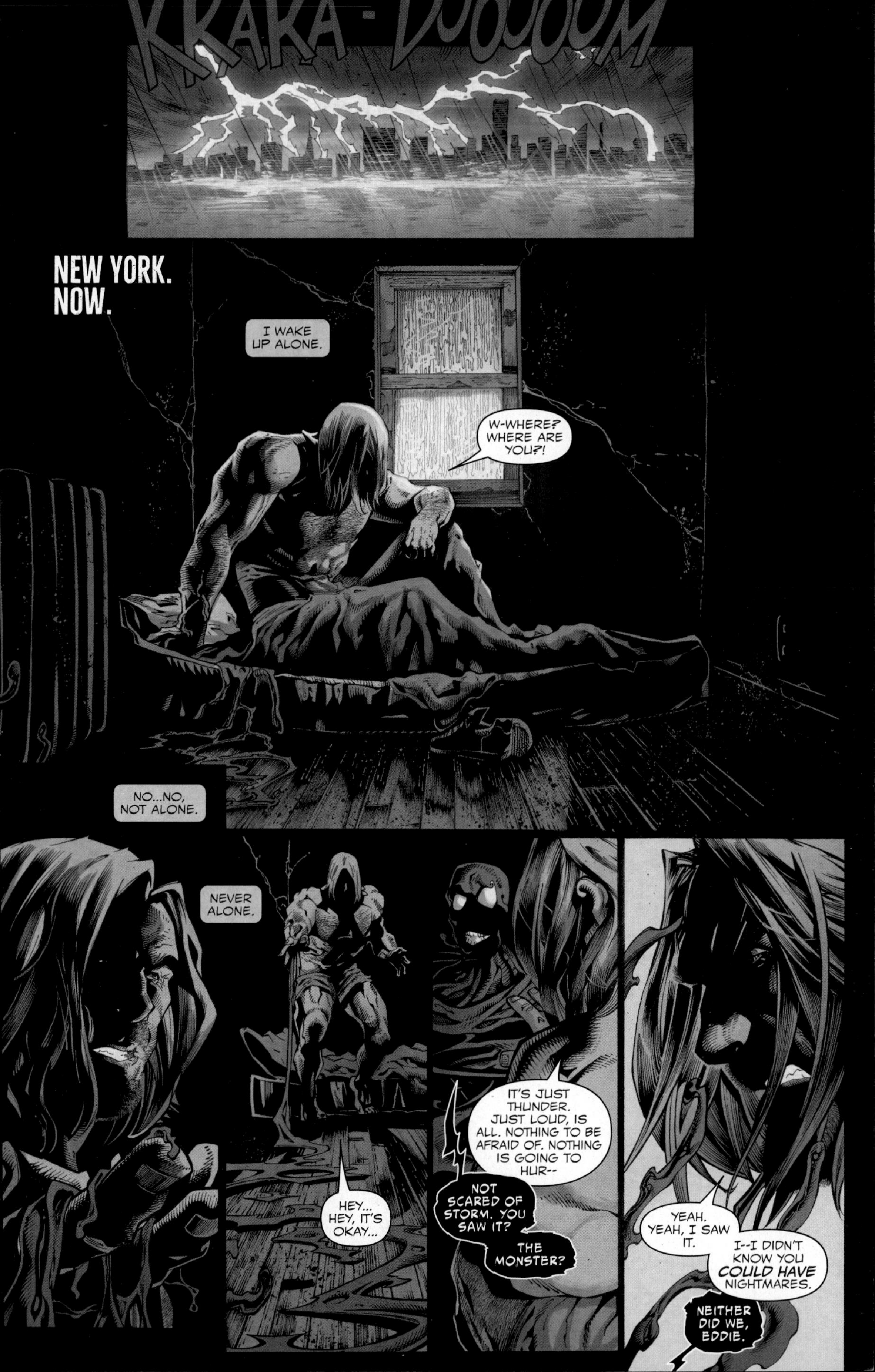
KRAKA-DOOOOOOM
NEW YORK. NOW.
I WAKE UP ALONE.
W-WHERE? WHERE ARE YOU?!
NO...NO, NOT ALONE.
NEVER ALONE.
HEY... HEY, IT'S OKAY...
IT'S JUST THUNDER. JUST LOUD, IS ALL. NOTHING TO BE AFRAID OF. NOTHING IS GOING TO HUR--
NOT SCARED OF STORM. YOU SAW IT?
THE MONSTER?
YEAH. YEAH, I SAW IT.
I--I DIDN'T KNOW YOU COULD HAVE NIGHTMARES.
NEITHER DID WE, EDDIE.

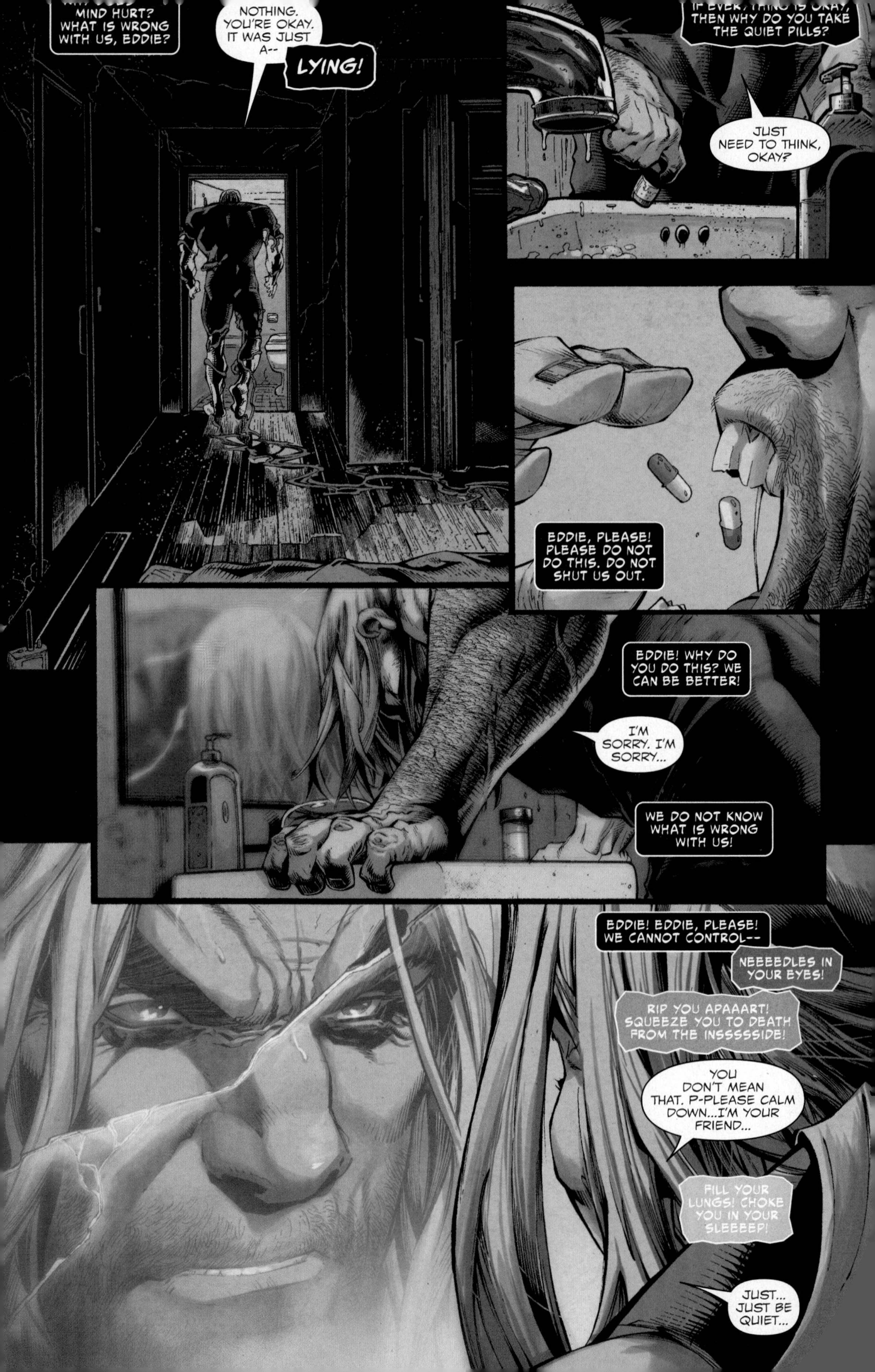
MIND HURT? WHAT IS WRONG WITH US, EDDIE?
NOTHING. YOU'RE OKAY. IT WAS JUST A--
LYING!
THEN WHY DO YOU TAKE THE QUIET PILLS?
JUST NEED TO THINK, OKAY?
EDDIE, PLEASE! PLEASE DO NOT DO THIS. DO NOT SHUT US OUT.
EDDIE! WHY DO YOU DO THIS? WE CAN BE BETTER!
I'M SORRY. I'M SORRY...
WE DO NOT KNOW WHAT IS WRONG WITH US!
EDDIE! EDDIE, PLEASE! WE CANNOT CONTROL--
NEEEEDLES IN YOUR EYES!
RIP YOU APAAART! SQUEEZE YOU TO DEATH FROM THE INSSSSSIDE!
YOU DON'T MEAN THAT. P-PLEASE CALM DOWN...I'M YOUR FRIEND...
FILL YOUR LUNGS! CHOKE YOU IN YOUR SLEEEEP!
JUST... JUST BE QUIET...

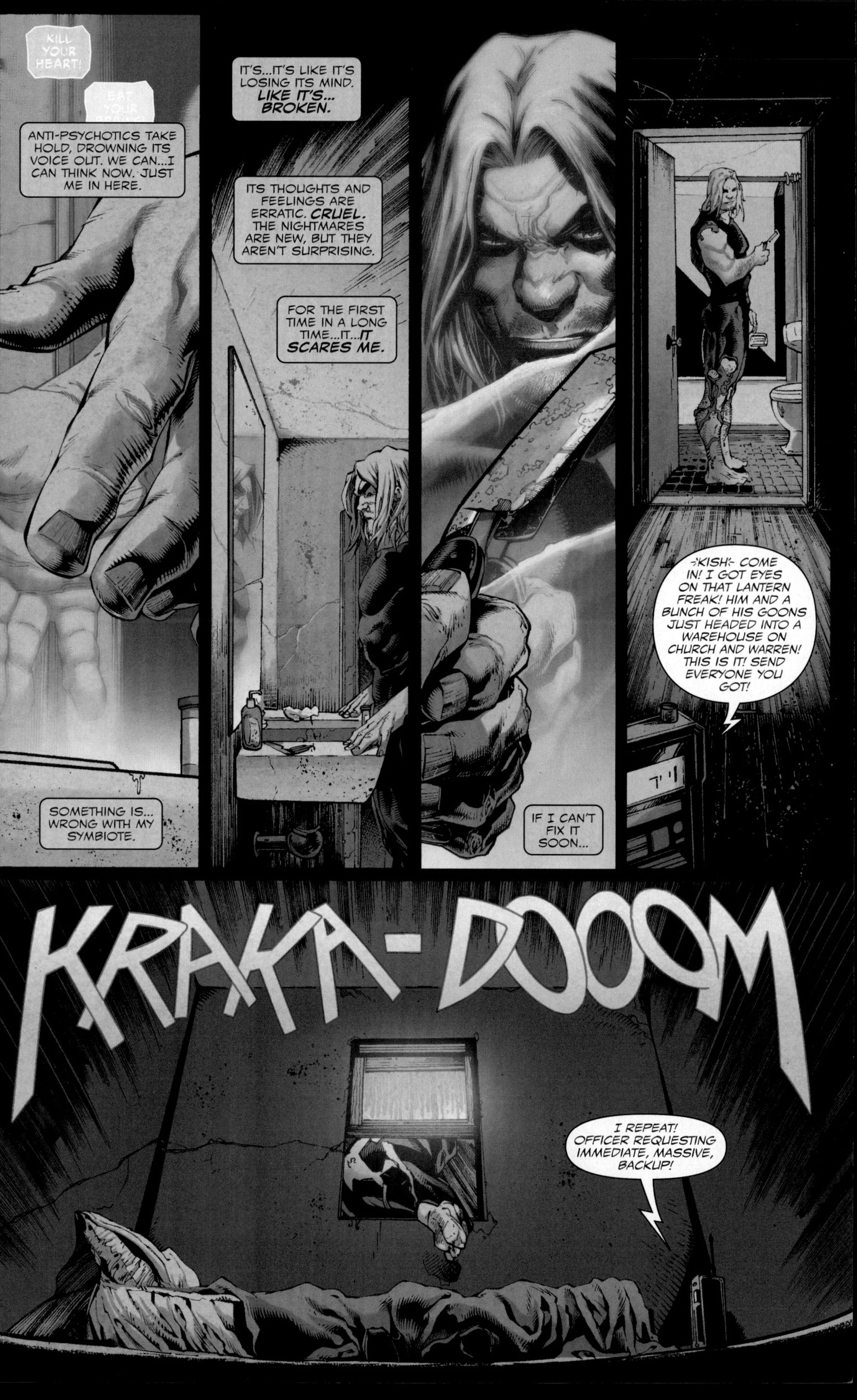
KILL YOUR HEART!
EAT YOUR
ANTI-PSYCHOTICS TAKE HOLD, DROWNING ITS VOICE OUT. WE CAN...I CAN THINK NOW. JUST ME IN HERE.
SOMETHING IS... WRONG WITH MY SYMBIOTE.
IT'S...IT'S LIKE IT'S LOSING ITS MIND. LIKE IT'S... BROKEN.
ITS THOUGHTS AND FEELINGS ARE ERRATIC. CRUEL. THE NIGHTMARES ARE NEW, BUT THEY AREN'T SURPRISING.
FOR THE FIRST TIME IN A LONG TIME...IT...IT SCARES ME.
IF I CAN'T FIX IT SOON...
-KISH- COME IN! I GOT EYES ON THAT LANTERN FREAK! HIM AND A BUNCH OF HIS GOONS JUST HEADED INTO A WAREHOUSE ON CHURCH AND WARREN! THIS IS IT! SEND EVERYONE YOU GOT!
KRAKA-DOOOM
I REPEAT! OFFICER REQUESTING IMMEDIATE, MASSIVE, BACKUP!

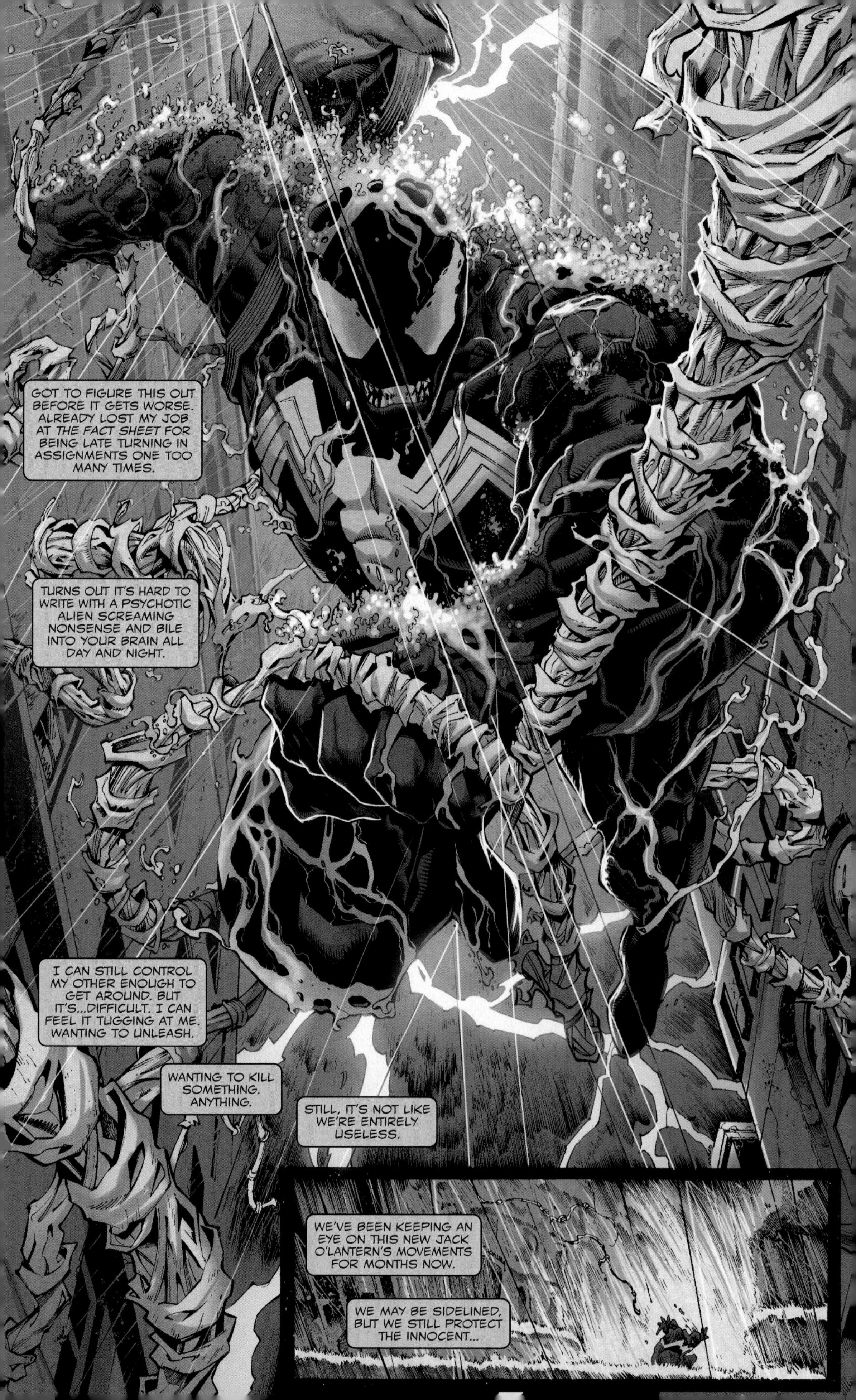
GOT TO FIGURE THIS OUT BEFORE IT GETS WORSE. ALREADY LOST MY JOB AT *THE FACT SHEET* FOR BEING LATE TURNING IN ASSIGNMENTS ONE TOO MANY TIMES.
TURNS OUT IT'S HARD TO WRITE WITH A PSYCHOTIC ALIEN SCREAMING NONSENSE AND BILE INTO YOUR BRAIN ALL DAY AND NIGHT.
I CAN STILL CONTROL MY OTHER ENOUGH TO GET AROUND. BUT IT'S...DIFFICULT. I CAN FEEL IT TUGGING AT ME. WANTING TO UNLEASH.
WANTING TO KILL SOMETHING. ANYTHING.
STILL, IT'S NOT LIKE WE'RE ENTIRELY USELESS.
WE'VE BEEN KEEPING AN EYE ON THIS NEW JACK O'LANTERN'S MOVEMENTS FOR MONTHS NOW.
WE MAY BE SIDELINED, BUT WE STILL PROTECT THE INNOCENT...

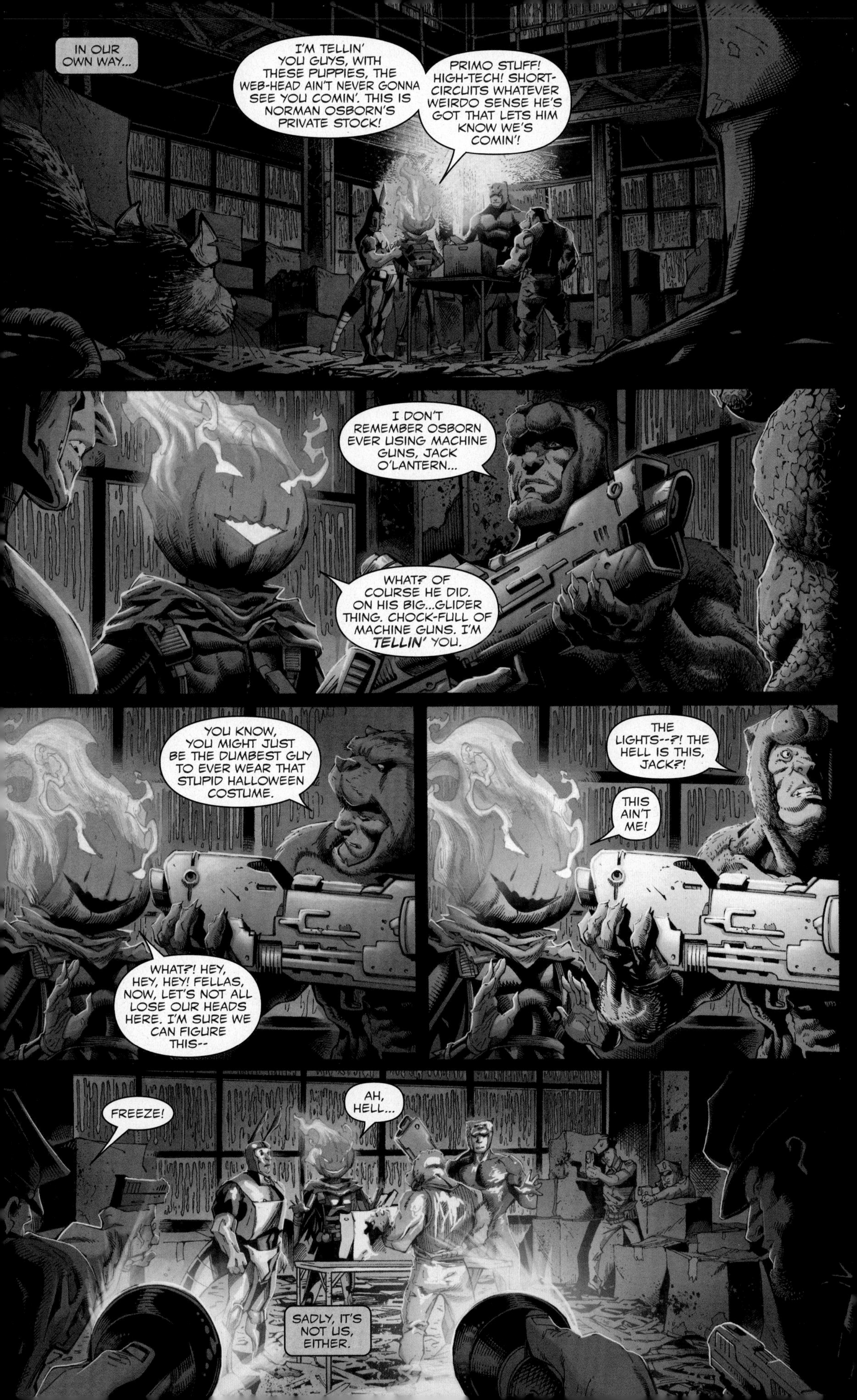
IN OUR OWN WAY...
I'M TELLIN' YOU GUYS, WITH THESE PUPPIES, THE WEB-HEAD AIN'T NEVER GONNA SEE YOU COMIN'. THIS IS NORMAN OSBORN'S PRIVATE STOCK!
PRIMO STUFF! HIGH-TECH! SHORT-CIRCUITS WHATEVER WEIRDO SENSE HE'S GOT THAT LETS HIM KNOW WE'S COMIN'!
I DON'T REMEMBER OSBORN EVER USING MACHINE GUNS, JACK O'LANTERN...
WHAT? OF COURSE HE DID. ON HIS BIG...GLIDER THING. CHOCK-FULL OF MACHINE GUNS. I'M TELLIN' YOU.
YOU KNOW, YOU MIGHT JUST BE THE DUMBEST GUY TO EVER WEAR THAT STUPID HALLOWEEN COSTUME.
WHAT?! HEY, HEY, HEY! FELLAS, NOW, LET'S NOT ALL LOSE OUR HEADS HERE. I'M SURE WE CAN FIGURE THIS--
THE LIGHTS--?! THE HELL IS THIS, JACK?!
THIS AIN'T ME!
FREEZE!
AH, HELL...
SADLY, IT'S NOT US, EITHER.

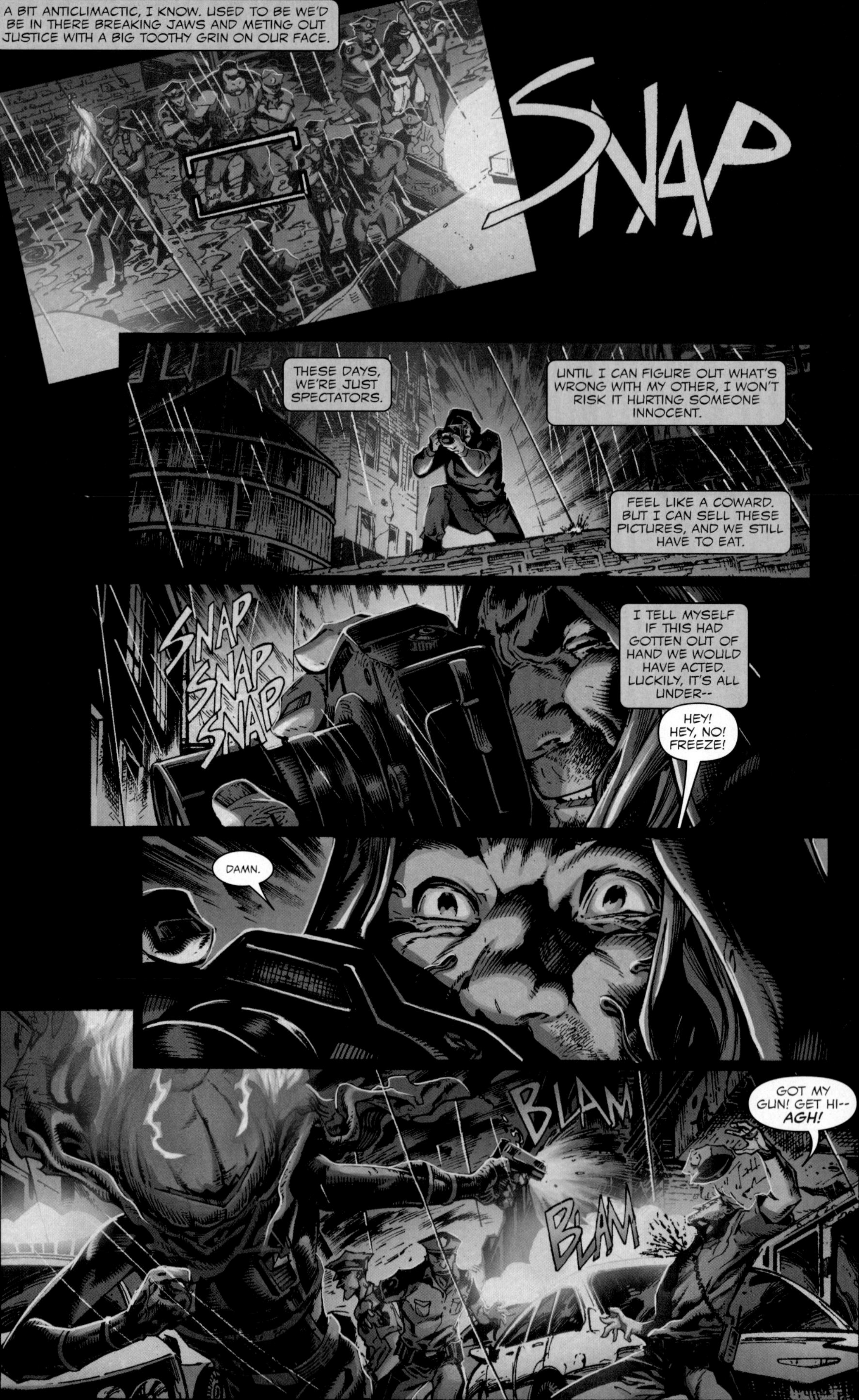

A BIT ANTICLIMACTIC, I KNOW. USED TO BE WE'D BE IN THERE BREAKING JAWS AND METING OUT JUSTICE WITH A BIG TOOTHY GRIN ON OUR FACE.
SNAP
THESE DAYS, WE'RE JUST SPECTATORS.
UNTIL I CAN FIGURE OUT WHAT'S WRONG WITH MY OTHER, I WON'T RISK IT HURTING SOMEONE INNOCENT.
FEEL LIKE A COWARD. BUT I CAN SELL THESE PICTURES, AND WE STILL HAVE TO EAT.
SNAP SNAP SNAP SNAP
I TELL MYSELF IF THIS HAD GOTTEN OUT OF HAND WE WOULD HAVE ACTED. LUCKILY, IT'S ALL UNDER--
HEY! HEY, NO! FREEZE!
DAMN.
BLAM
GOT MY GUN! GET HI-- *AGH!*
BLAM

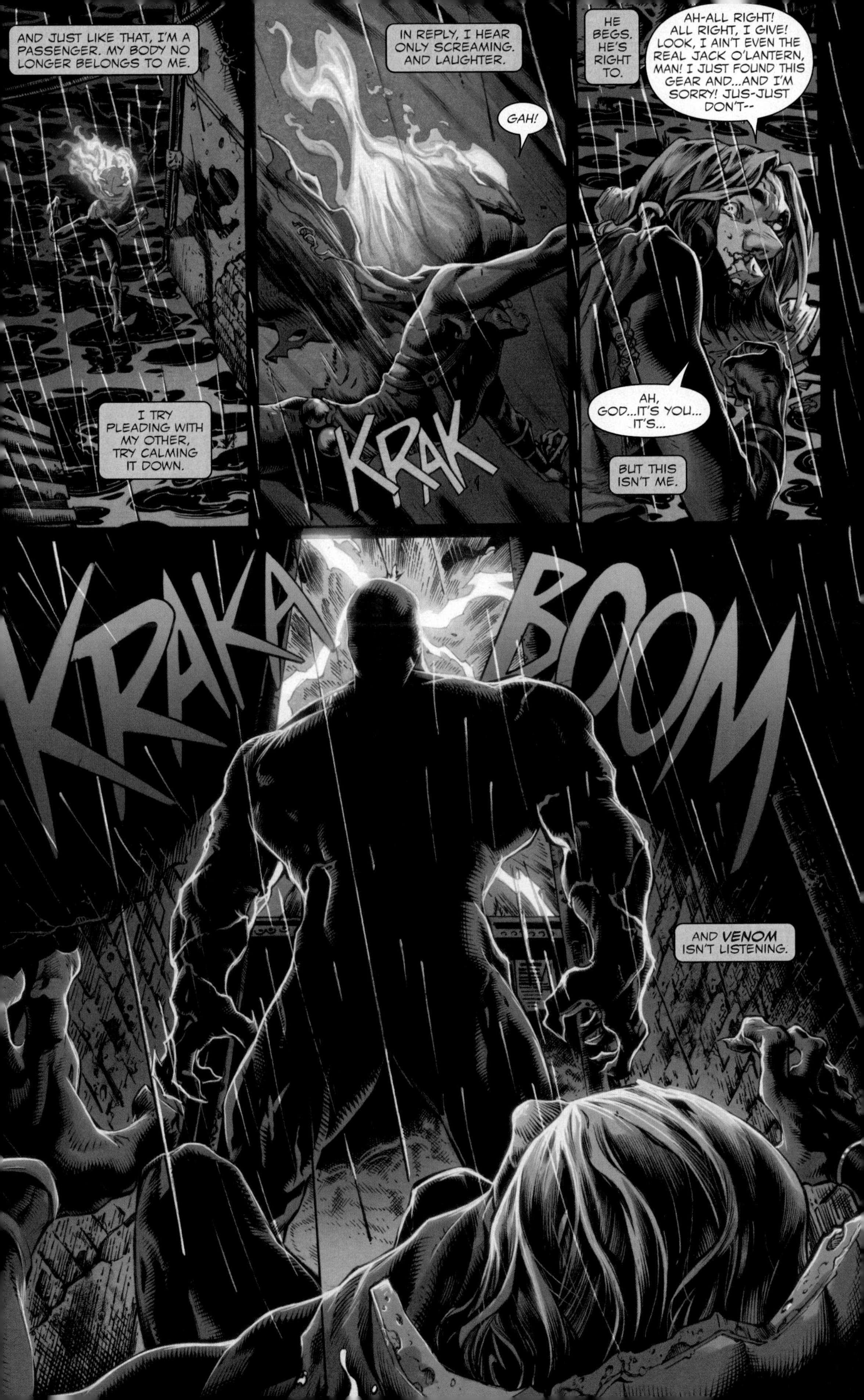
AND JUST LIKE THAT, I'M A PASSENGER. MY BODY NO LONGER BELONGS TO ME.
I TRY PLEADING WITH MY OTHER, TRY CALMING IT DOWN.
IN REPLY, I HEAR ONLY SCREAMING. AND LAUGHTER.
GAH!
KRAK
HE BEGS. HE'S RIGHT TO.
AH-ALL RIGHT! ALL RIGHT, I GIVE! LOOK, I AIN'T EVEN THE REAL JACK O'LANTERN, MAN! I JUST FOUND THIS GEAR AND...AND I'M SORRY! JUS-JUST DON'T--
AH, GOD...IT'S YOU... IT'S...
BUT THIS ISN'T ME.
KRAKABOOM
AND VENOM ISN'T LISTENING.

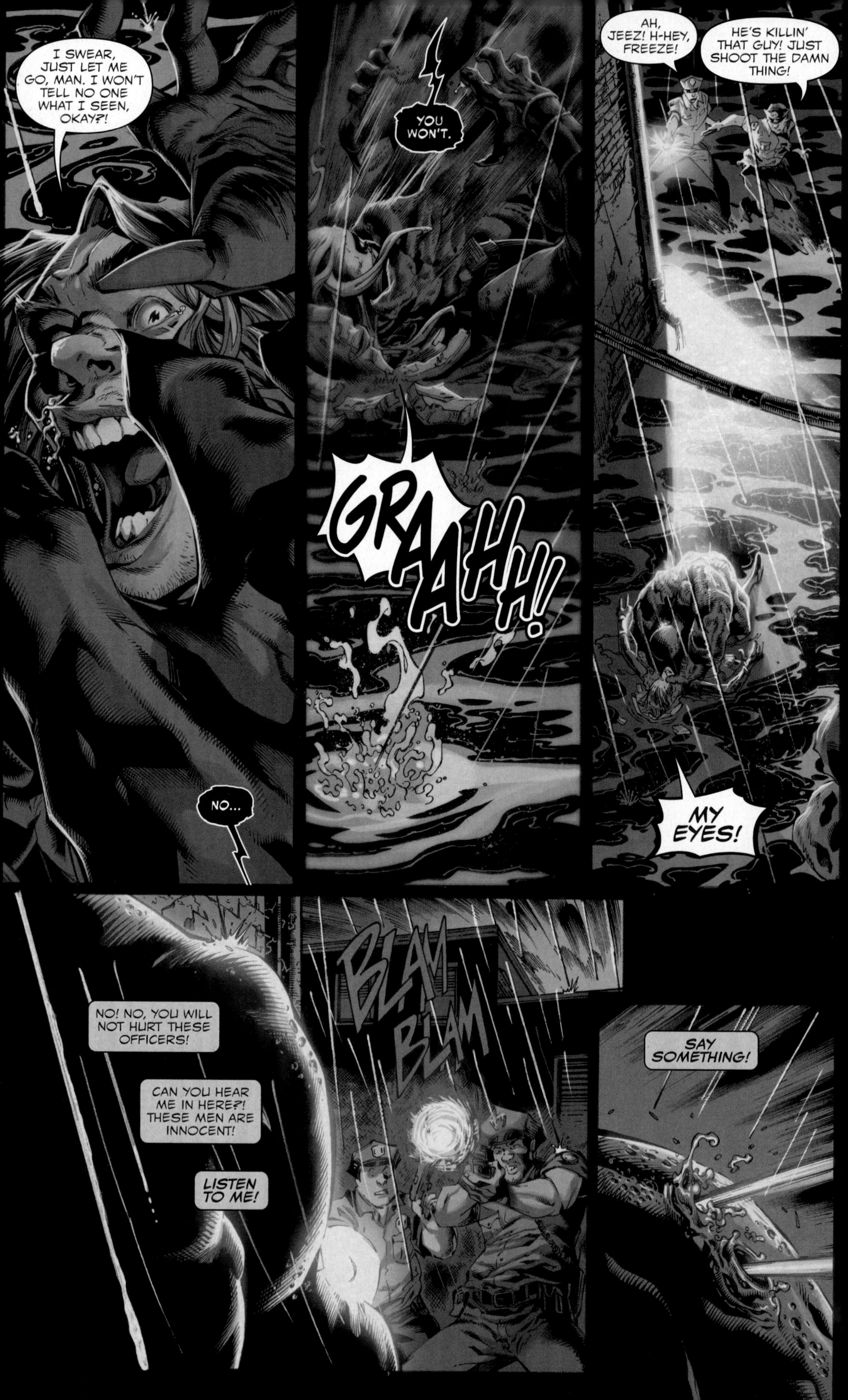
I SWEAR, JUST LET ME GO, MAN. I WON'T TELL NO ONE WHAT I SEEN, OKAY?!
NO...
YOU WON'T.
GRAAHH!
AH, JEEZ! H-HEY, FREEZE!
HE'S KILLIN' THAT GUY! JUST SHOOT THE DAMN THING!
MY EYES!
NO! NO, YOU WILL NOT HURT THESE OFFICERS!
CAN YOU HEAR ME IN HERE?! THESE MEN ARE INNOCENT!
LISTEN TO ME!
BLAM BLAM BLAM
SAY SOMETHING!

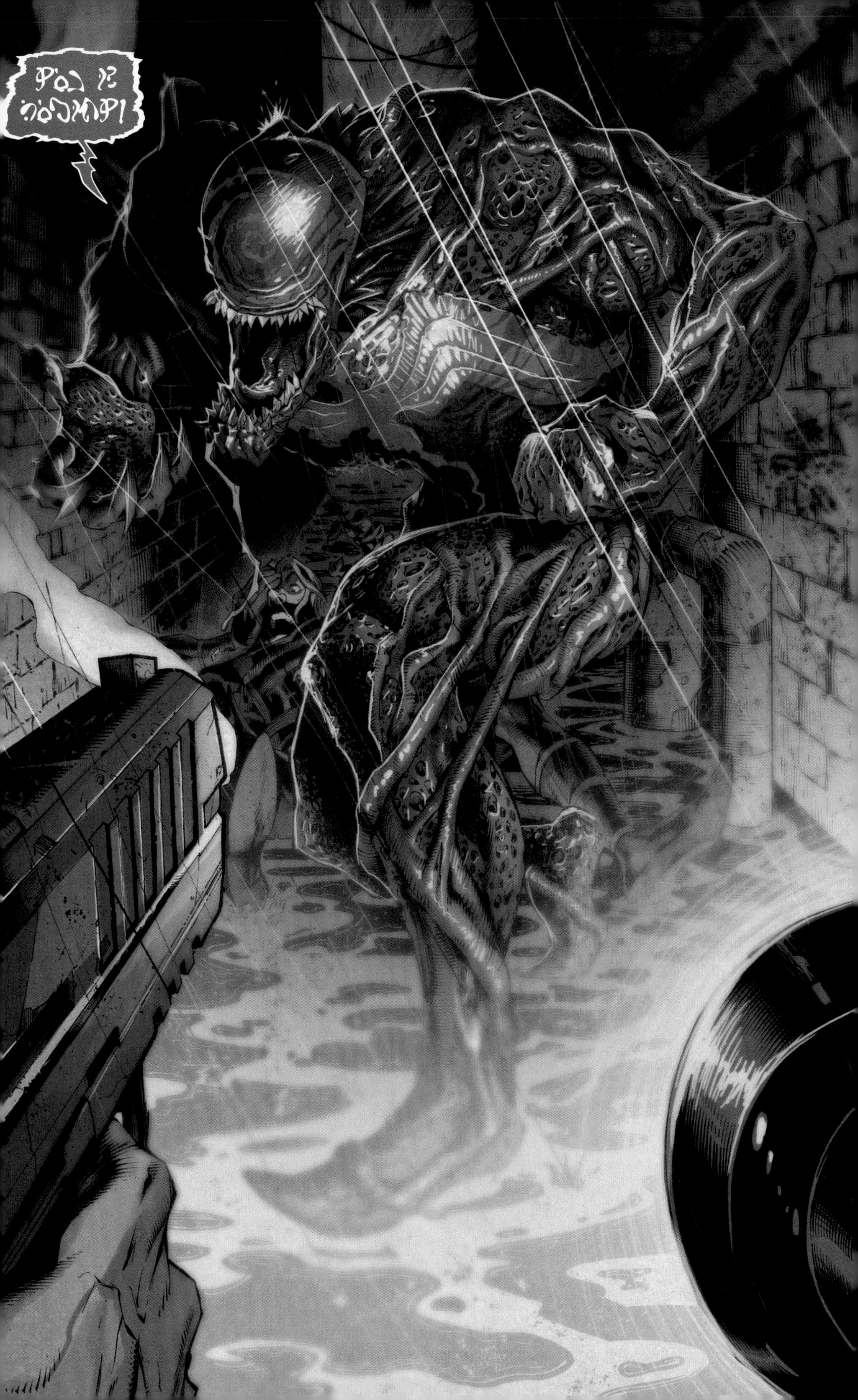

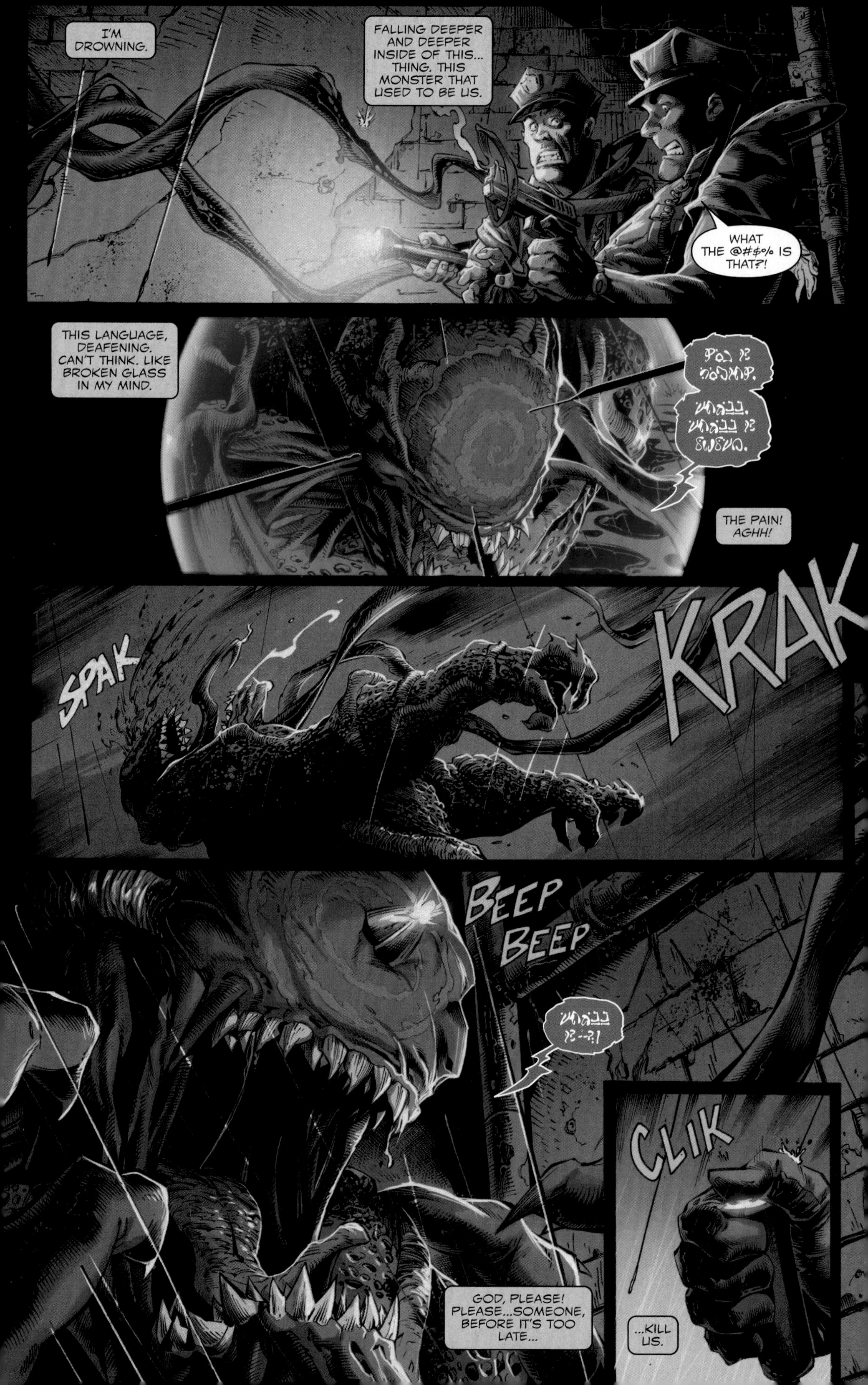
I'M DROWNING.
FALLING DEEPER AND DEEPER INSIDE OF THIS... THING. THIS MONSTER THAT USED TO BE US.
WHAT THE @#$% IS THAT?!
THIS LANGUAGE, DEAFENING. CAN'T THINK. LIKE BROKEN GLASS IN MY MIND.
THE PAIN! AGHH!
SPAK
KRAK
BEEP BEEP
CLIK
GOD, PLEASE! PLEASE...SOMEONE, BEFORE IT'S TOO LATE...
...KILL US.

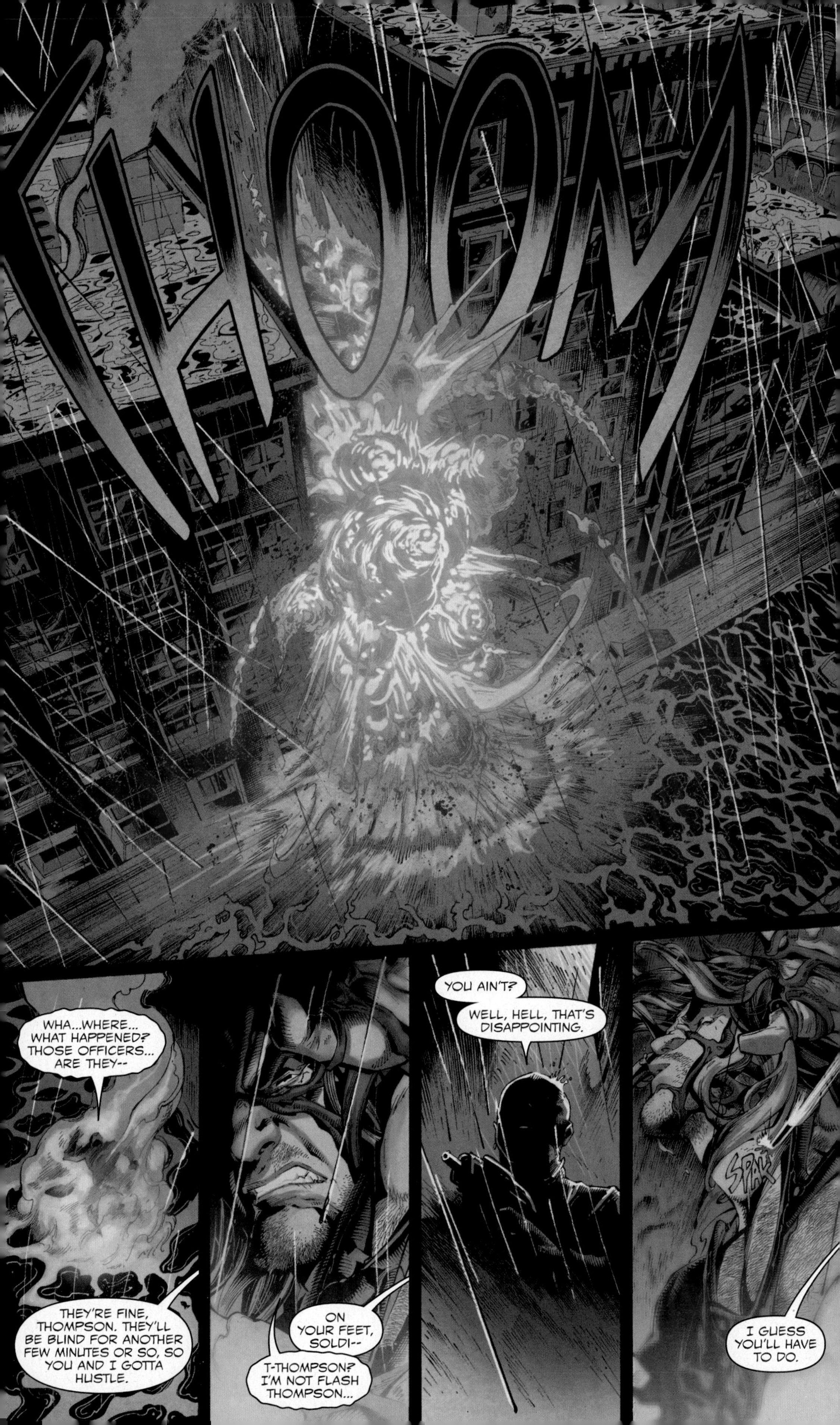
CHOOM
WHA...WHERE... WHAT HAPPENED? THOSE OFFICERS... ARE THEY--
THEY'RE FINE, THOMPSON. THEY'LL BE BLIND FOR ANOTHER FEW MINUTES OR SO, SO YOU AND I GOTTA HUSTLE.
ON YOUR FEET, SOLDI--
T-THOMPSON? I'M NOT FLASH THOMPSON...
YOU AIN'T?
WELL, HELL, THAT'S DISAPPOINTING.
SPAK
I GUESS YOU'LL HAVE TO DO.

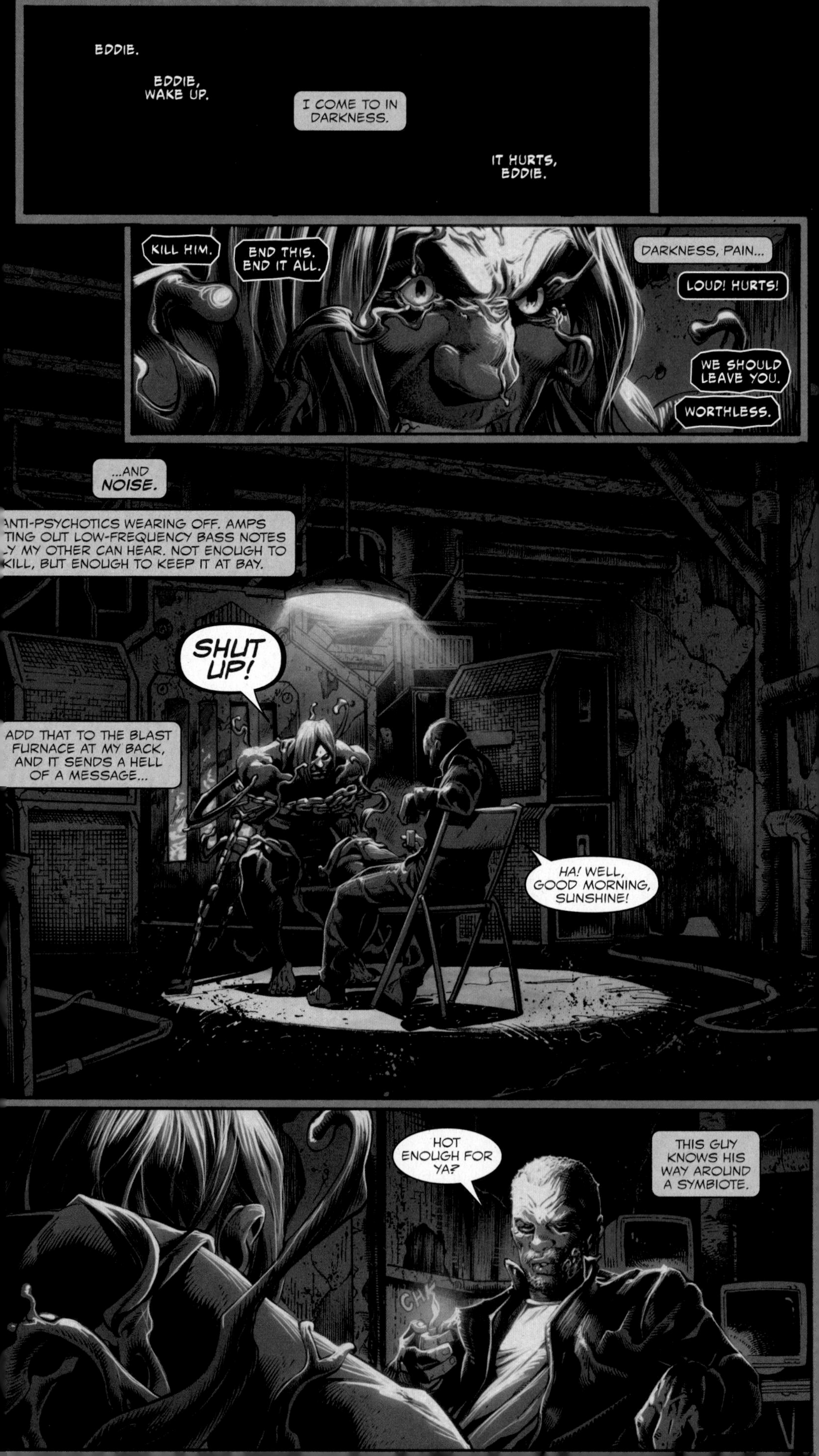
EDDIE.
EDDIE, WAKE UP.
I COME TO IN DARKNESS.
IT HURTS, EDDIE.
KILL HIM.
END THIS. END IT ALL.
DARKNESS, PAIN...
LOUD! HURTS!
WE SHOULD LEAVE YOU.
WORTHLESS.
...AND NOISE.
ANTI-PSYCHOTICS WEARING OFF. AMPS TING OUT LOW-FREQUENCY BASS NOTES Y MY OTHER CAN HEAR. NOT ENOUGH TO KILL, BUT ENOUGH TO KEEP IT AT BAY.
SHUT UP!
ADD THAT TO THE BLAST FURNACE AT MY BACK, AND IT SENDS A HELL OF A MESSAGE...
HA! WELL, GOOD MORNING, SUNSHINE!
HOT ENOUGH FOR YA?
THIS GUY KNOWS HIS WAY AROUND A SYMBIOTE.
CHK

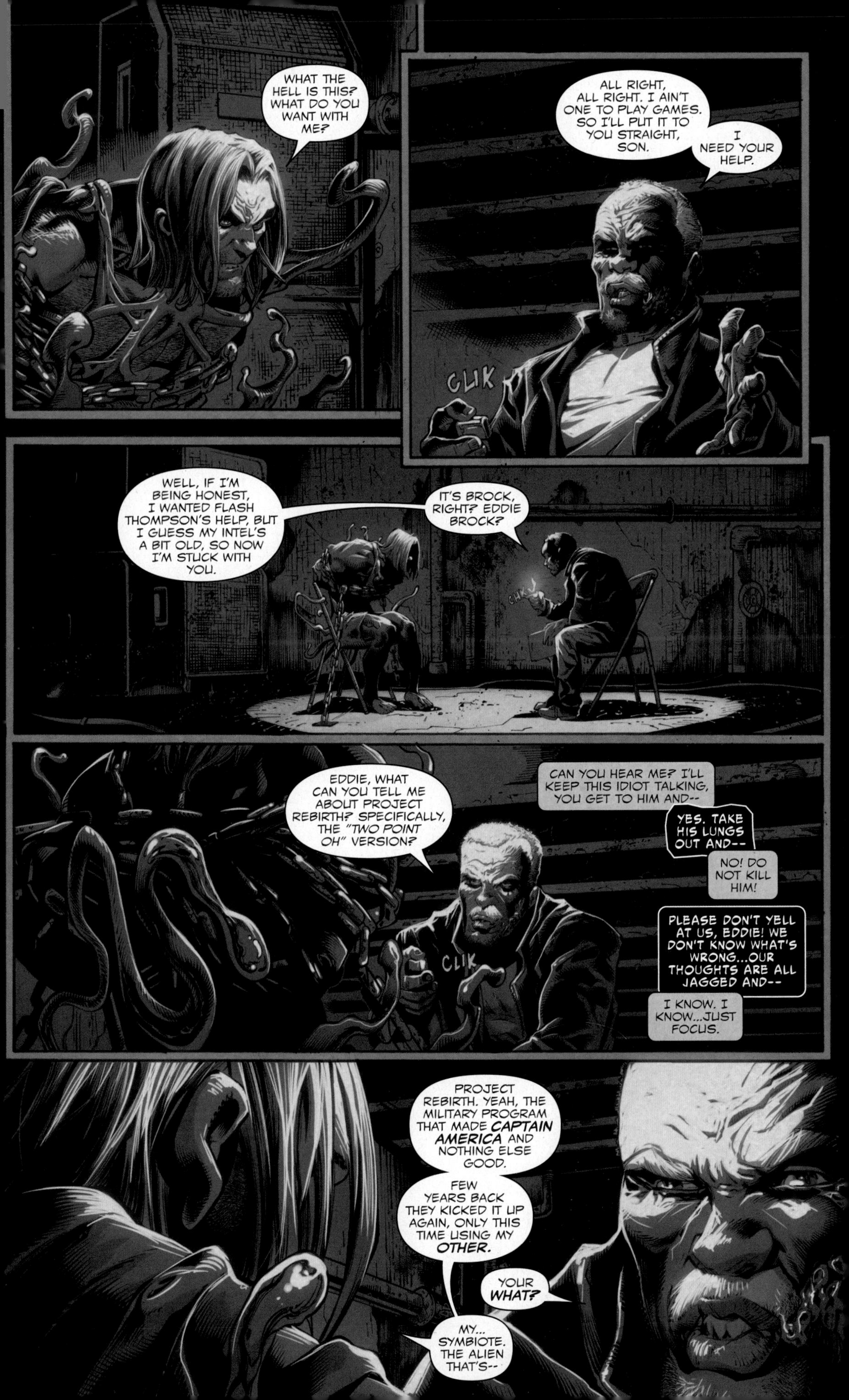
WHAT THE HELL IS THIS? WHAT DO YOU WANT WITH ME?
ALL RIGHT, ALL RIGHT. I AIN'T ONE TO PLAY GAMES. SO I'LL PUT IT TO YOU STRAIGHT, SON.
I NEED YOUR HELP.
CLIK
WELL, IF I'M BEING HONEST, I WANTED FLASH THOMPSON'S HELP, BUT I GUESS MY INTEL'S A BIT OLD, SO NOW I'M STUCK WITH YOU.
IT'S BROCK, RIGHT? EDDIE BROCK?
CLIK
EDDIE, WHAT CAN YOU TELL ME ABOUT PROJECT REBIRTH? SPECIFICALLY, THE "TWO POINT OH" VERSION?
CLIK
CAN YOU HEAR ME? I'LL KEEP THIS IDIOT TALKING, YOU GET TO HIM AND--
YES. TAKE HIS LUNGS OUT AND--
NO! DO NOT KILL HIM!
PLEASE DON'T YELL AT US, EDDIE! WE DON'T KNOW WHAT'S WRONG...OUR THOUGHTS ARE ALL JAGGED AND--
I KNOW. I KNOW...JUST FOCUS.
PROJECT REBIRTH. YEAH, THE MILITARY PROGRAM THAT MADE CAPTAIN AMERICA AND NOTHING ELSE GOOD.
FEW YEARS BACK THEY KICKED IT UP AGAIN, ONLY THIS TIME USING MY OTHER.
YOUR WHAT?
MY... SYMBIOTE. THE ALIEN THAT'S--

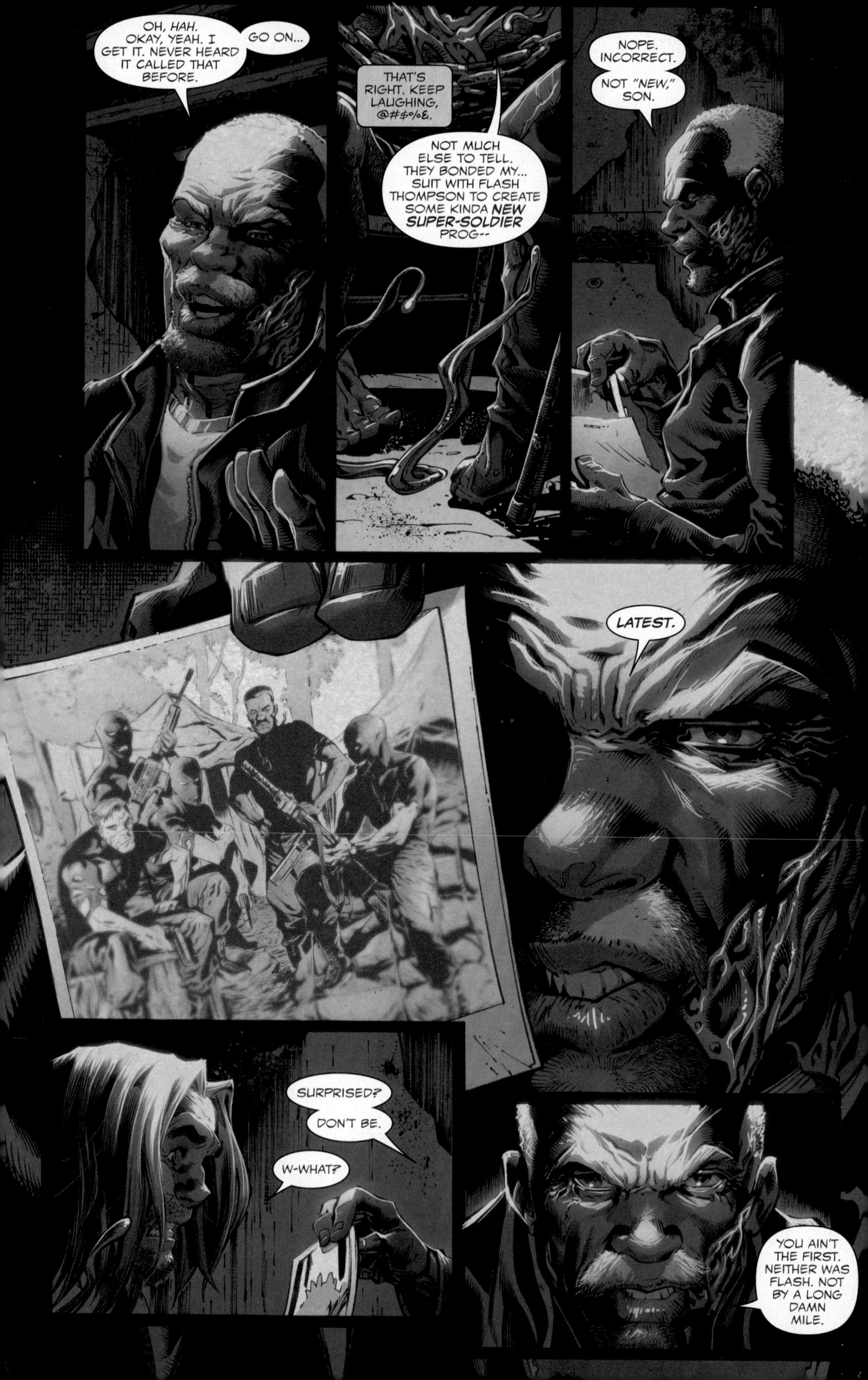
OH, HAH. OKAY, YEAH. I GET IT. NEVER HEARD IT CALLED THAT BEFORE.
GO ON...
THAT'S RIGHT. KEEP LAUGHING, @#$%&.
NOT MUCH ELSE TO TELL. THEY BONDED MY... SUIT WITH FLASH THOMPSON TO CREATE SOME KINDA NEW SUPER-SOLDIER PROG--
NOPE. INCORRECT.
NOT "NEW," SON.
LATEST.
SURPRISED?
DON'T BE.
W-WHAT?
YOU AIN'T THE FIRST. NEITHER WAS FLASH. NOT BY A LONG DAMN MILE.

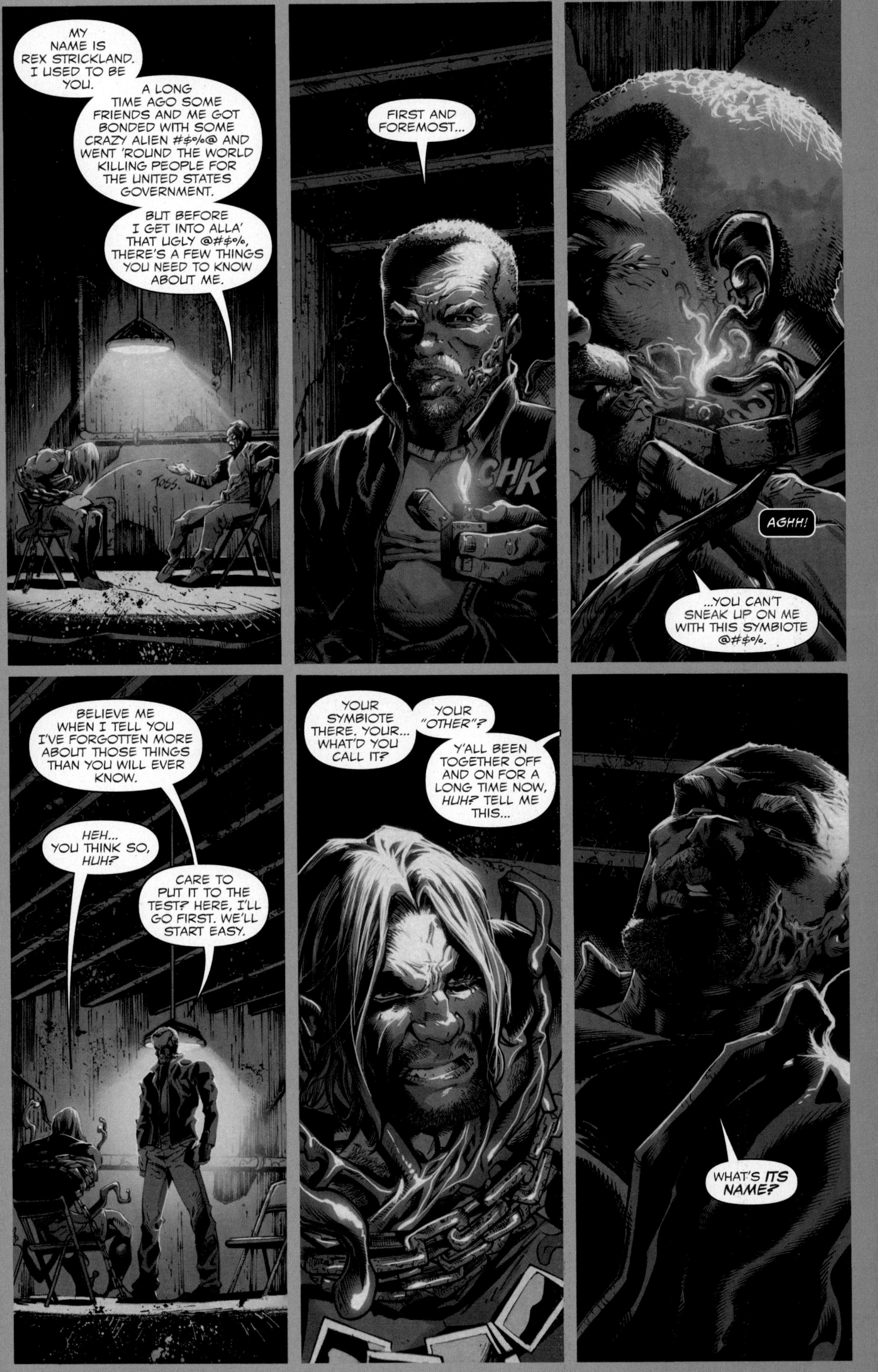

MY NAME IS REX STRICKLAND. I USED TO BE YOU.
A LONG TIME AGO SOME FRIENDS AND ME GOT BONDED WITH SOME CRAZY ALIEN #$%@ AND WENT 'ROUND THE WORLD KILLING PEOPLE FOR THE UNITED STATES GOVERNMENT.
BUT BEFORE I GET INTO ALLA' THAT UGLY @#$%, THERE'S A FEW THINGS YOU NEED TO KNOW ABOUT ME.
TOSS.
FIRST AND FOREMOST...
CHK
AGHH!
...YOU CAN'T SNEAK UP ON ME WITH THIS SYMBIOTE @#$%.
BELIEVE ME WHEN I TELL YOU I'VE FORGOTTEN MORE ABOUT THOSE THINGS THAN YOU WILL EVER KNOW.
HEH... YOU THINK SO, HUH?
CARE TO PUT IT TO THE TEST? HERE, I'LL GO FIRST. WE'LL START EASY.
YOUR SYMBIOTE THERE. YOUR... WHAT'D YOU CALL IT?
YOUR "OTHER"?
Y'ALL BEEN TOGETHER OFF AND ON FOR A LONG TIME NOW, HUH? TELL ME THIS...
WHAT'S ITS NAME?

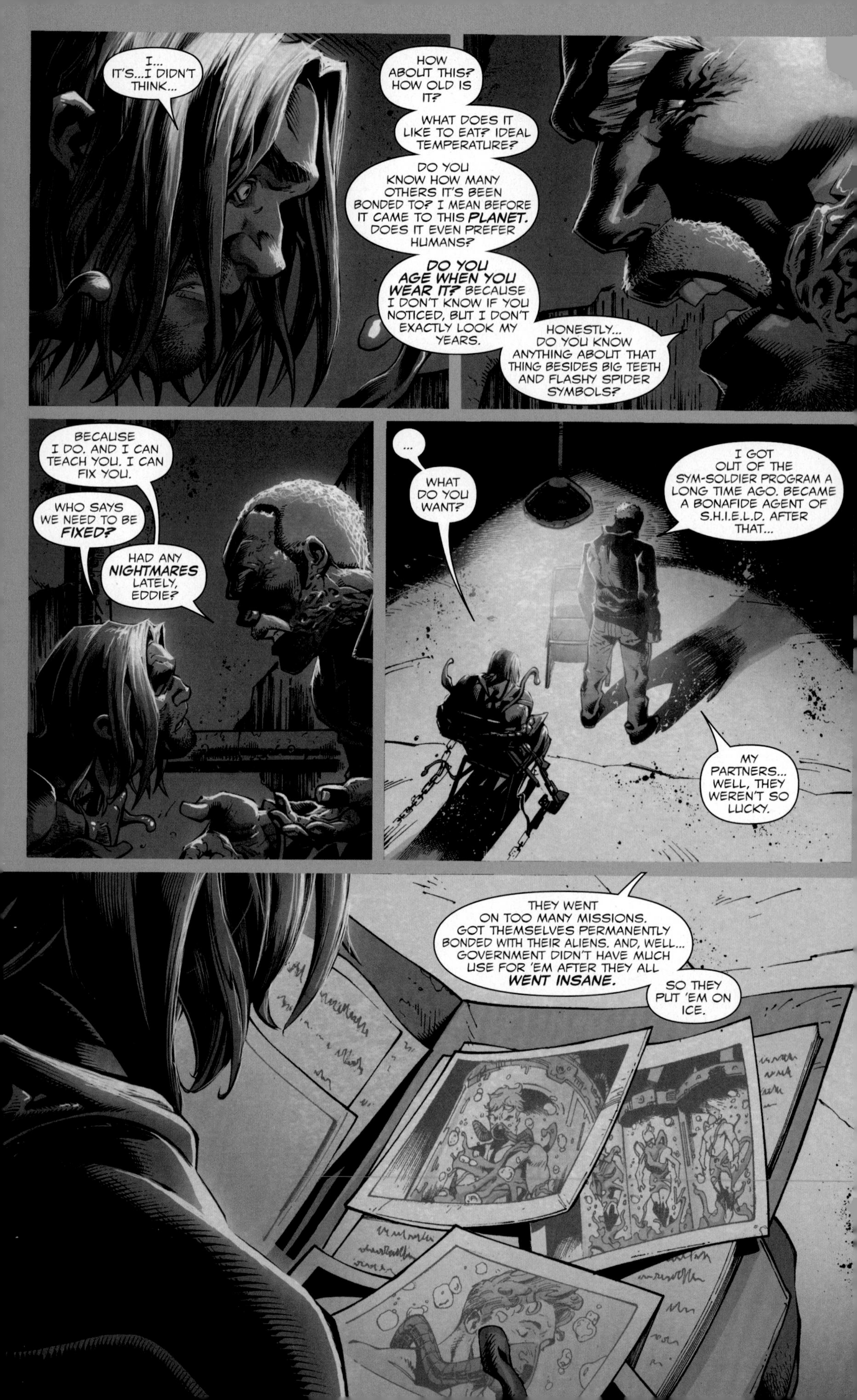

I... IT'S...I DIDN'T THINK...
HOW ABOUT THIS? HOW OLD IS IT?
WHAT DOES IT LIKE TO EAT? IDEAL TEMPERATURE?
DO YOU KNOW HOW MANY OTHERS IT'S BEEN BONDED TO? I MEAN BEFORE IT CAME TO THIS PLANET. DOES IT EVEN PREFER HUMANS?
DO YOU AGE WHEN YOU WEAR IT? BECAUSE I DON'T KNOW IF YOU NOTICED, BUT I DON'T EXACTLY LOOK MY YEARS.
HONESTLY... DO YOU KNOW ANYTHING ABOUT THAT THING BESIDES BIG TEETH AND FLASHY SPIDER SYMBOLS?
BECAUSE I DO. AND I CAN TEACH YOU. I CAN FIX YOU.
WHO SAYS WE NEED TO BE FIXED?
HAD ANY NIGHTMARES LATELY, EDDIE?
...
WHAT DO YOU WANT?
I GOT OUT OF THE SYM-SOLDIER PROGRAM A LONG TIME AGO. BECAME A BONAFIDE AGENT OF S.H.I.E.L.D. AFTER THAT...
MY PARTNERS... WELL, THEY WEREN'T SO LUCKY.
THEY WENT ON TOO MANY MISSIONS. GOT THEMSELVES PERMANENTLY BONDED WITH THEIR ALIENS. AND, WELL... GOVERNMENT DIDN'T HAVE MUCH USE FOR 'EM AFTER THEY ALL WENT INSANE.
SO THEY PUT 'EM ON ICE.

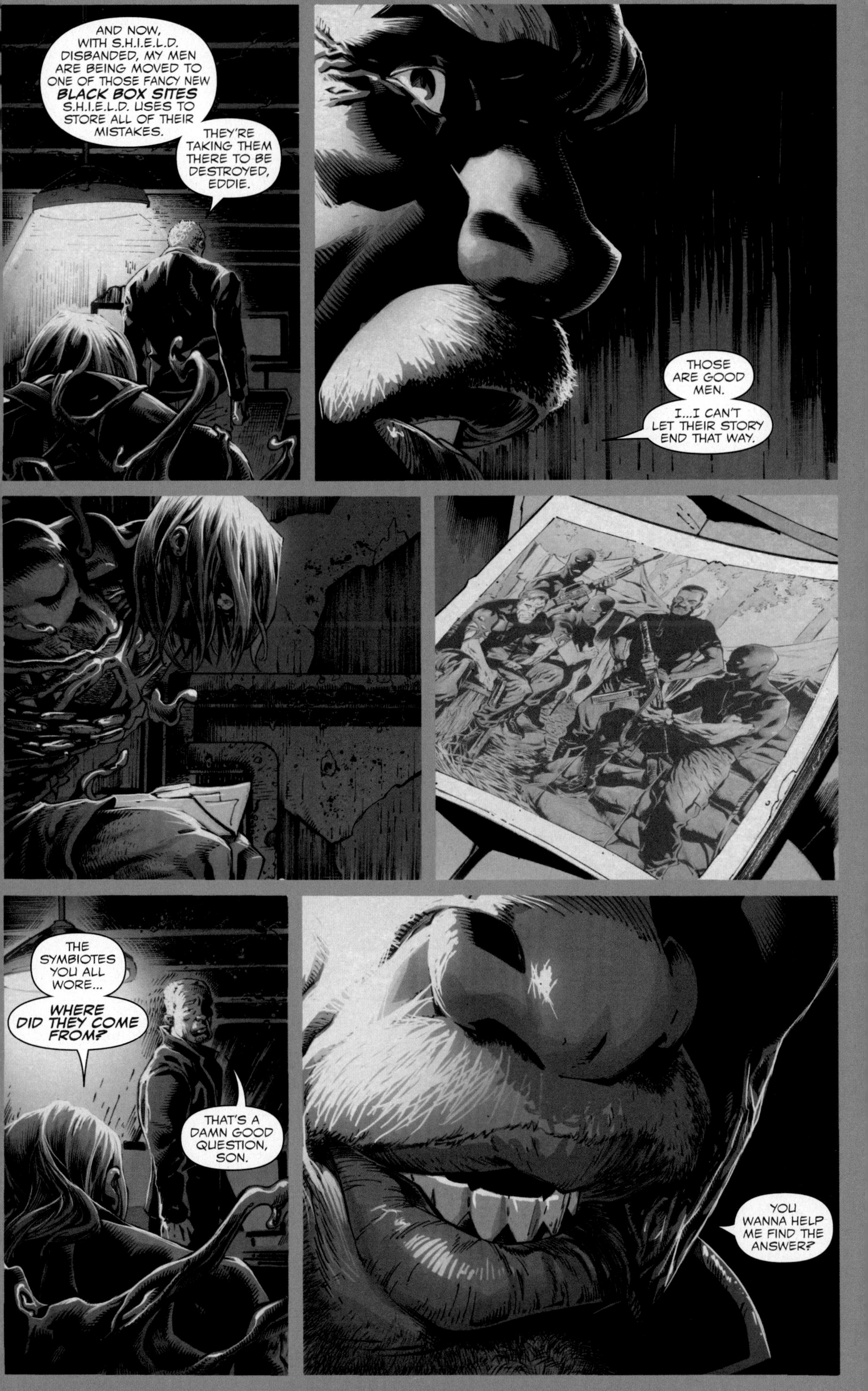
AND NOW, WITH S.H.I.E.L.D. DISBANDED, MY MEN ARE BEING MOVED TO ONE OF THOSE FANCY NEW BLACK BOX SITES S.H.I.E.L.D. USES TO STORE ALL OF THEIR MISTAKES.
THEY'RE TAKING THEM THERE TO BE DESTROYED, EDDIE.
THOSE ARE GOOD MEN.
I...I CAN'T LET THEIR STORY END THAT WAY.
THE SYMBIOTES YOU ALL WORE... WHERE DID THEY COME FROM?
THAT'S A DAMN GOOD QUESTION, SON.
YOU WANNA HELP ME FIND THE ANSWER?

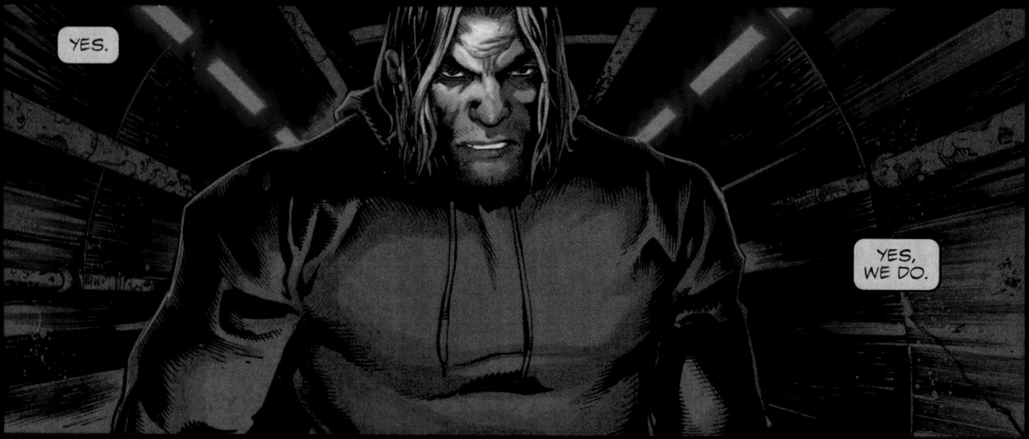
YES.
YES, WE DO.

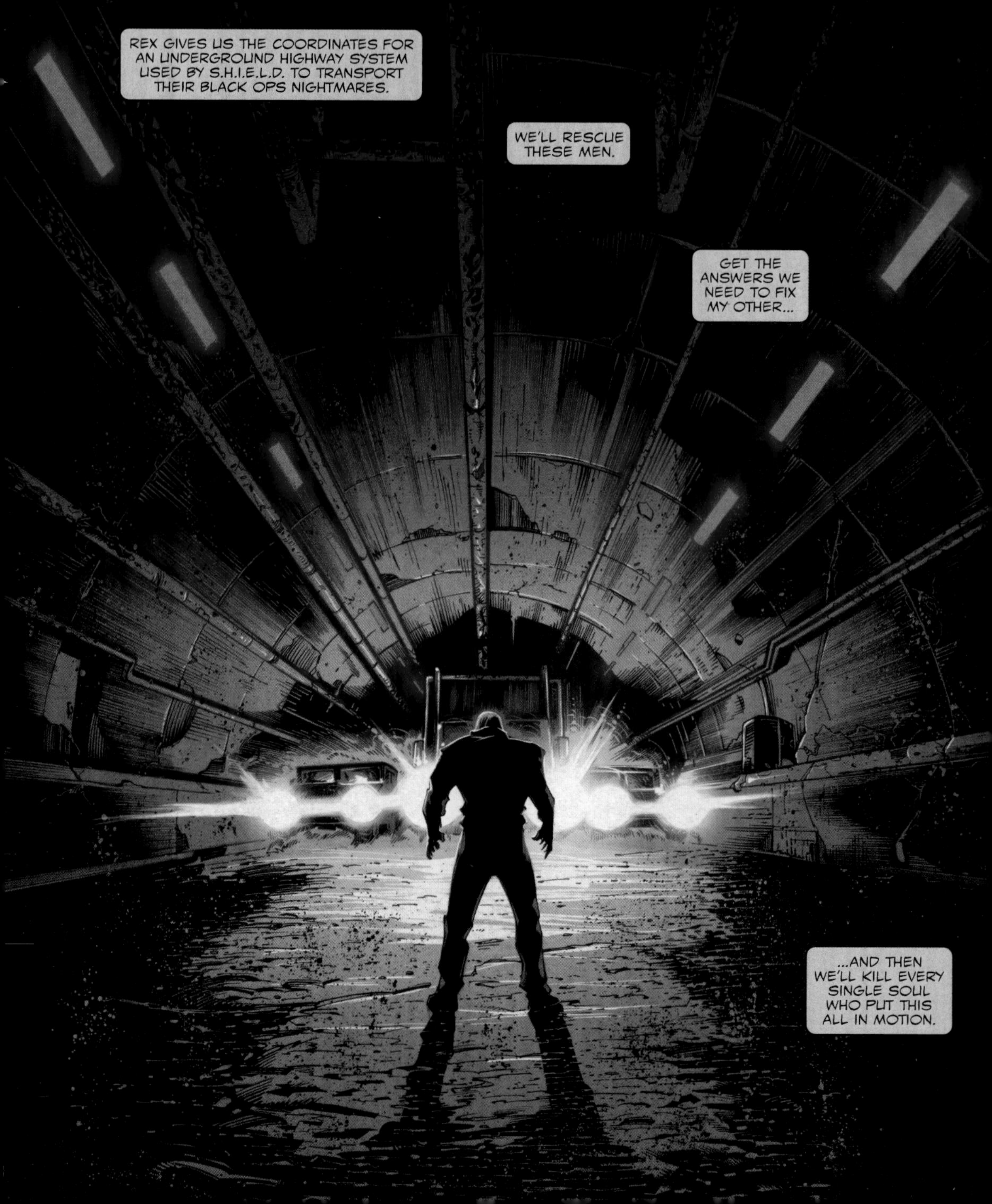
REX GIVES US THE COORDINATES FOR AN UNDERGROUND HIGHWAY SYSTEM USED BY S.H.I.E.L.D. TO TRANSPORT THEIR BLACK OPS NIGHTMARES.
WE'LL RESCUE THESE MEN.
GET THE ANSWERS WE NEED TO FIX MY OTHER...
...AND THEN WE'LL KILL EVERY SINGLE SOUL WHO PUT THIS ALL IN MOTION.

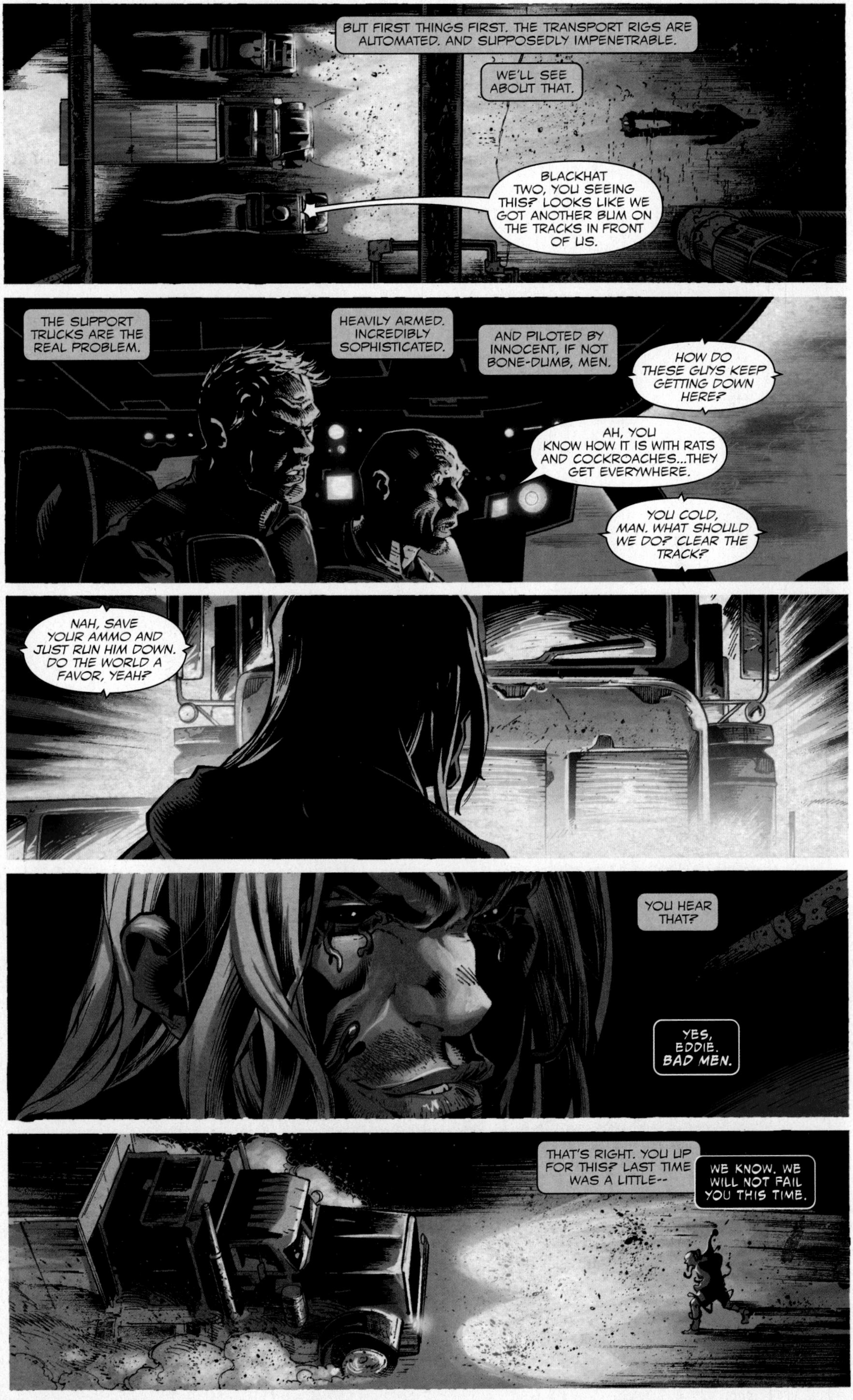
BUT FIRST THINGS FIRST. THE TRANSPORT RIGS ARE AUTOMATED. AND SUPPOSEDLY IMPENETRABLE.
WE'LL SEE ABOUT THAT.
BLACKHAT TWO, YOU SEEING THIS? LOOKS LIKE WE GOT ANOTHER BUM ON THE TRACKS IN FRONT OF US.
THE SUPPORT TRUCKS ARE THE REAL PROBLEM.
HEAVILY ARMED. INCREDIBLY SOPHISTICATED.
AND PILOTED BY INNOCENT, IF NOT BONE-DUMB, MEN.
HOW DO THESE GUYS KEEP GETTING DOWN HERE?
AH, YOU KNOW HOW IT IS WITH RATS AND COCKROACHES...THEY GET EVERYWHERE.
YOU COLD, MAN. WHAT SHOULD WE DO? CLEAR THE TRACK?
NAH, SAVE YOUR AMMO AND JUST RUN HIM DOWN. DO THE WORLD A FAVOR, YEAH?
YOU HEAR THAT?
YES, EDDIE. BAD MEN.
THAT'S RIGHT. YOU UP FOR THIS? LAST TIME WAS A LITTLE--
WE KNOW. WE WILL NOT FAIL YOU THIS TIME.

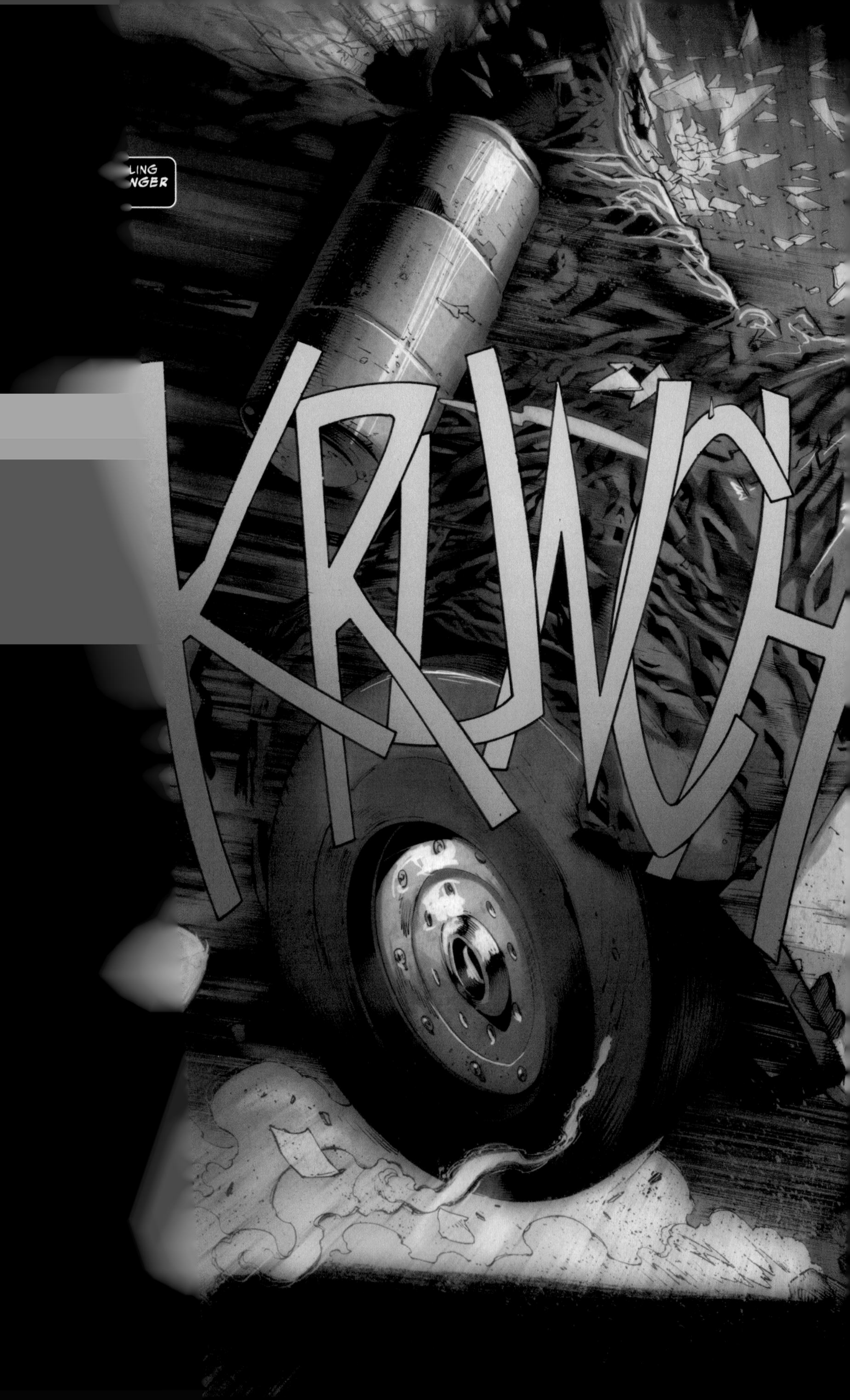
KRUNCH

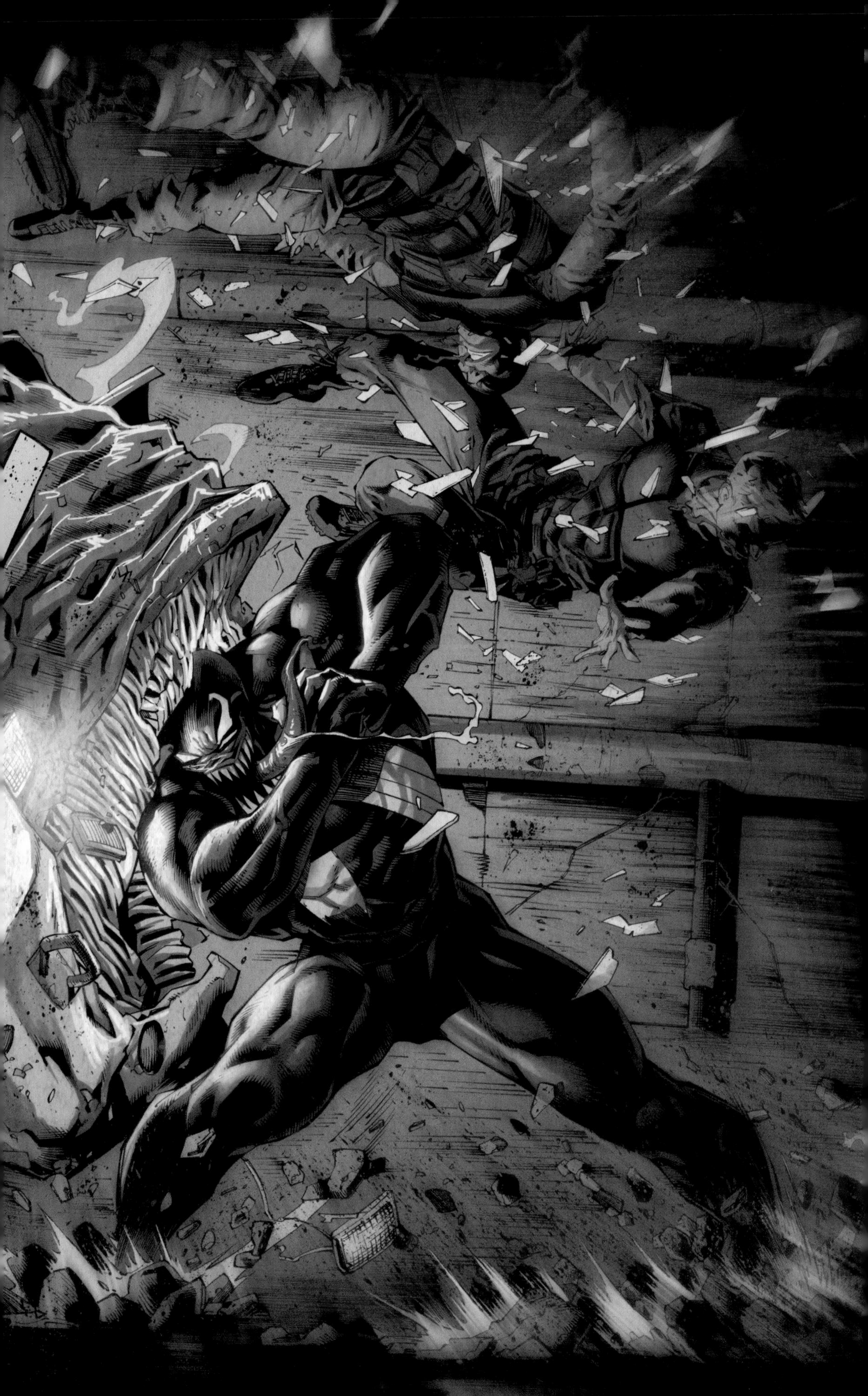

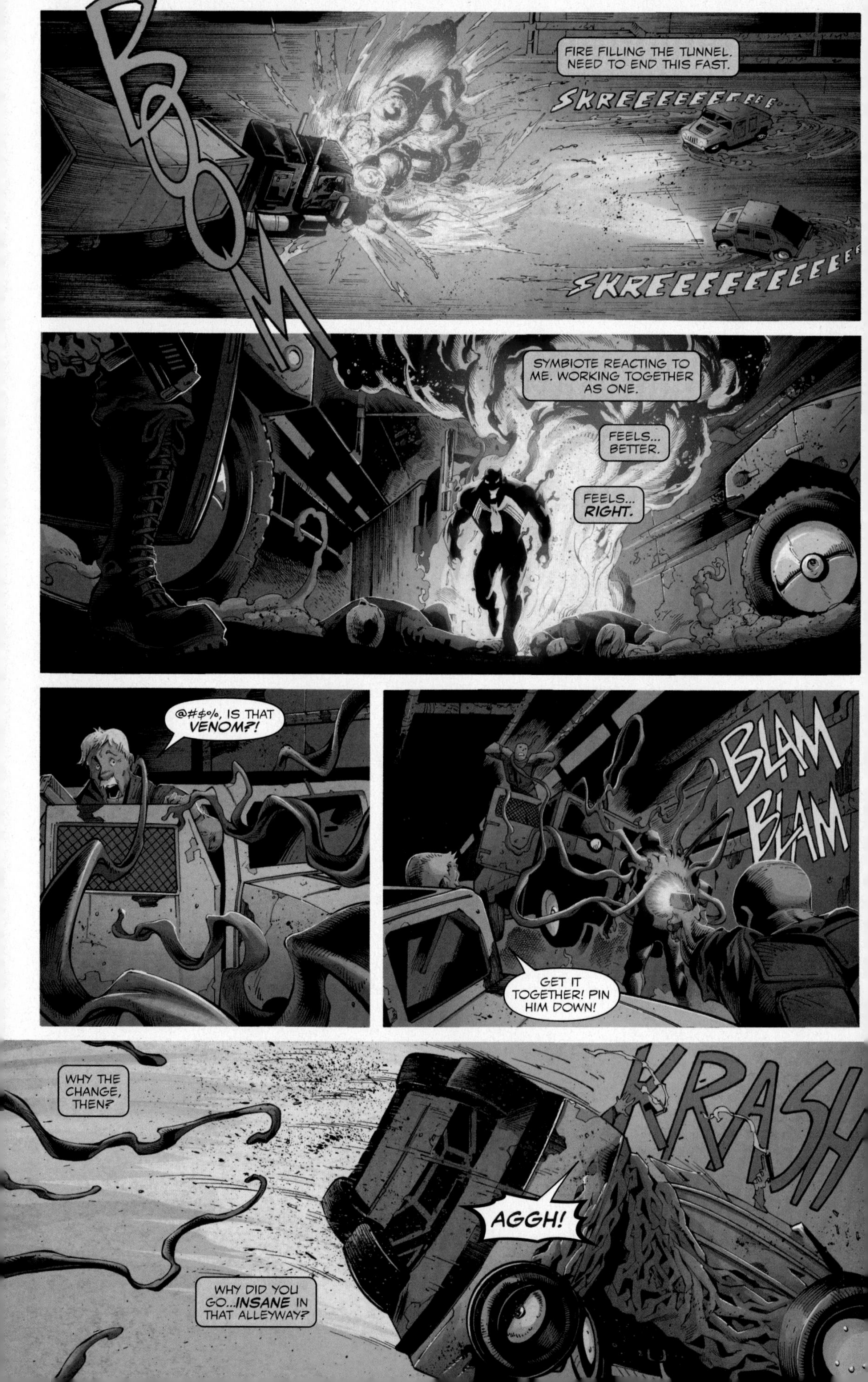
BOOM
FIRE FILLING THE TUNNEL. NEED TO END THIS FAST.
SKREEEEEEEEEE
SKREEEEEEEEEEE
SYMBIOTE REACTING TO ME. WORKING TOGETHER AS ONE.
FEELS... BETTER.
FEELS... RIGHT.
@#$%, IS THAT VENOM?!
BLAM BLAM
GET IT TOGETHER! PIN HIM DOWN!
WHY THE CHANGE, THEN?
KRASH
AGGH!
WHY DID YOU GO...INSANE IN THAT ALLEYWAY?

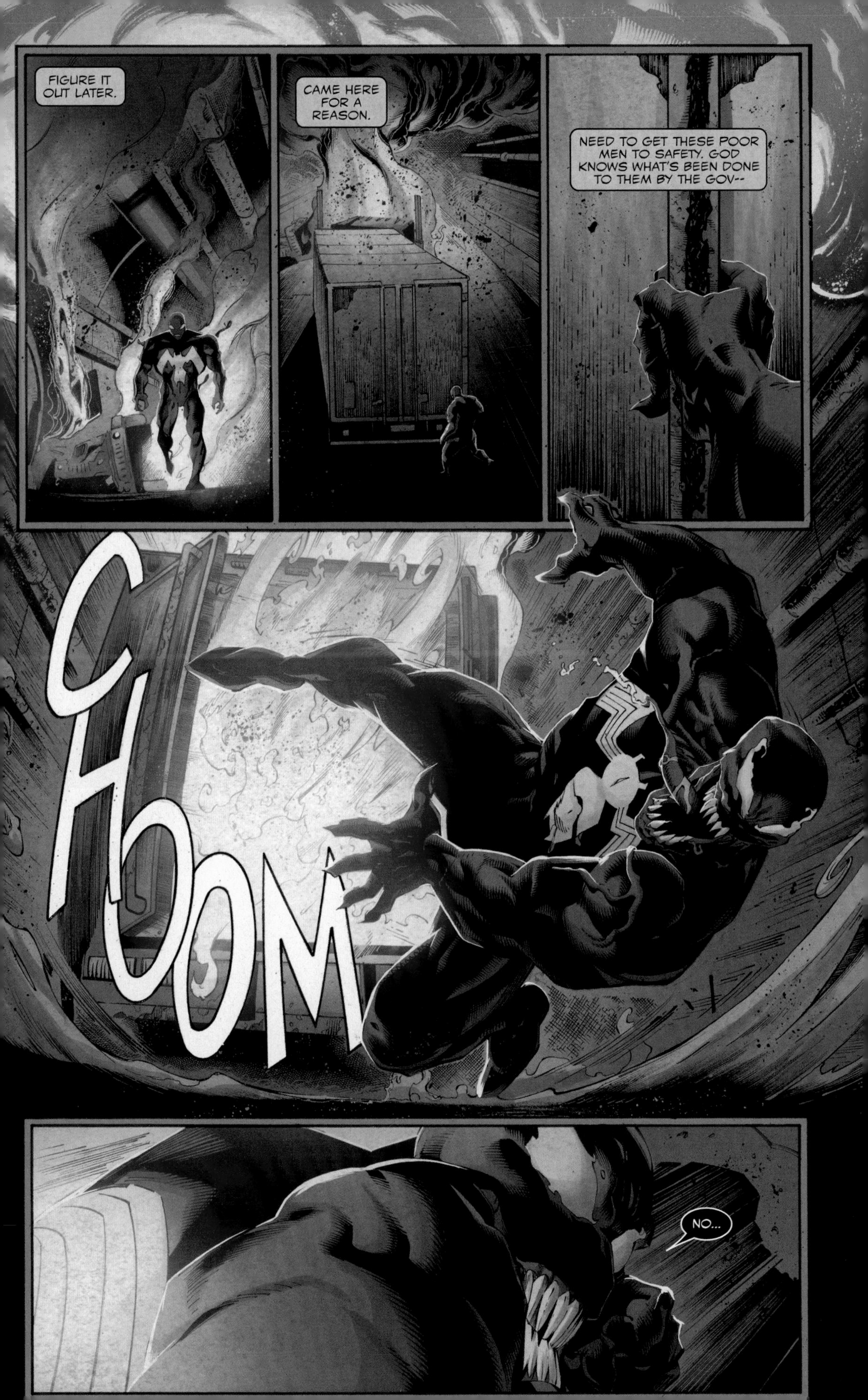

FIGURE IT OUT LATER.
CAME HERE FOR A REASON.
NEED TO GET THESE POOR MEN TO SAFETY. GOD KNOWS WHAT'S BEEN DONE TO THEM BY THE GOV--
CHOOM
NO...

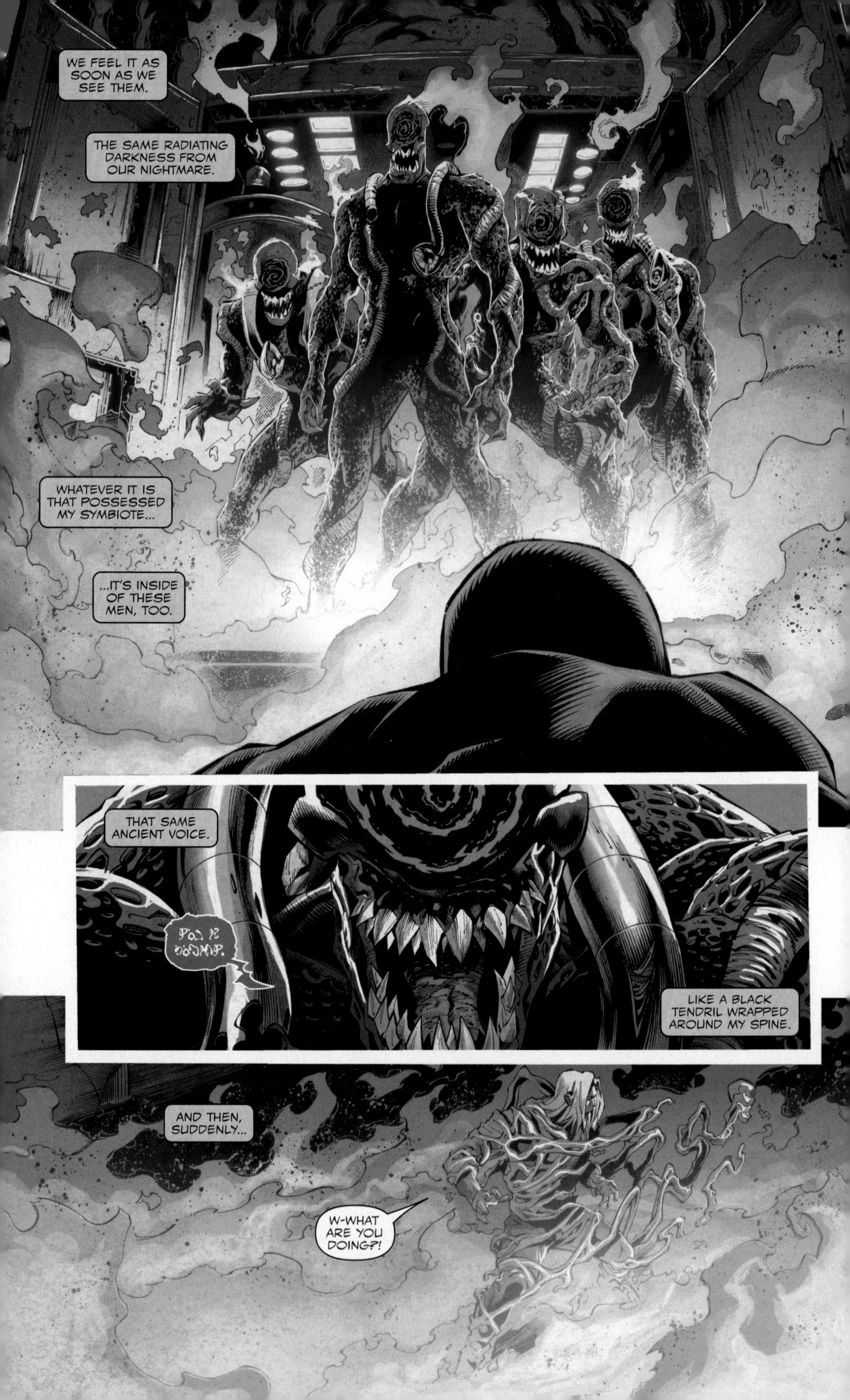
WE FEEL IT AS SOON AS WE SEE THEM.
THE SAME RADIATING DARKNESS FROM OUR NIGHTMARE.
WHATEVER IT IS THAT POSSESSED MY SYMBIOTE...
...IT'S INSIDE OF THESE MEN, TOO.
THAT SAME ANCIENT VOICE.
LIKE A BLACK TENDRIL WRAPPED AROUND MY SPINE.
AND THEN, SUDDENLY...
W-WHAT ARE YOU DOING?!

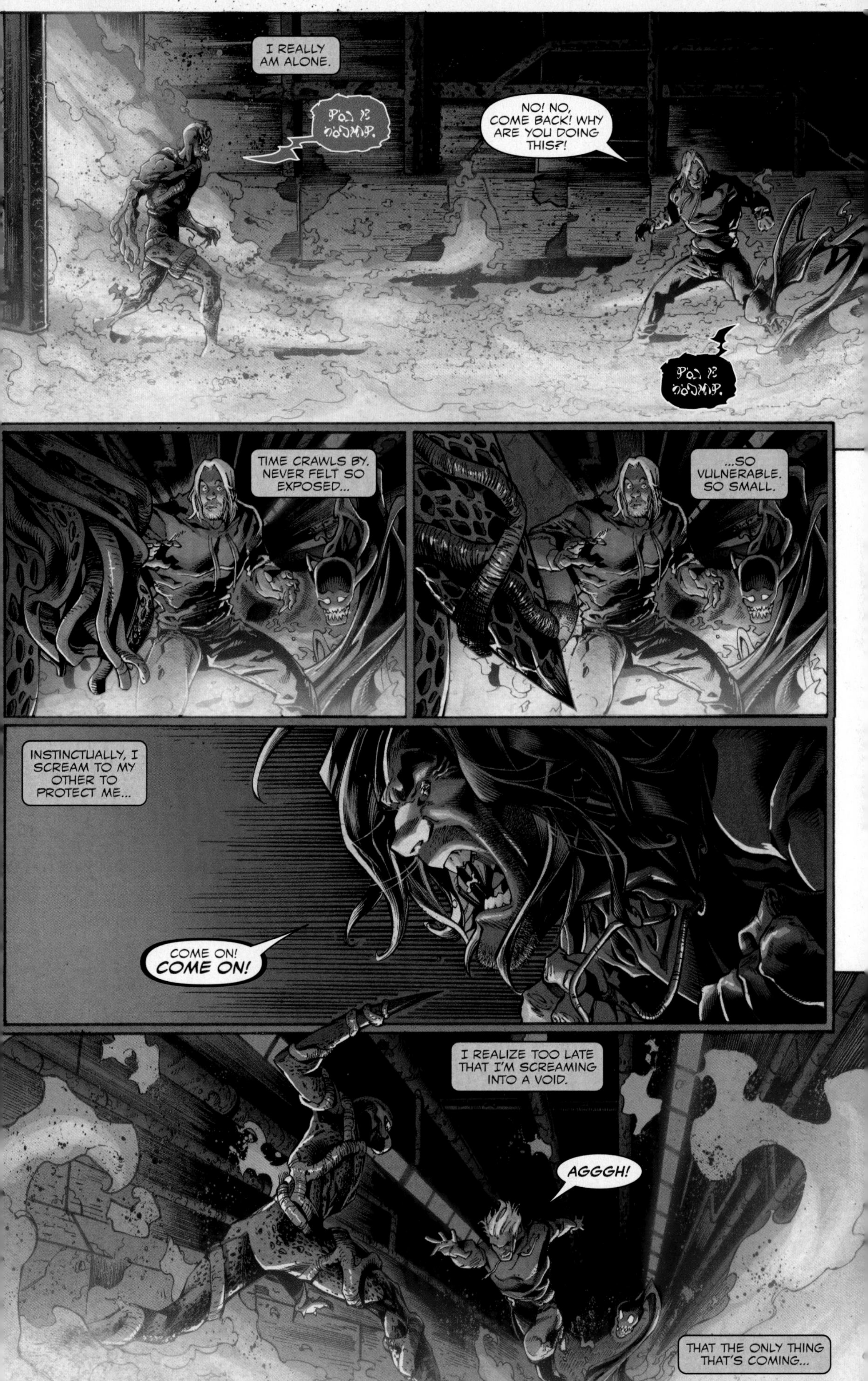
I REALLY AM ALONE.
NO! NO, COME BACK! WHY ARE YOU DOING THIS?!
TIME CRAWLS BY. NEVER FELT SO EXPOSED...
...SO VULNERABLE. SO SMALL.
INSTINCTUALLY, I SCREAM TO MY OTHER TO PROTECT ME...
COME ON! COME ON!
I REALIZE TOO LATE THAT I'M SCREAMING INTO A VOID.
AGGGH!
THAT THE ONLY THING THAT'S COMING...

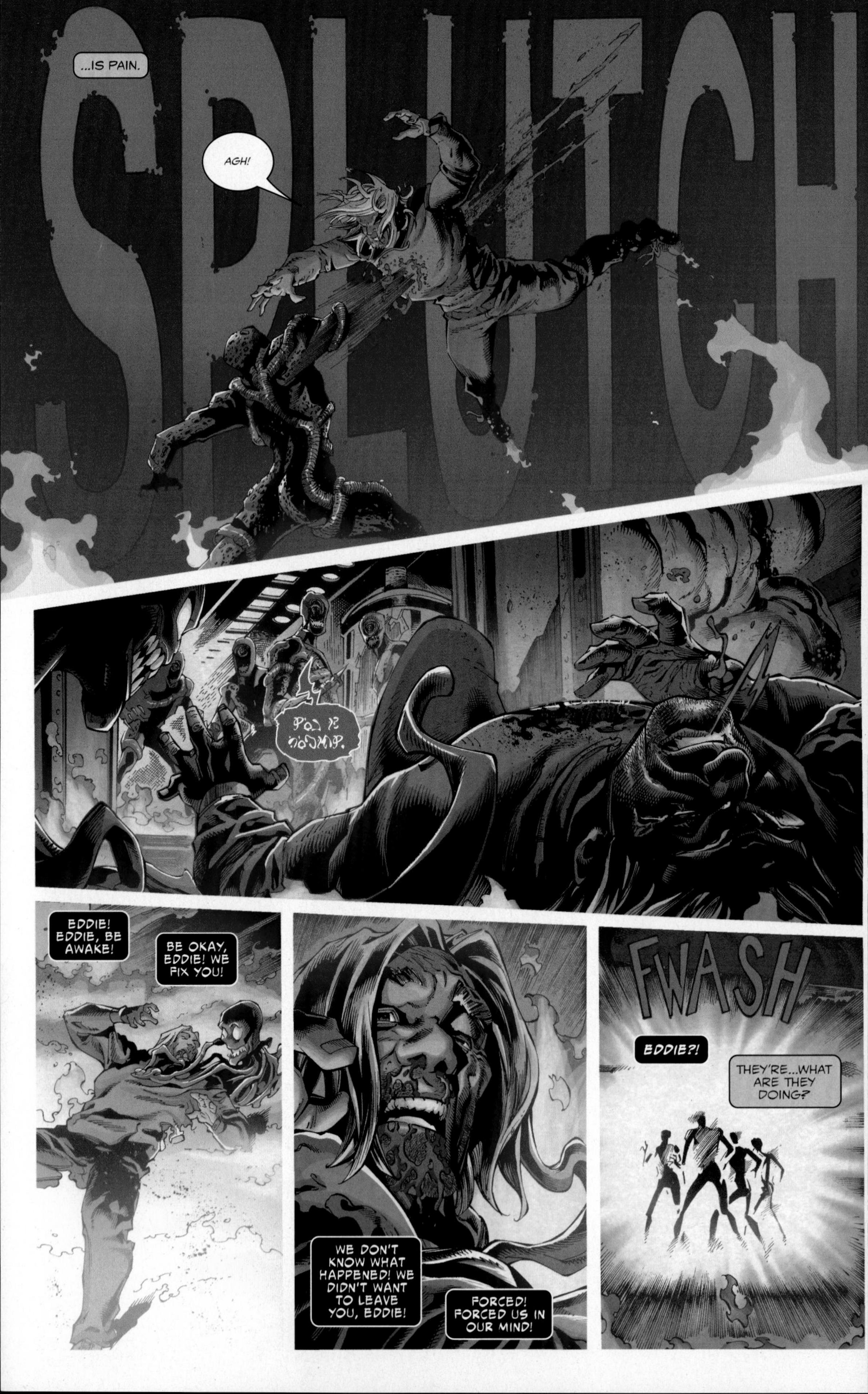
...IS PAIN.
SPLUTCH
AGH!
EDDIE! EDDIE, BE AWAKE!
BE OKAY, EDDIE! WE FIX YOU!
WE DON'T KNOW WHAT HAPPENED! WE DIDN'T WANT TO LEAVE YOU, EDDIE!
FORCED! FORCED US IN OUR MIND!
FWASH
EDDIE?!
THEY'RE...WHAT ARE THEY DOING?

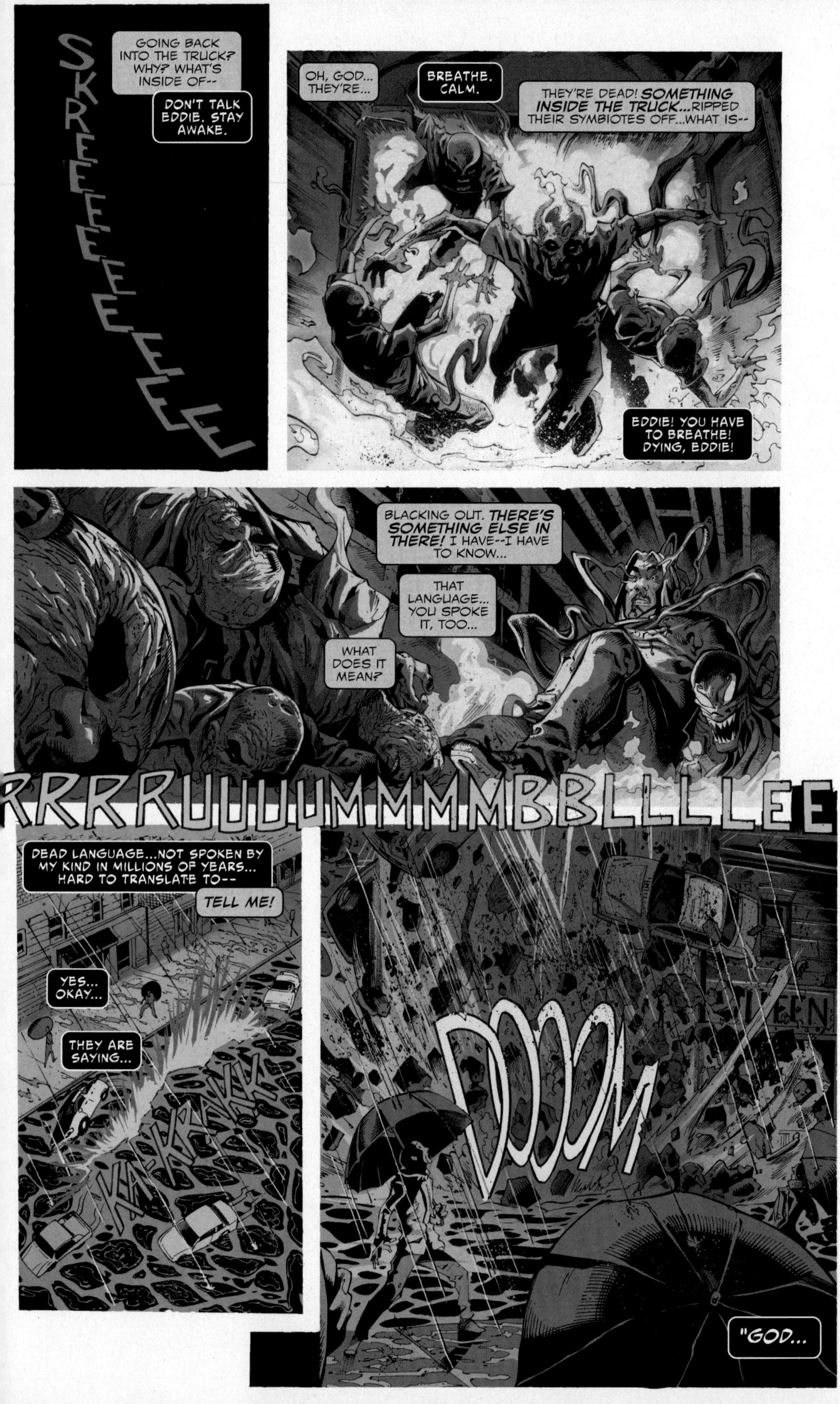
SKREEEEEEEEEE
GOING BACK INTO THE TRUCK? WHY? WHAT'S INSIDE OF--
DON'T TALK EDDIE. STAY AWAKE.
OH, GOD... THEY'RE...
BREATHE. CALM.
THEY'RE DEAD! SOMETHING INSIDE THE TRUCK...RIPPED THEIR SYMBIOTES OFF...WHAT IS--
EDDIE! YOU HAVE TO BREATHE! DYING, EDDIE!
BLACKING OUT. THERE'S SOMETHING ELSE IN THERE! I HAVE--I HAVE TO KNOW...
THAT LANGUAGE... YOU SPOKE IT, TOO...
WHAT DOES IT MEAN?
RRRRUUUUMMMMBBLLLEE
DEAD LANGUAGE...NOT SPOKEN BY MY KIND IN MILLIONS OF YEARS... HARD TO TRANSLATE TO--
TELL ME!
YES... OKAY...
THEY ARE SAYING...
DOOOM
"GOD...

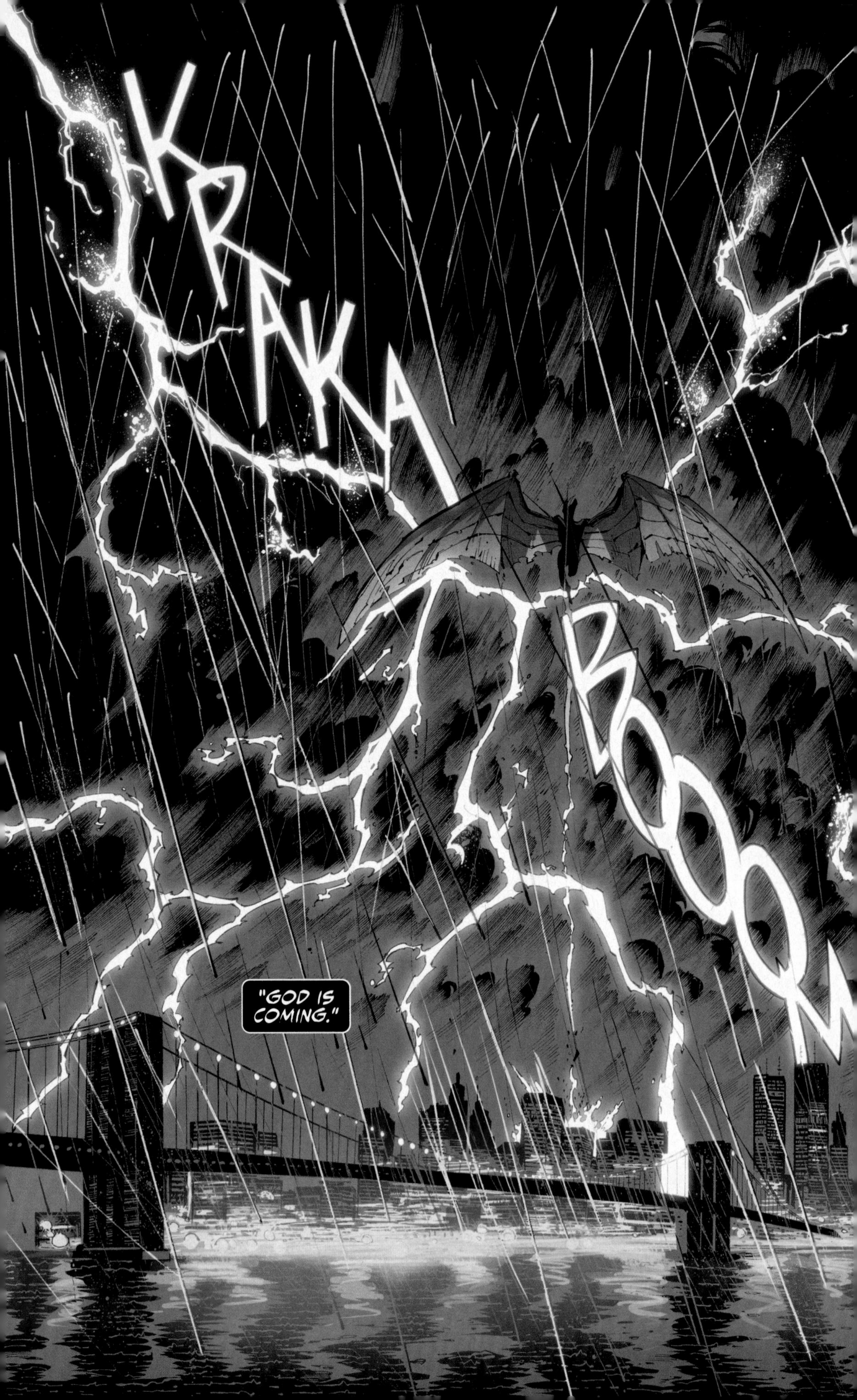
KRAKA
BOOOOM
"GOD IS COMING."

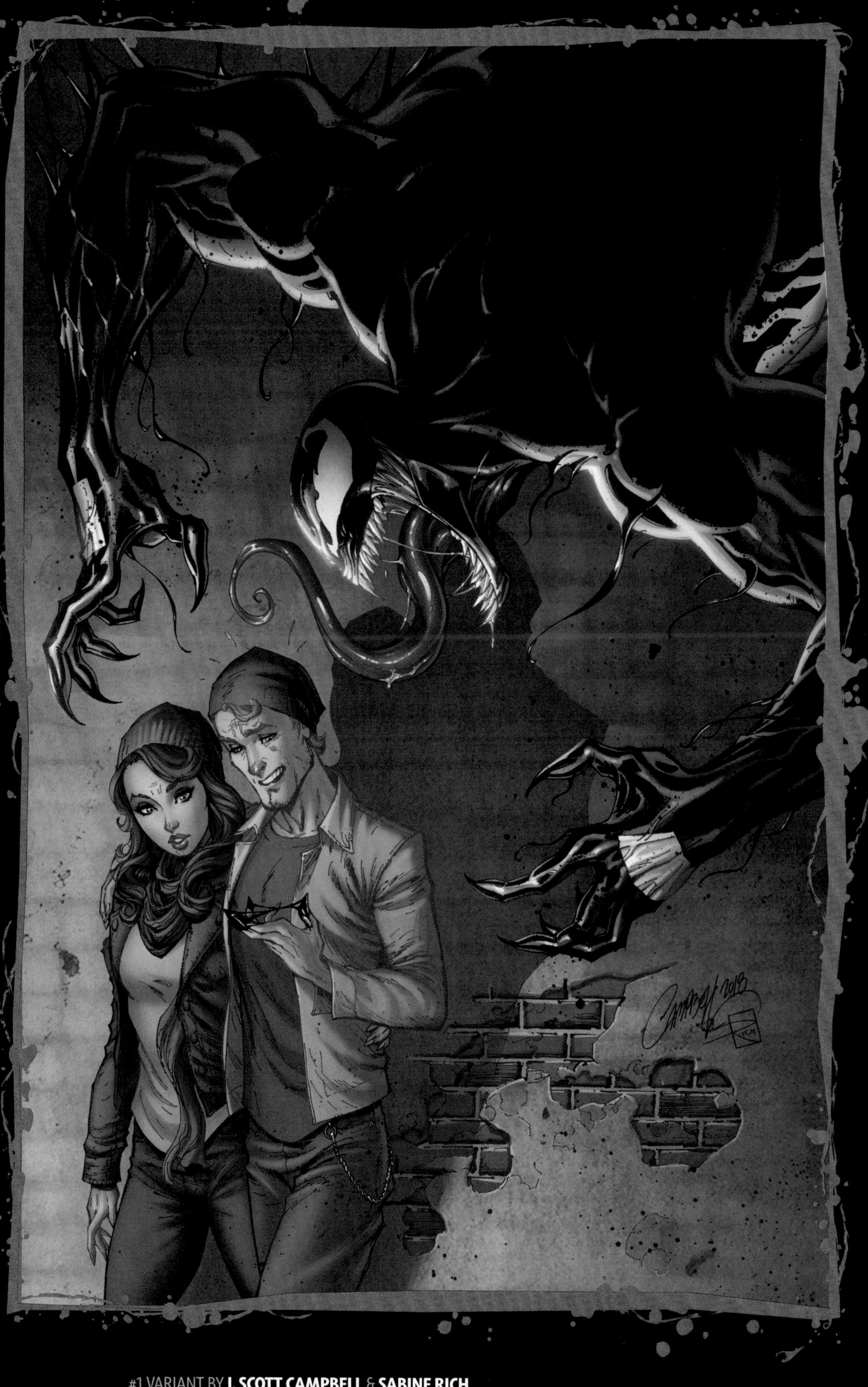

#1 VARIANT BY **J. SCOTT CAMPBELL** & **SABINE RICH**

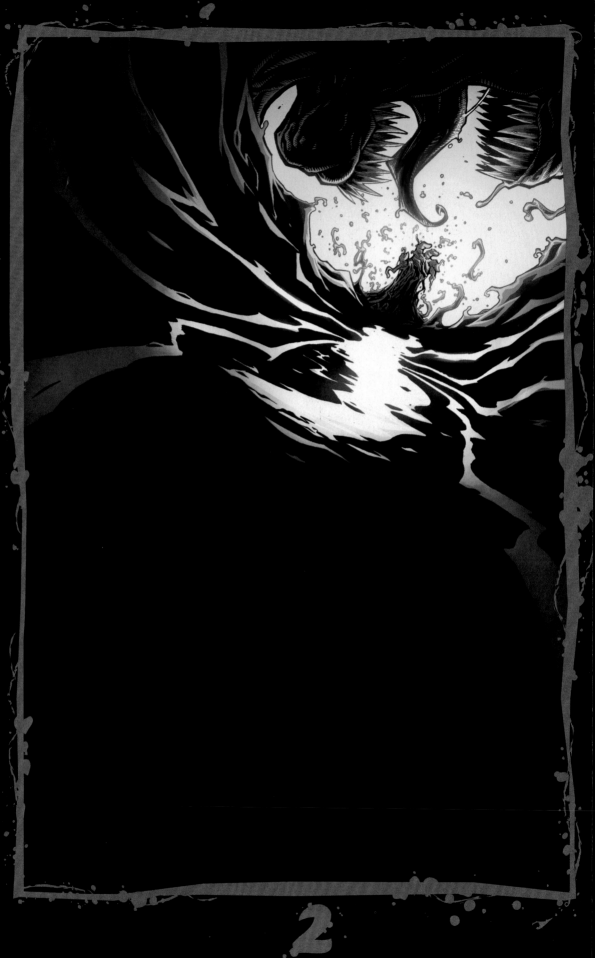

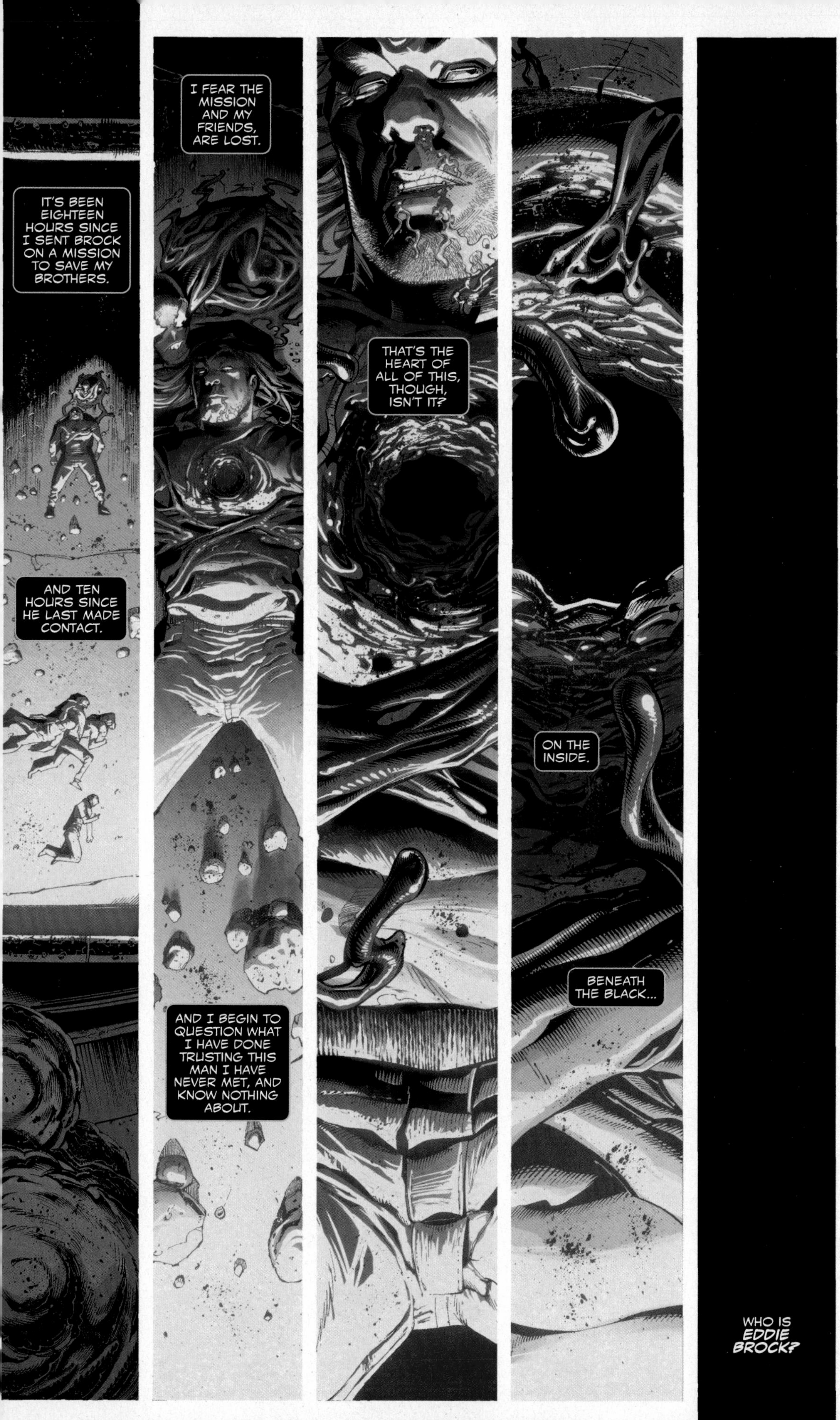
IT'S BEEN EIGHTEEN HOURS SINCE I SENT BROCK ON A MISSION TO SAVE MY BROTHERS.
AND TEN HOURS SINCE HE LAST MADE CONTACT.
I FEAR THE MISSION AND MY FRIENDS, ARE LOST.
AND I BEGIN TO QUESTION WHAT I HAVE DONE TRUSTING THIS MAN I HAVE NEVER MET, AND KNOW NOTHING ABOUT.
THAT'S THE HEART OF ALL OF THIS, THOUGH, ISN'T IT?
ON THE INSIDE.
BENEATH THE BLACK...
WHO IS EDDIE BROCK?

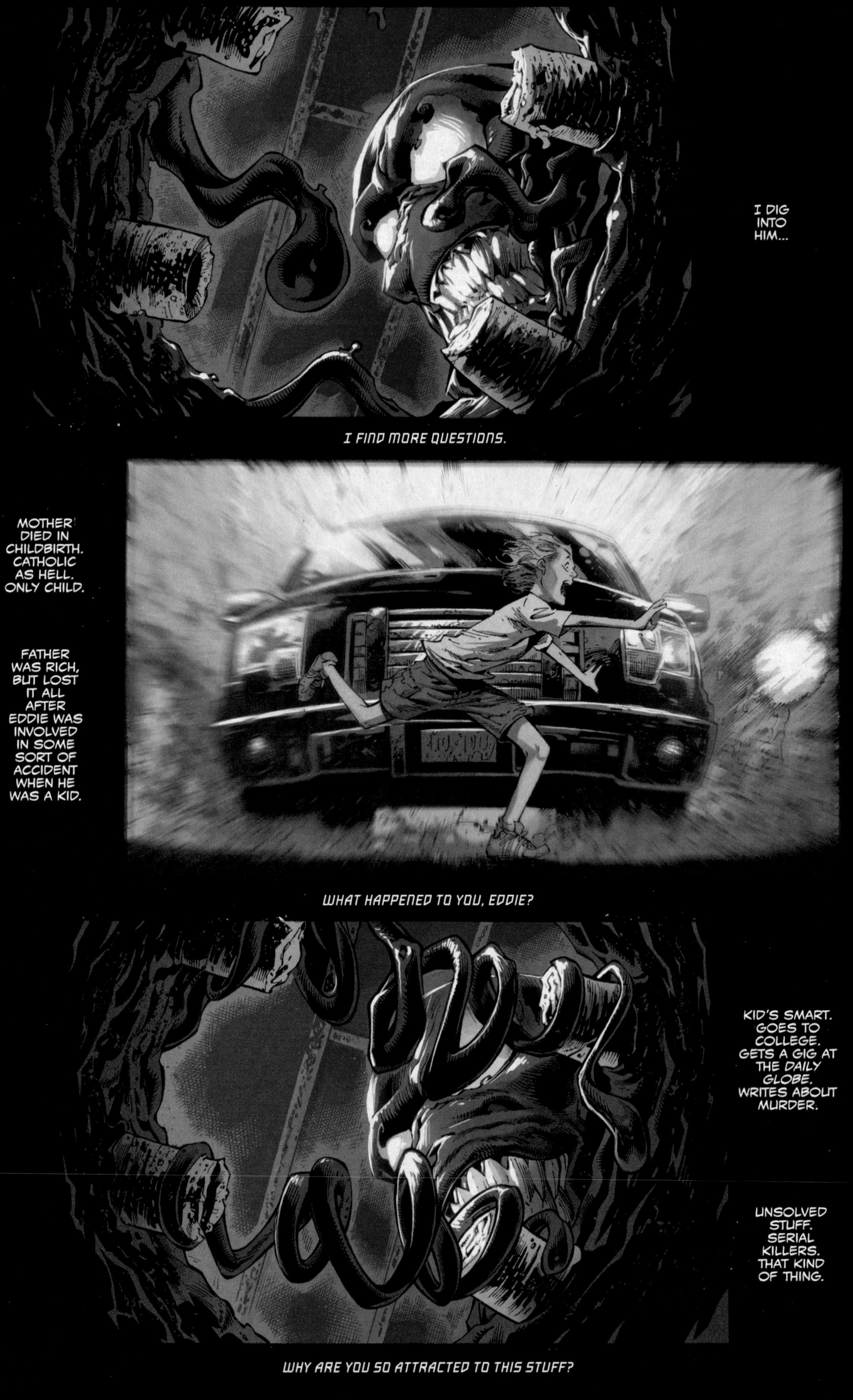
I DIG INTO HIM...
I FIND MORE QUESTIONS.
MOTHER DIED IN CHILDBIRTH. CATHOLIC AS HELL. ONLY CHILD.
FATHER WAS RICH, BUT LOST IT ALL AFTER EDDIE WAS INVOLVED IN SOME SORT OF ACCIDENT WHEN HE WAS A KID.
WHAT HAPPENED TO YOU, EDDIE?
KID'S SMART. GOES TO COLLEGE. GETS A GIG AT THE *DAILY GLOBE*. WRITES ABOUT MURDER.
UNSOLVED STUFF. SERIAL KILLERS. THAT KIND OF THING.
WHY ARE YOU SO ATTRACTED TO THIS STUFF?

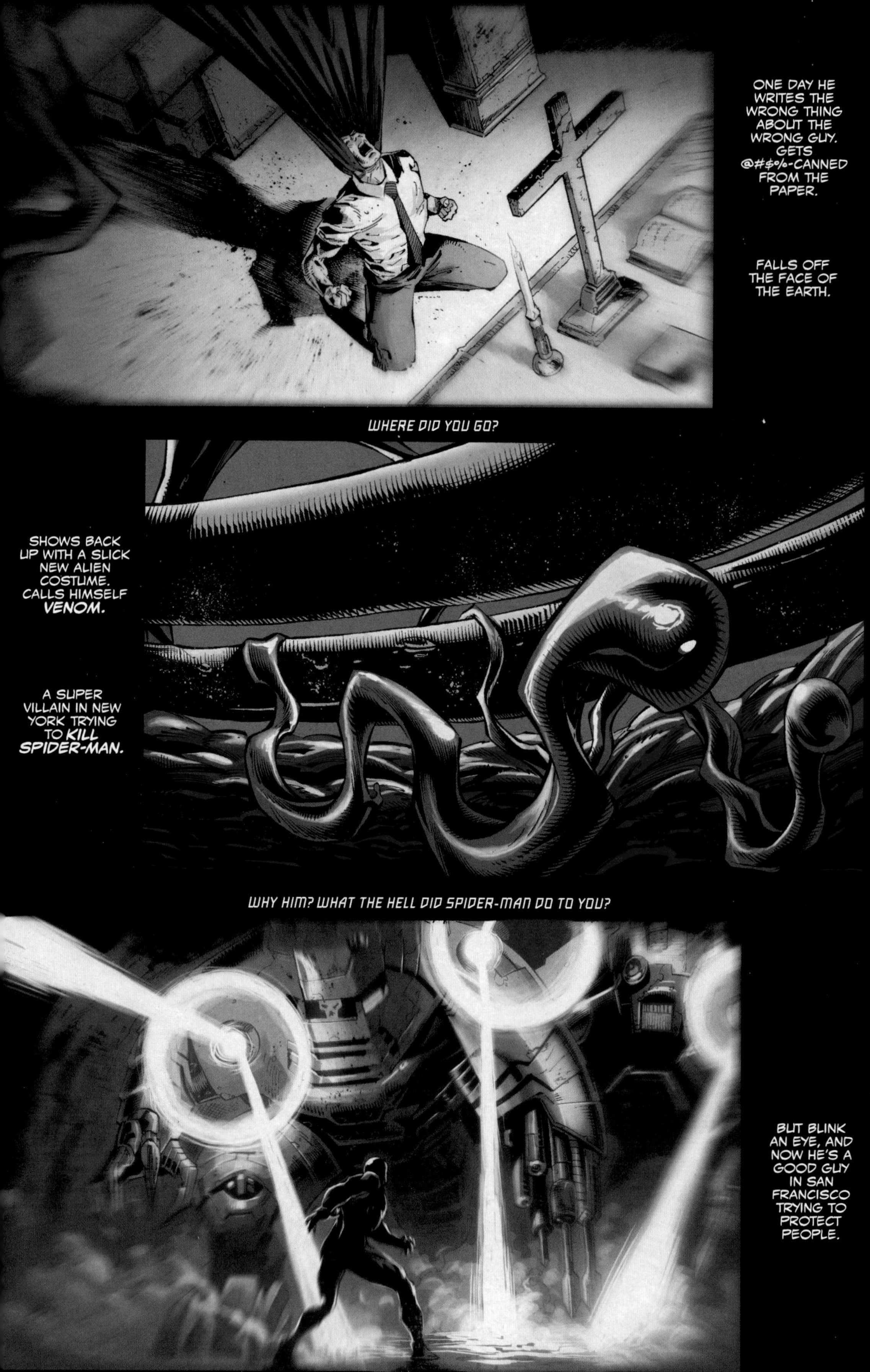
ONE DAY HE WRITES THE WRONG THING ABOUT THE WRONG GUY. GETS @#$%-CANNED FROM THE PAPER.
FALLS OFF THE FACE OF THE EARTH.
WHERE DID YOU GO?
SHOWS BACK UP WITH A SLICK NEW ALIEN COSTUME. CALLS HIMSELF VENOM.
A SUPER VILLAIN IN NEW YORK TRYING TO KILL SPIDER-MAN.
WHY HIM? WHAT THE HELL DID SPIDER-MAN DO TO YOU?
BUT BLINK AN EYE, AND NOW HE'S A GOOD GUY IN SAN FRANCISCO TRYING TO PROTECT PEOPLE.
WHY DO YOU CARE SO MUCH FOR THE INNOCENT?

LOTS MORE THINGS LIKE
THAT, IN BETWEEN AND AFTER.

CARNAGE.

CANCER.

TOXIN.

ANTI-VENOM.

BORN AND
UNBORN AND
REBORN.

OVER AND
OVER AND
OVER AGAIN.

MAYBE *THAT'S*
THE REAL STORY
OF EDWARD
ALLAN BROCK...

...THE MAN OF A
THOUSAND
SECOND CHANCES.

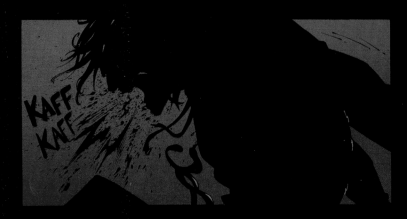

KAFF
KAFF

THE
COMEBACK
KING.

TROUBLE IS I KNOW EXACTLY WHO HE IS.

I'M JUST TOO DAMNED SCARED TO ADMIT IT.

EDDIE BROCK IS NO ONE.

AND ONE OF THESE DAYS THEM CHANCES ARE GONNA RUN DRY.

COULD BE TODAY, COULD BE A HUNDRED YEARS FROM NOW.

EITHER WHICH WAY IT DON'T CHANGE THE TRUTH.

HE'S JUST ANOTHER DEAD MAN WEARING HIS OWN COFFIN.

I'M SORRY, BOYS. IT SHOULD'A BEEN--

YOUR MEN ARE GONE.

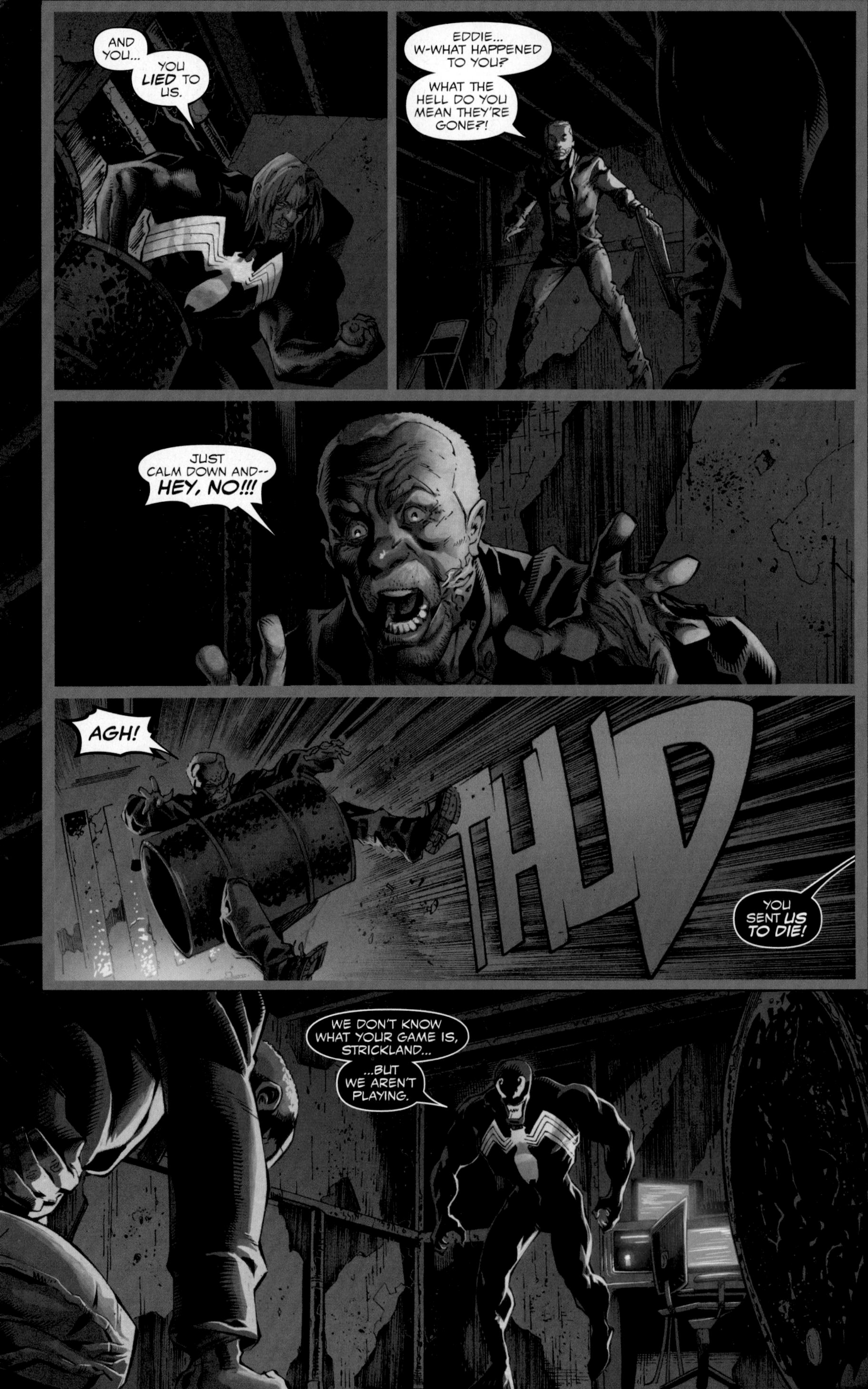

AND YOU... YOU LIED TO US.
EDDIE... W-WHAT HAPPENED TO YOU?
WHAT THE HELL DO YOU MEAN THEY'RE GONE?!
JUST CALM DOWN AND-- HEY, NO!!!
AGH!
THUD
YOU SENT US TO DIE!
WE DON'T KNOW WHAT YOUR GAME IS, STRICKLAND...
...BUT WE AREN'T PLAYING.

I FEEL IT COMING THIS TIME. THE DARKNESS SLIDING UP MY SPINE AND TAKING CONTROL.

USED TO THINK IT WAS MY OTHER TAKING OVER...BUT NO...

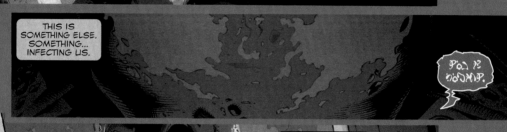

THIS IS SOMETHING ELSE. SOMETHING... INFECTING US.

SOMETHING EVIL.

W-WHAT? WHAT DID YOU JUST SAY?!

GOT TO STOP US. NEED TO FOCUS.

REGAIN CONTROL BEFORE WE KILL THIS MAN.

LOSING GROUND. DARK...SEEPING IN... AROUND...EDGE...

FIGHT THIS! BE STRONGER, BROCK!

TSSS

R-REX!

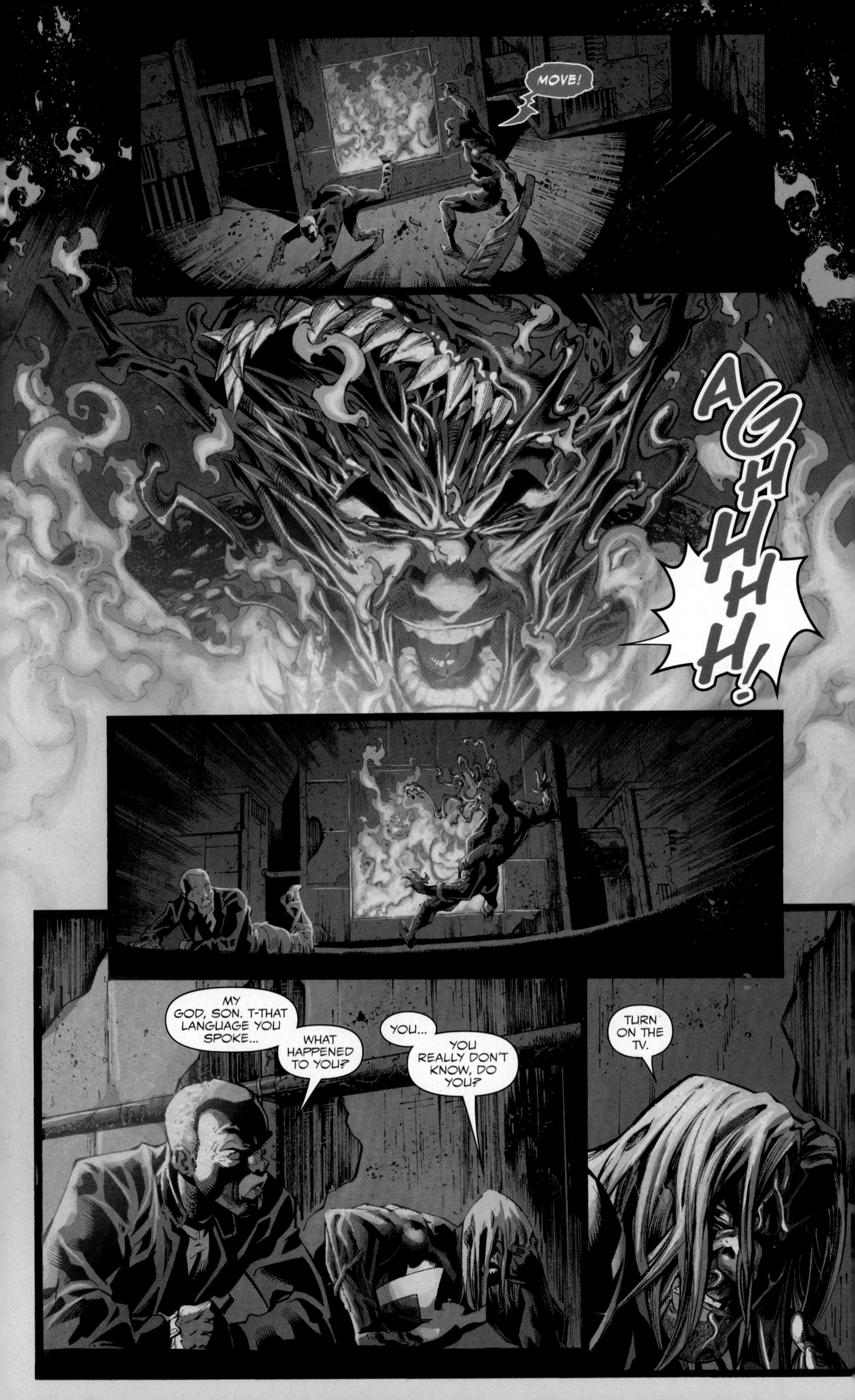
MOVE!
AGHHHHH!
MY GOD, SON. T-THAT LANGUAGE YOU SPOKE...
WHAT HAPPENED TO YOU?
YOU...
YOU REALLY DON'T KNOW, DO YOU?
TURN ON THE TV.

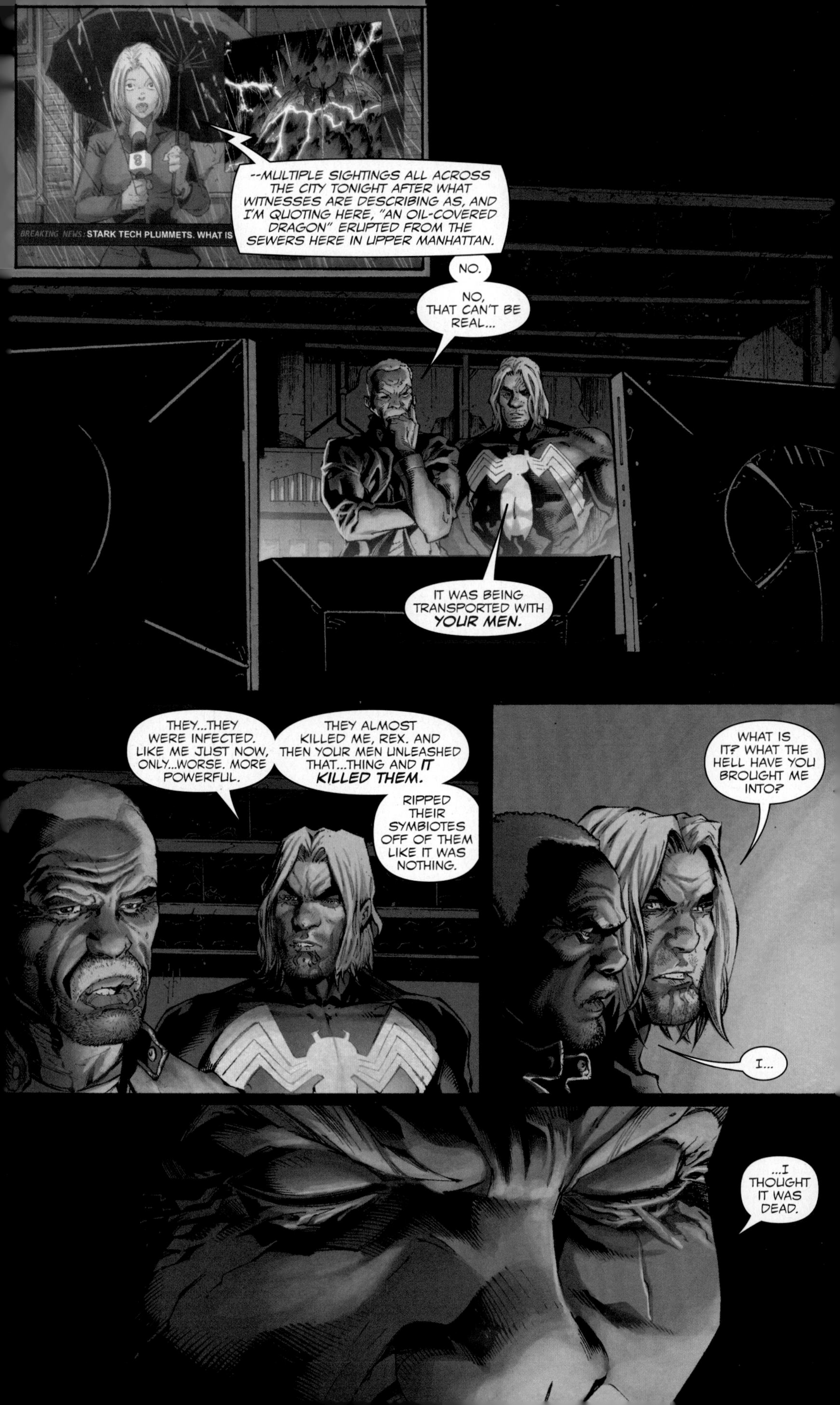
BREAKING NEWS: STARK TECH PLUMMETS. WHAT IS
--MULTIPLE SIGHTINGS ALL ACROSS THE CITY TONIGHT AFTER WHAT WITNESSES ARE DESCRIBING AS, AND I'M QUOTING HERE, "AN OIL-COVERED DRAGON" ERUPTED FROM THE SEWERS HERE IN UPPER MANHATTAN.
NO.
NO, THAT CAN'T BE REAL...
IT WAS BEING TRANSPORTED WITH YOUR MEN.
THEY...THEY WERE INFECTED. LIKE ME JUST NOW, ONLY...WORSE. MORE POWERFUL.
THEY ALMOST KILLED ME, REX. AND THEN YOUR MEN UNLEASHED THAT...THING AND IT KILLED THEM.
RIPPED THEIR SYMBIOTES OFF OF THEM LIKE IT WAS NOTHING.
WHAT IS IT? WHAT THE HELL HAVE YOU BROUGHT ME INTO?
I...
...I THOUGHT IT WAS DEAD.

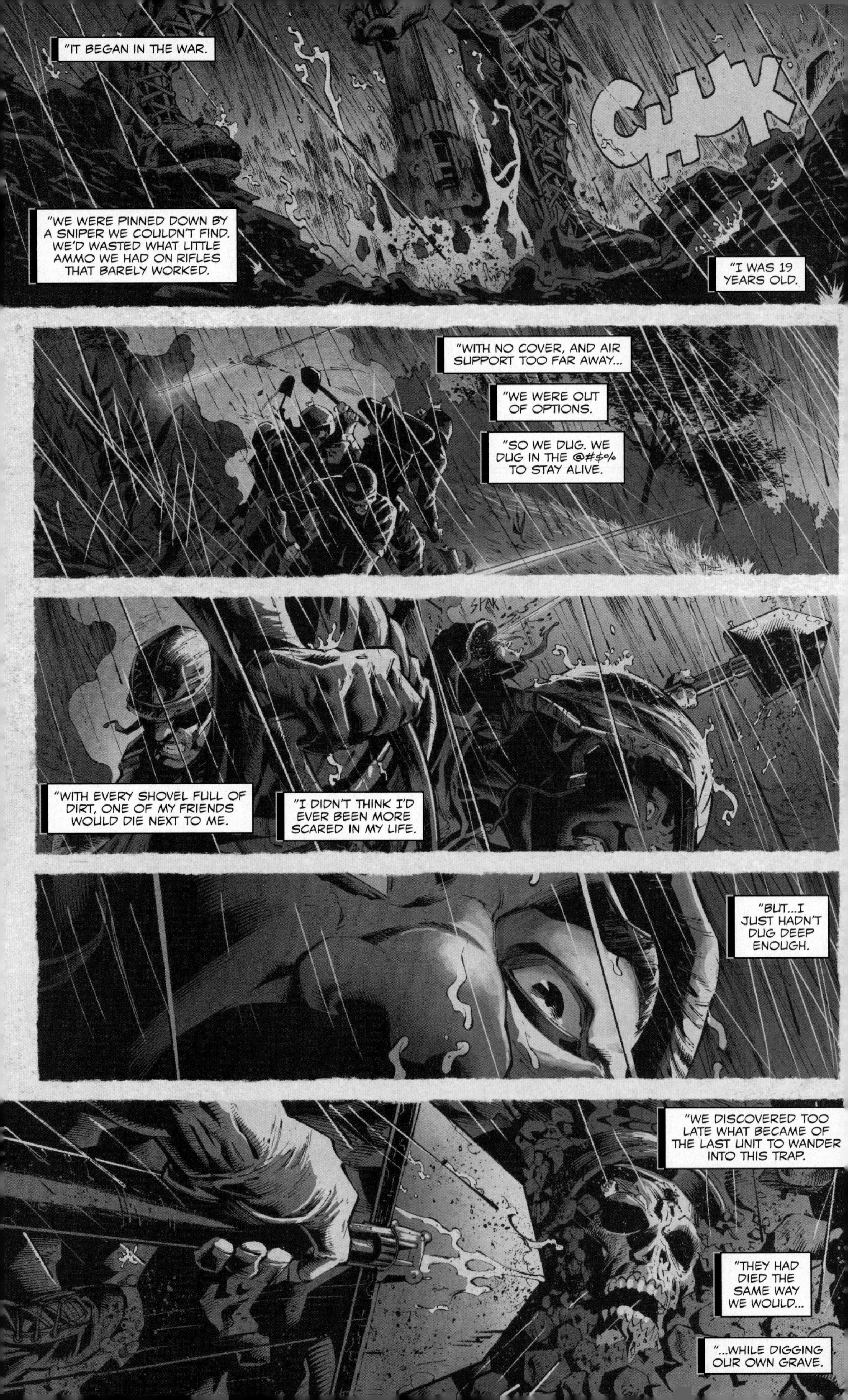
"IT BEGAN IN THE WAR.
CHUK
"WE WERE PINNED DOWN BY A SNIPER WE COULDN'T FIND. WE'D WASTED WHAT LITTLE AMMO WE HAD ON RIFLES THAT BARELY WORKED.
"I WAS 19 YEARS OLD.
"WITH NO COVER, AND AIR SUPPORT TOO FAR AWAY...
"WE WERE OUT OF OPTIONS.
"SO WE DUG. WE DUG IN THE @#$% TO STAY ALIVE.
SPAK
"WITH EVERY SHOVEL FULL OF DIRT, ONE OF MY FRIENDS WOULD DIE NEXT TO ME.
"I DIDN'T THINK I'D EVER BEEN MORE SCARED IN MY LIFE.
"BUT...I JUST HADN'T DUG DEEP ENOUGH.
"WE DISCOVERED TOO LATE WHAT BECAME OF THE LAST UNIT TO WANDER INTO THIS TRAP.
"THEY HAD DIED THE SAME WAY WE WOULD...
"...WHILE DIGGING OUR OWN GRAVE.

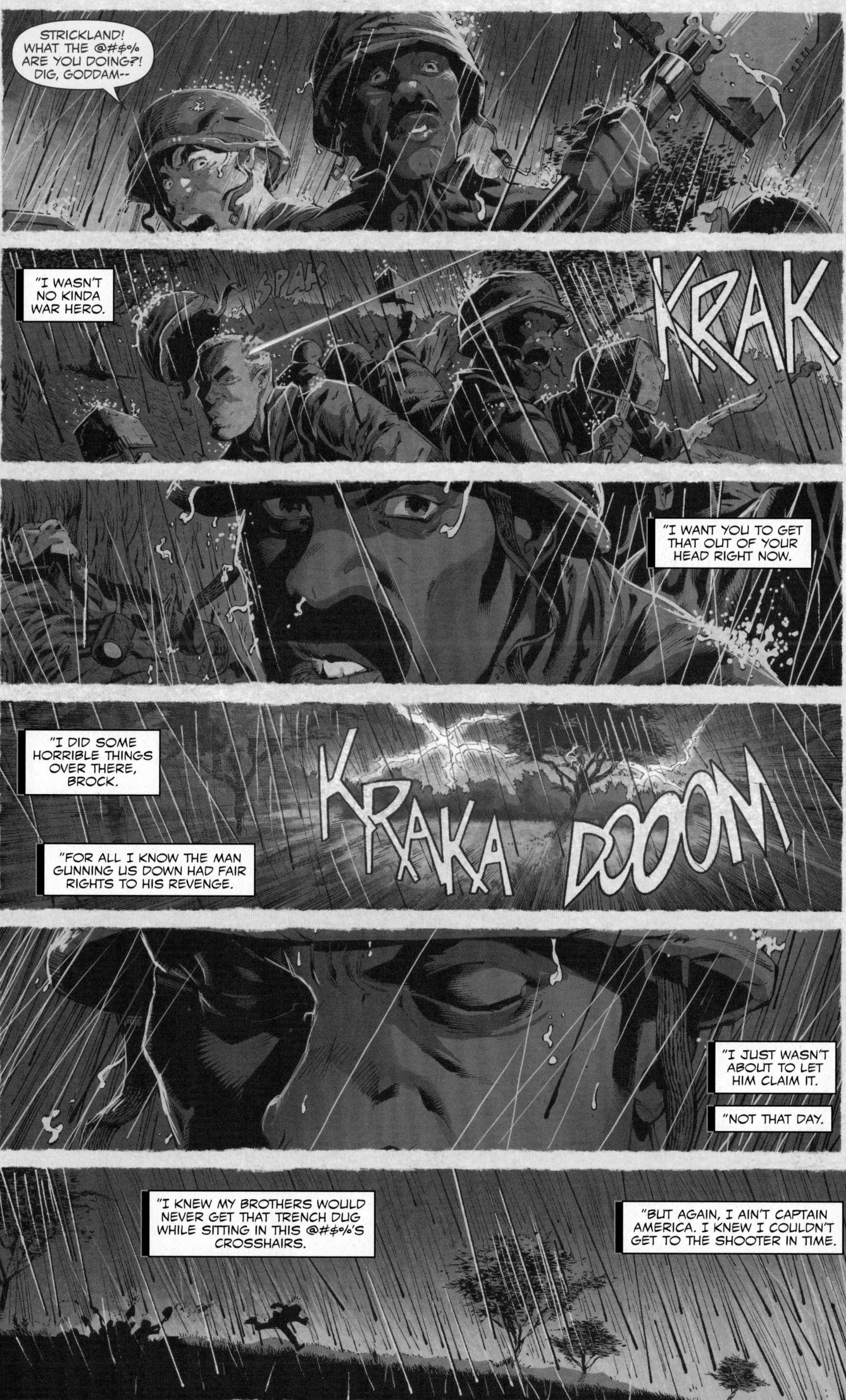
STRICKLAND! WHAT THE @#$% ARE YOU DOING?! DIG, GODDAM--
"I WASN'T NO KINDA WAR HERO.
KRAK
"I WANT YOU TO GET THAT OUT OF YOUR HEAD RIGHT NOW.
"I DID SOME HORRIBLE THINGS OVER THERE, BROCK.
"FOR ALL I KNOW THE MAN GUNNING US DOWN HAD FAIR RIGHTS TO HIS REVENGE.
KRAKA DOOOM
"I JUST WASN'T ABOUT TO LET HIM CLAIM IT.
"NOT THAT DAY.
"I KNEW MY BROTHERS WOULD NEVER GET THAT TRENCH DUG WHILE SITTING IN THIS @#$%'S CROSSHAIRS.
"BUT AGAIN, I AIN'T CAPTAIN AMERICA. I KNEW I COULDN'T GET TO THE SHOOTER IN TIME.

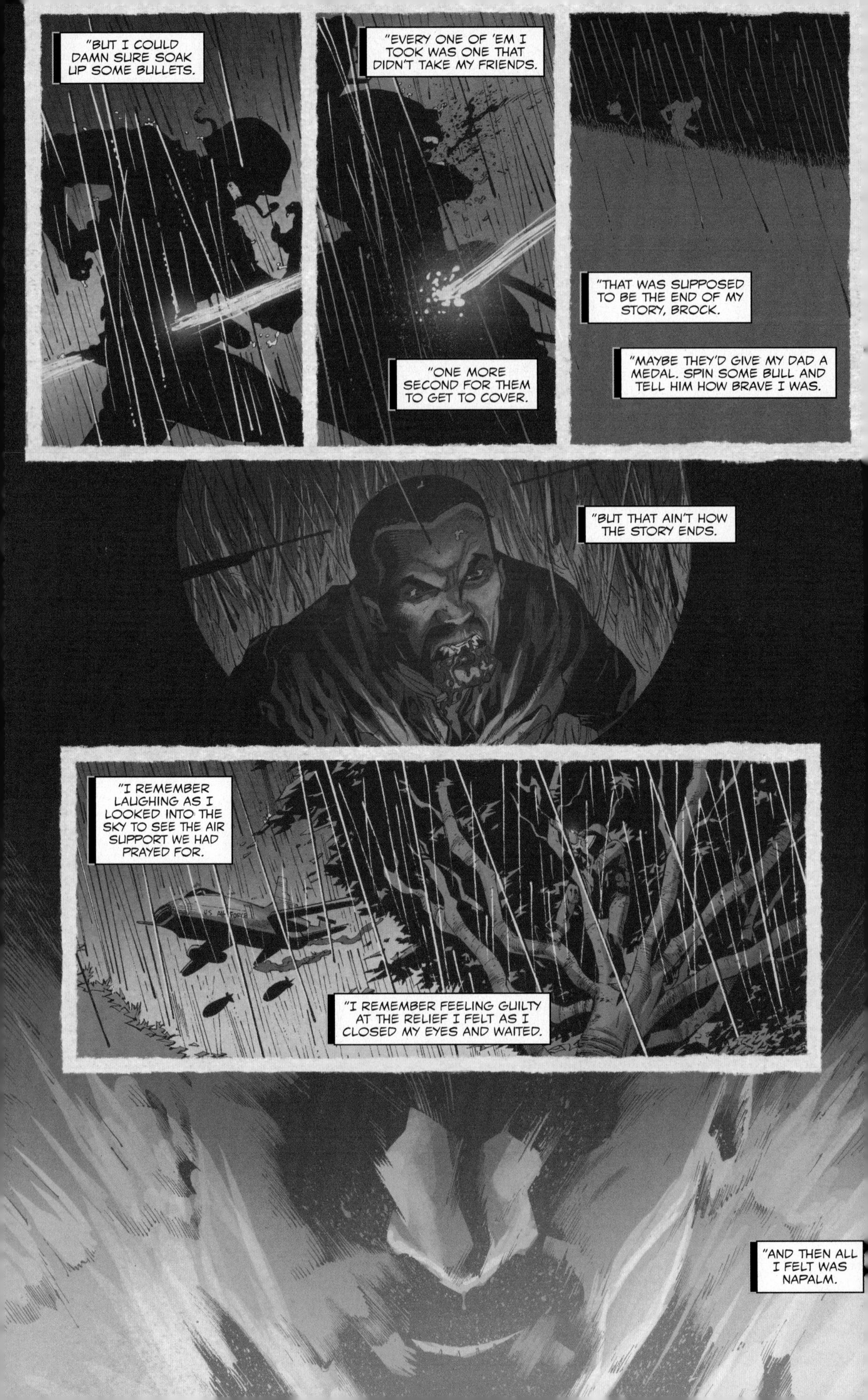
"BUT I COULD DAMN SURE SOAK UP SOME BULLETS.
"EVERY ONE OF 'EM I TOOK WAS ONE THAT DIDN'T TAKE MY FRIENDS.
"ONE MORE SECOND FOR THEM TO GET TO COVER.
"THAT WAS SUPPOSED TO BE THE END OF MY STORY, BROCK.
"MAYBE THEY'D GIVE MY DAD A MEDAL. SPIN SOME BULL AND TELL HIM HOW BRAVE I WAS.
"BUT THAT AIN'T HOW THE STORY ENDS.
"I REMEMBER LAUGHING AS I LOOKED INTO THE SKY TO SEE THE AIR SUPPORT WE HAD PRAYED FOR.
"I REMEMBER FEELING GUILTY AT THE RELIEF I FELT AS I CLOSED MY EYES AND WAITED.
"AND THEN ALL I FELT WAS NAPALM.

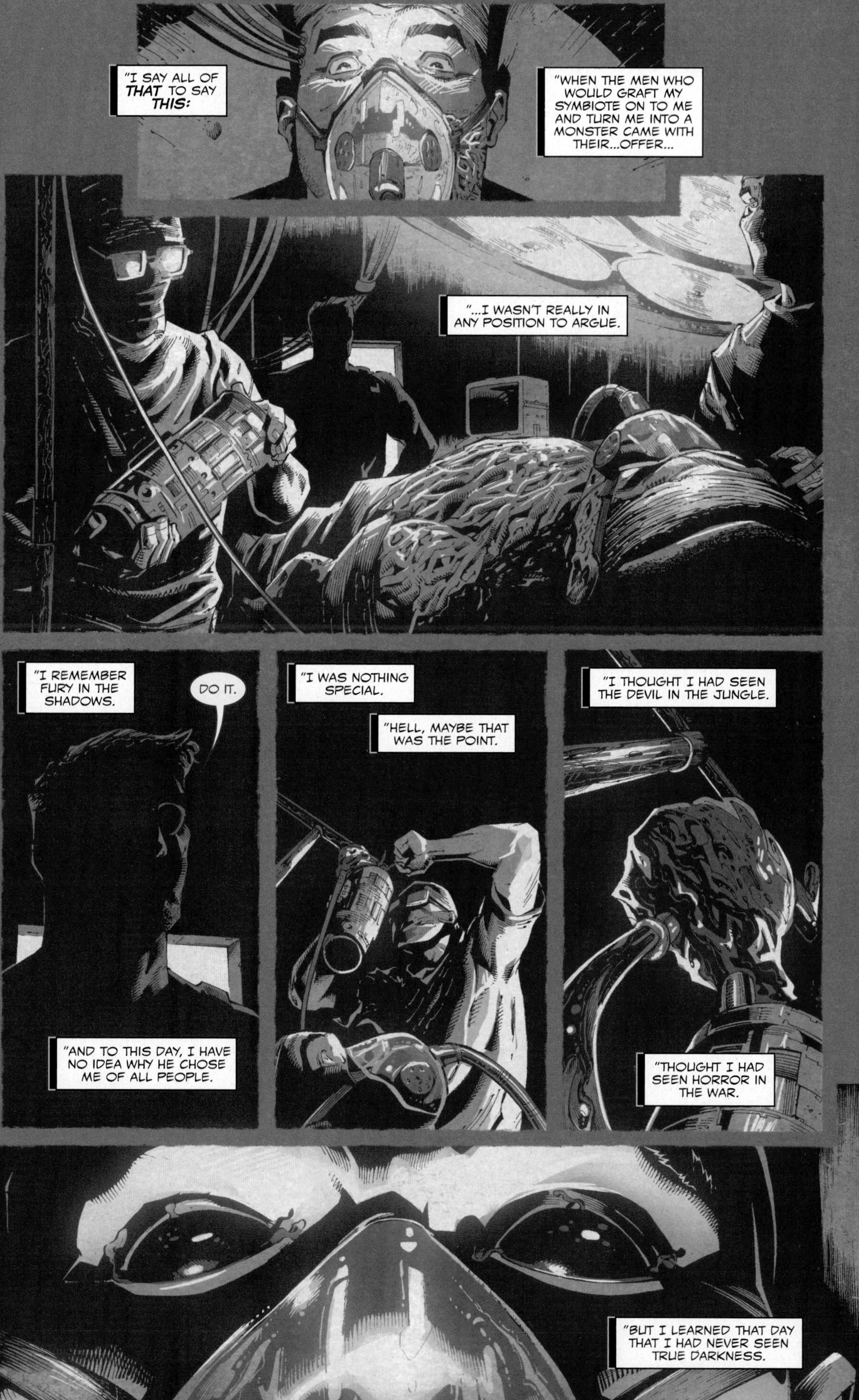
"I SAY ALL OF THAT TO SAY THIS:
"WHEN THE MEN WHO WOULD GRAFT MY SYMBIOTE ON TO ME AND TURN ME INTO A MONSTER CAME WITH THEIR...OFFER...
"...I WASN'T REALLY IN ANY POSITION TO ARGUE.
"I REMEMBER FURY IN THE SHADOWS.
DO IT.
"AND TO THIS DAY, I HAVE NO IDEA WHY HE CHOSE ME OF ALL PEOPLE.
"I WAS NOTHING SPECIAL.
"HELL, MAYBE THAT WAS THE POINT.
"I THOUGHT I HAD SEEN THE DEVIL IN THE JUNGLE.
"THOUGHT I HAD SEEN HORROR IN THE WAR.
"BUT I LEARNED THAT DAY THAT I HAD NEVER SEEN TRUE DARKNESS.

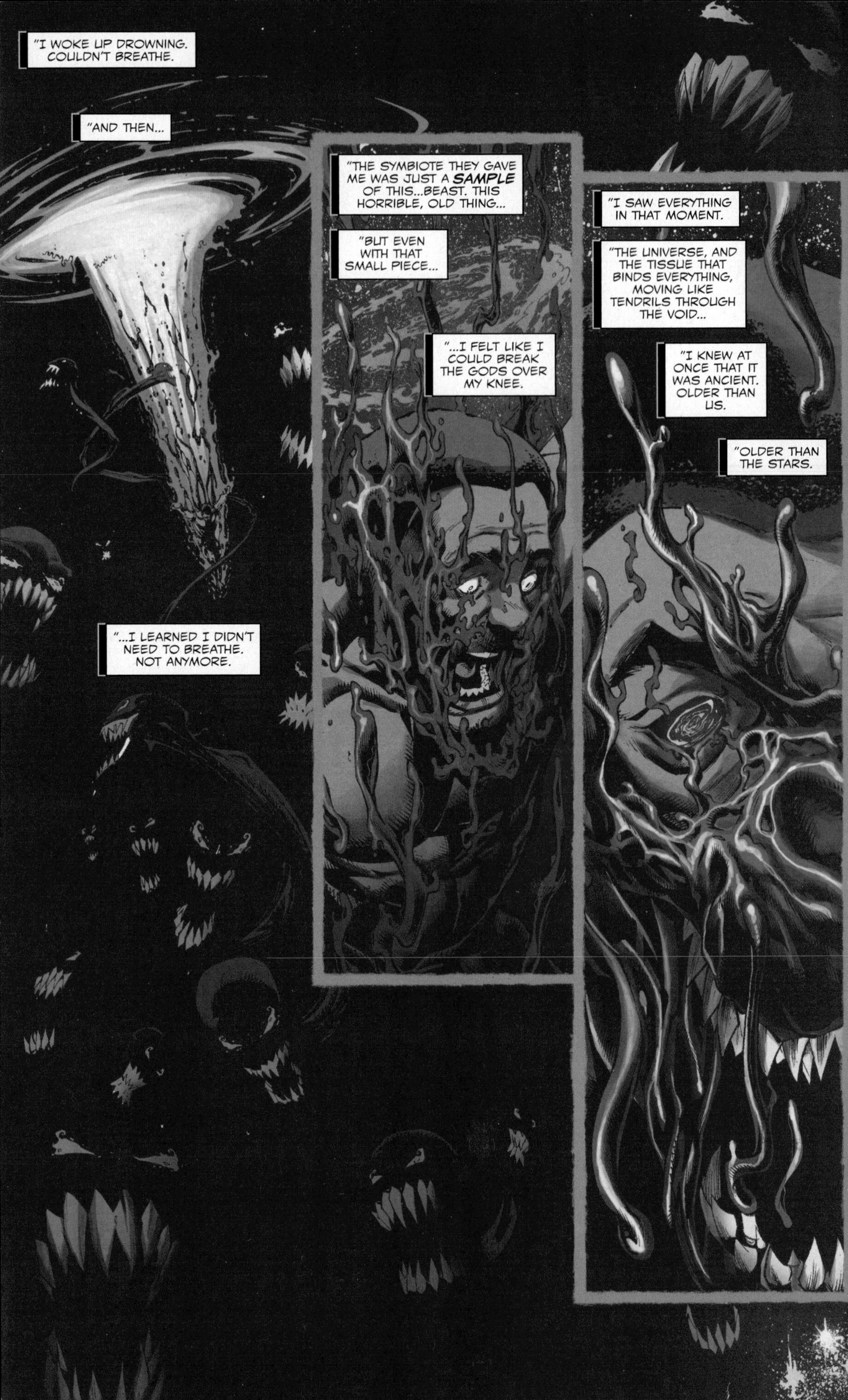
"I WOKE UP DROWNING. COULDN'T BREATHE.
"AND THEN...
"...I LEARNED I DIDN'T NEED TO BREATHE. NOT ANYMORE.
"THE SYMBIOTE THEY GAVE ME WAS JUST A SAMPLE OF THIS...BEAST. THIS HORRIBLE, OLD THING...
"BUT EVEN WITH THAT SMALL PIECE...
"...I FELT LIKE I COULD BREAK THE GODS OVER MY KNEE.
"I SAW EVERYTHING IN THAT MOMENT.
"THE UNIVERSE, AND THE TISSUE THAT BINDS EVERYTHING, MOVING LIKE TENDRILS THROUGH THE VOID...
"I KNEW AT ONCE THAT IT WAS ANCIENT. OLDER THAN US.
"OLDER THAN THE STARS.

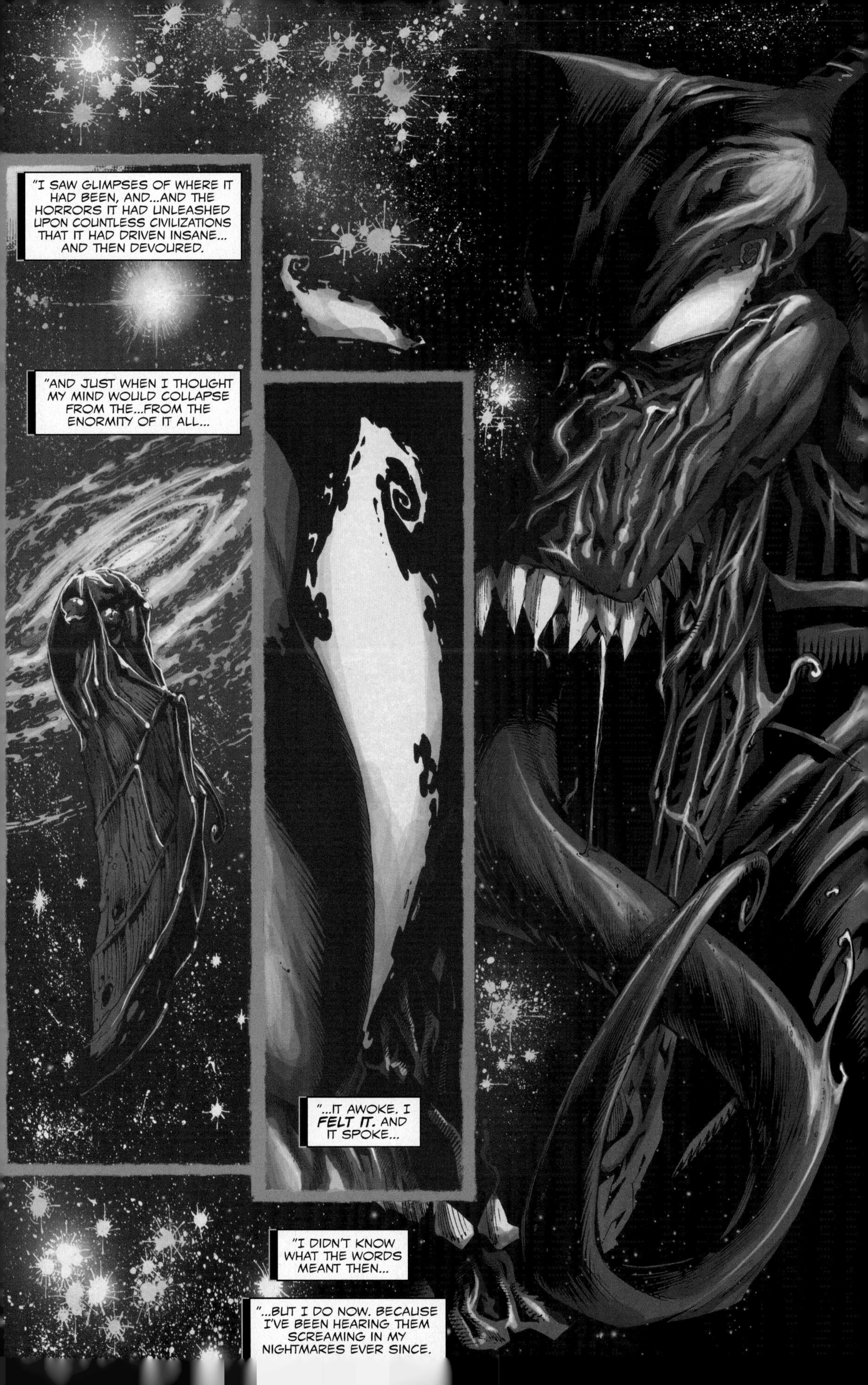
"I SAW GLIMPSES OF WHERE IT HAD BEEN, AND...AND THE HORRORS IT HAD UNLEASHED UPON COUNTLESS CIVILIZATIONS THAT IT HAD DRIVEN INSANE... AND THEN DEVOURED.
"AND JUST WHEN I THOUGHT MY MIND WOULD COLLAPSE FROM THE...FROM THE ENORMITY OF IT ALL...
"...IT AWOKE. I FELT IT. AND IT SPOKE...
"I DIDN'T KNOW WHAT THE WORDS MEANT THEN...
"...BUT I DO NOW. BECAUSE I'VE BEEN HEARING THEM SCREAMING IN MY NIGHTMARES EVER SINCE.

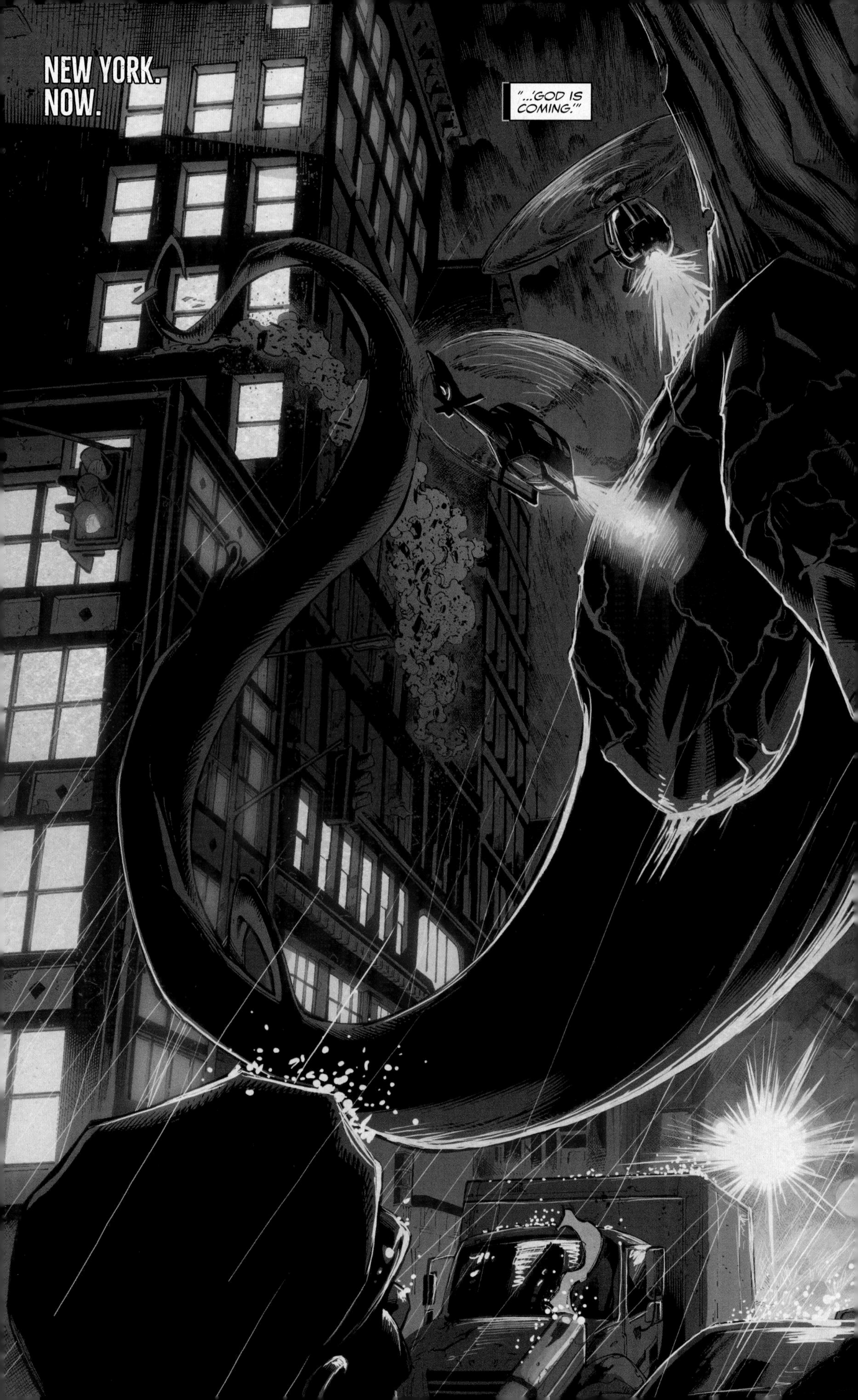
NEW YORK.
NOW.
"...'GOD IS COMING.'"

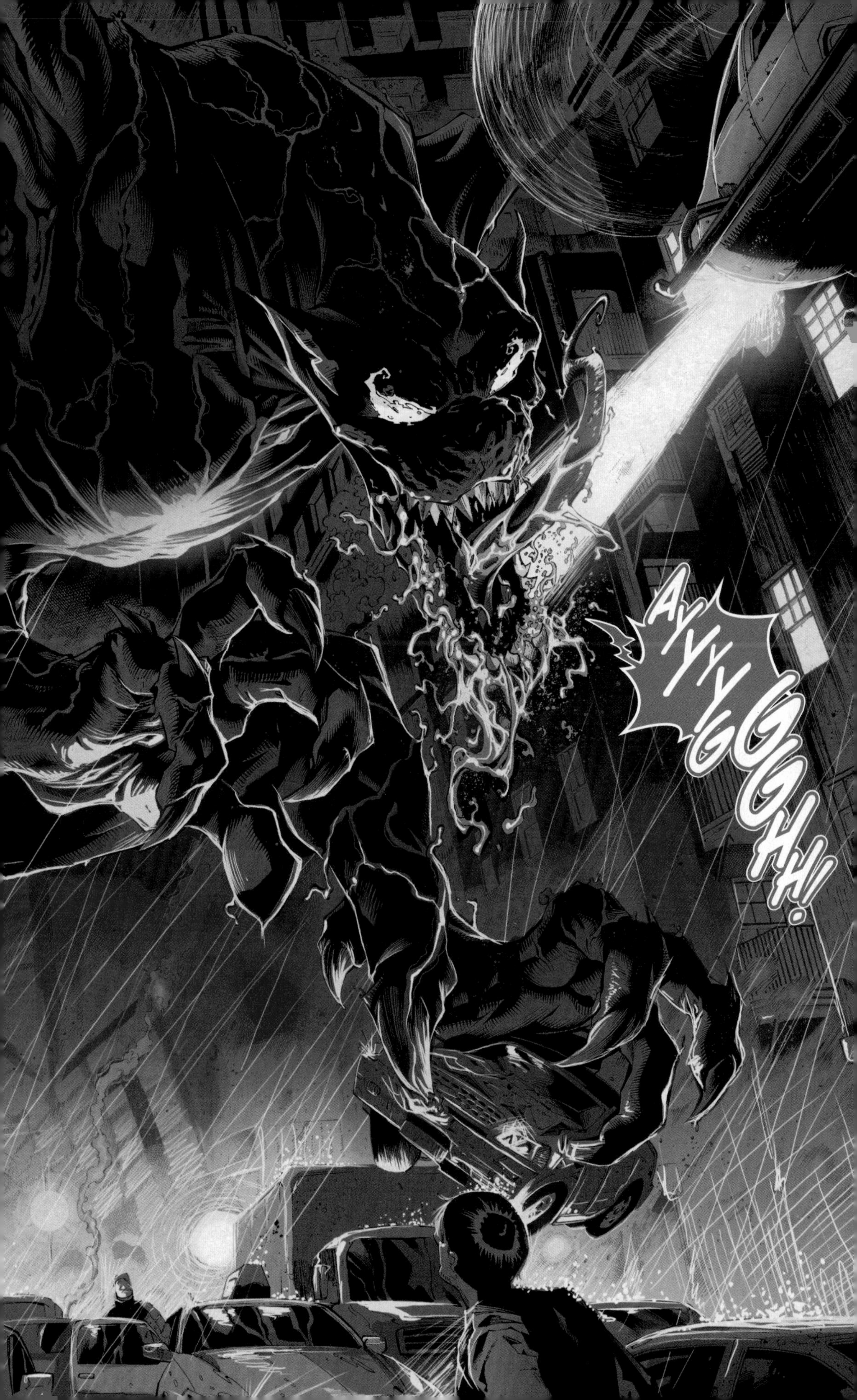
AYYYYGGGHH!

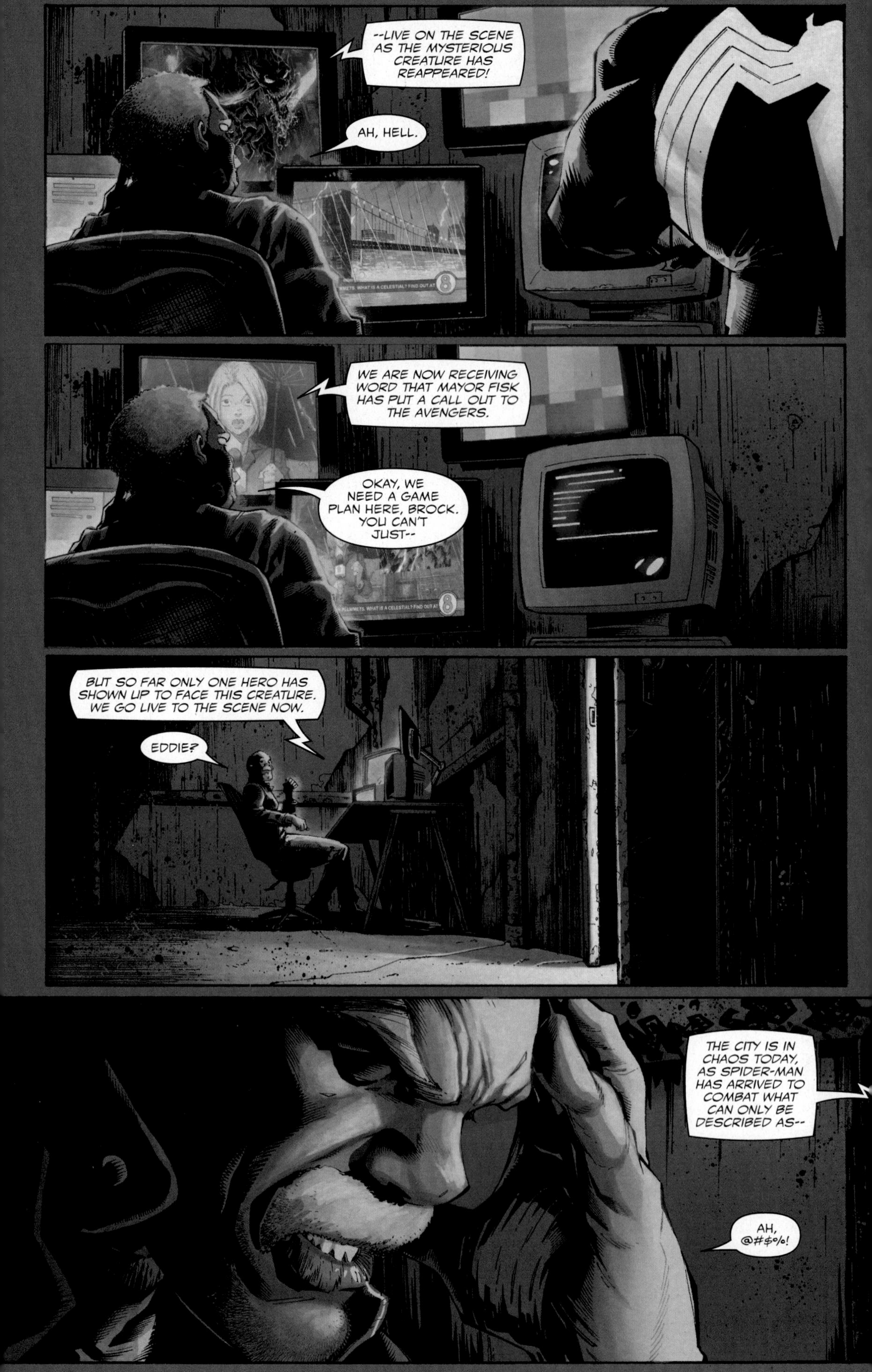
--LIVE ON THE SCENE AS THE MYSTERIOUS CREATURE HAS REAPPEARED!
AH, HELL.
WE ARE NOW RECEIVING WORD THAT MAYOR FISK HAS PUT A CALL OUT TO THE AVENGERS.
OKAY, WE NEED A GAME PLAN HERE, BROCK. YOU CAN'T JUST--
BUT SO FAR ONLY ONE HERO HAS SHOWN UP TO FACE THIS CREATURE. WE GO LIVE TO THE SCENE NOW.
EDDIE?
THE CITY IS IN CHAOS TODAY, AS SPIDER-MAN HAS ARRIVED TO COMBAT WHAT CAN ONLY BE DESCRIBED AS--
AH, @#$%!

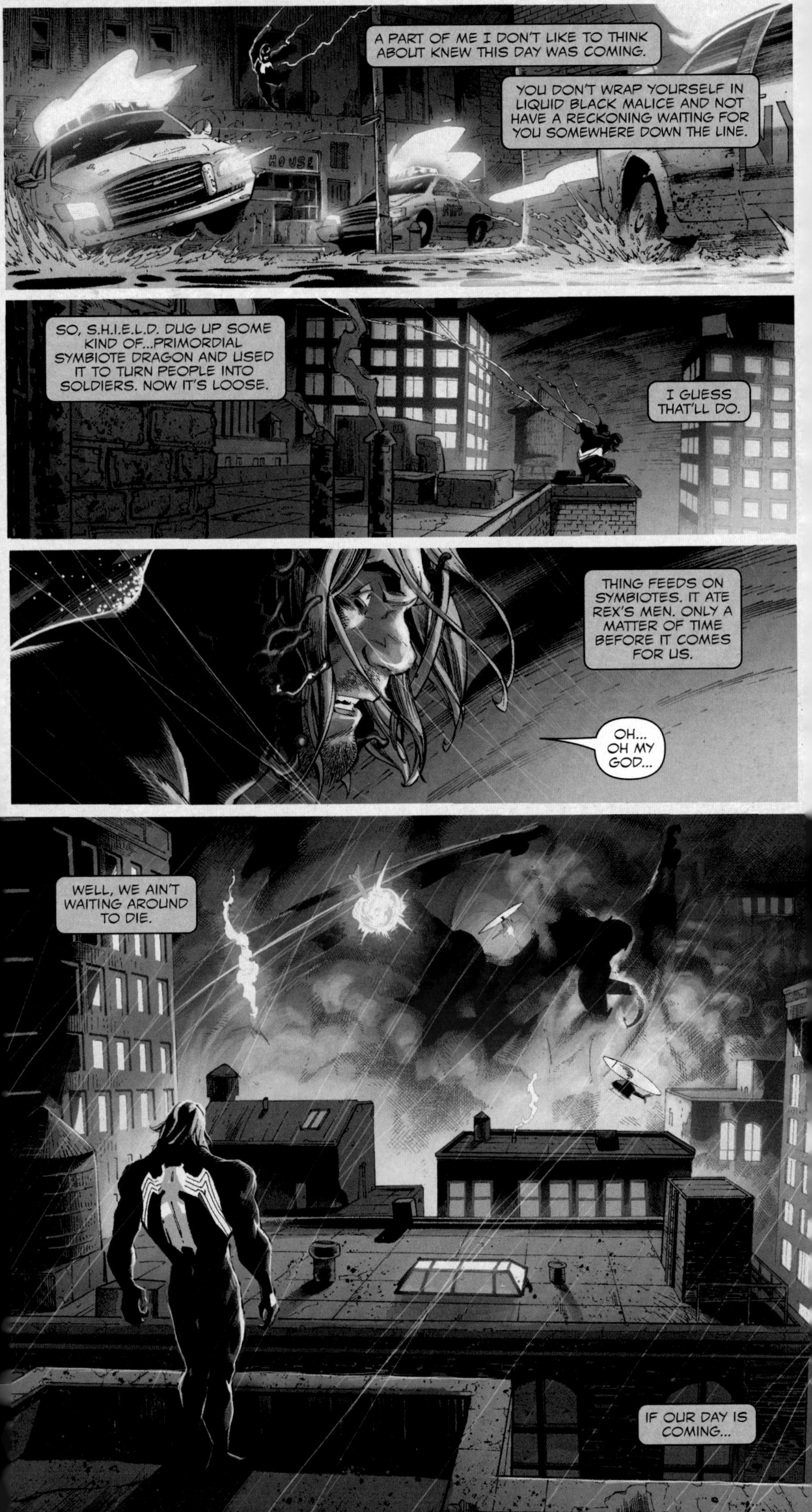
A PART OF ME I DON'T LIKE TO THINK ABOUT KNEW THIS DAY WAS COMING.
YOU DON'T WRAP YOURSELF IN LIQUID BLACK MALICE AND NOT HAVE A RECKONING WAITING FOR YOU SOMEWHERE DOWN THE LINE.
HOUSE
SO, S.H.I.E.L.D. DUG UP SOME KIND OF...PRIMORDIAL SYMBIOTE DRAGON AND USED IT TO TURN PEOPLE INTO SOLDIERS. NOW IT'S LOOSE.
I GUESS THAT'LL DO.
THING FEEDS ON SYMBIOTES. IT ATE REX'S MEN. ONLY A MATTER OF TIME BEFORE IT COMES FOR US.
OH... OH MY GOD...
WELL, WE AIN'T WAITING AROUND TO DIE.
IF OUR DAY IS COMING...

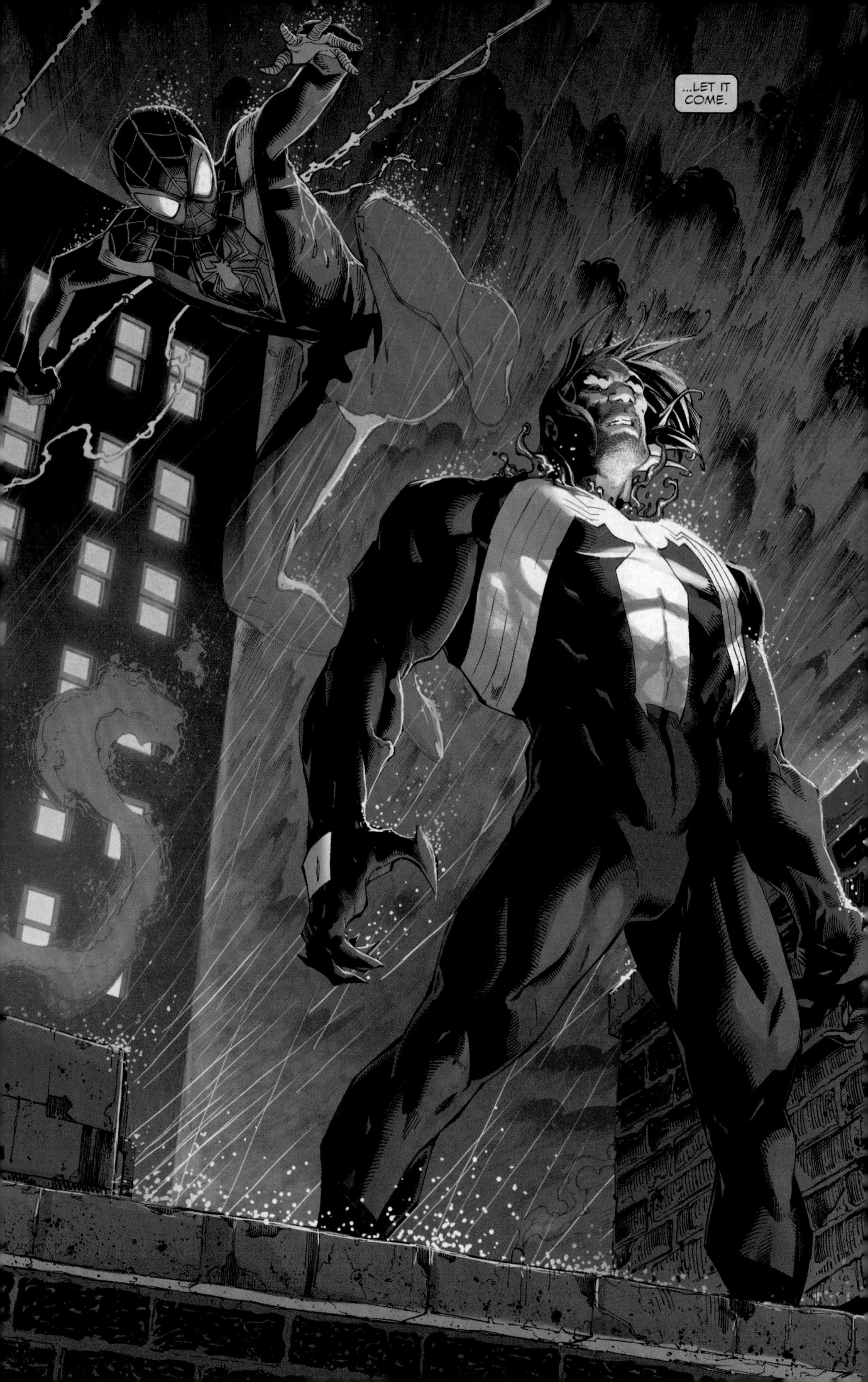
...LET IT COME.

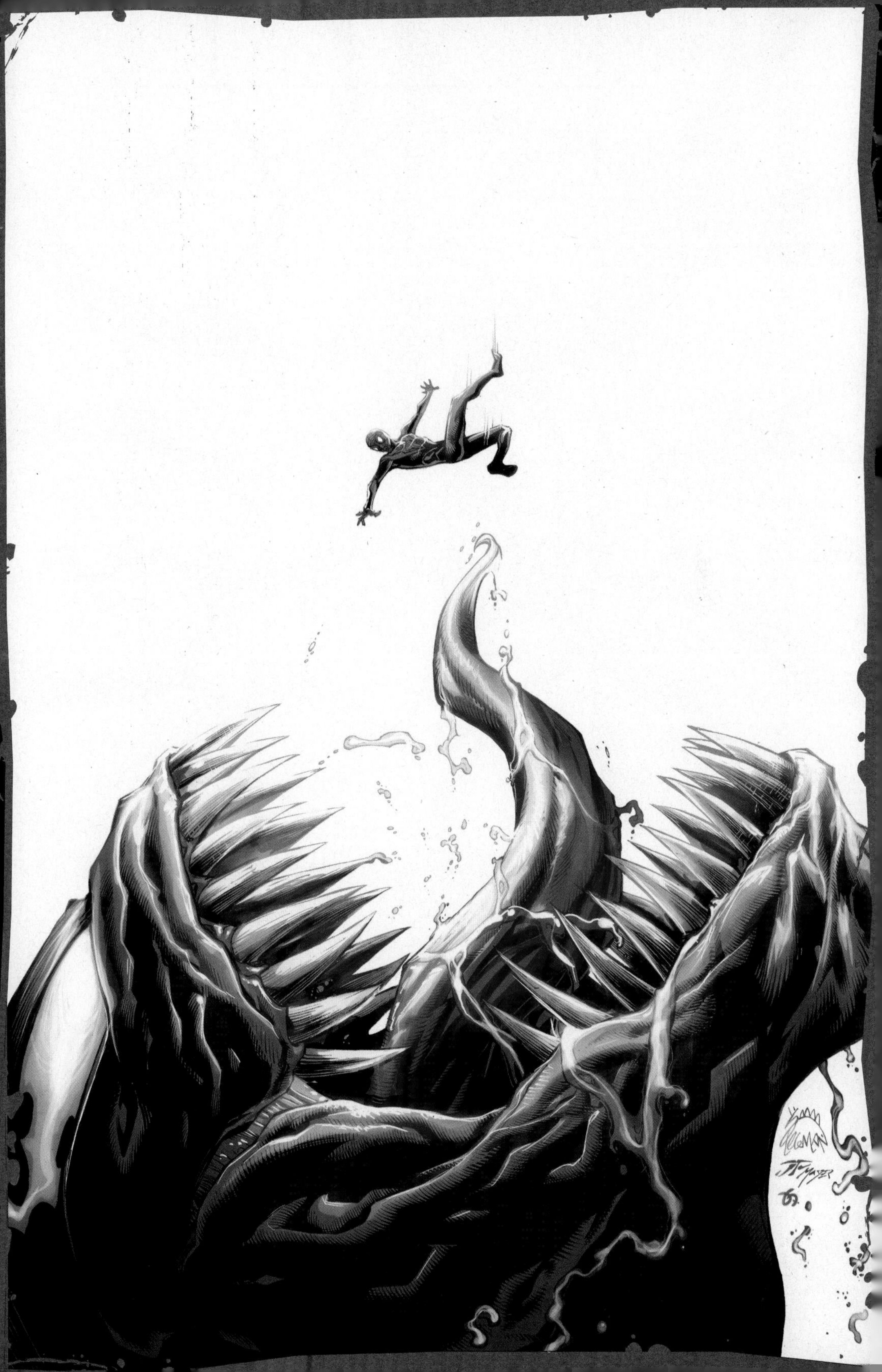

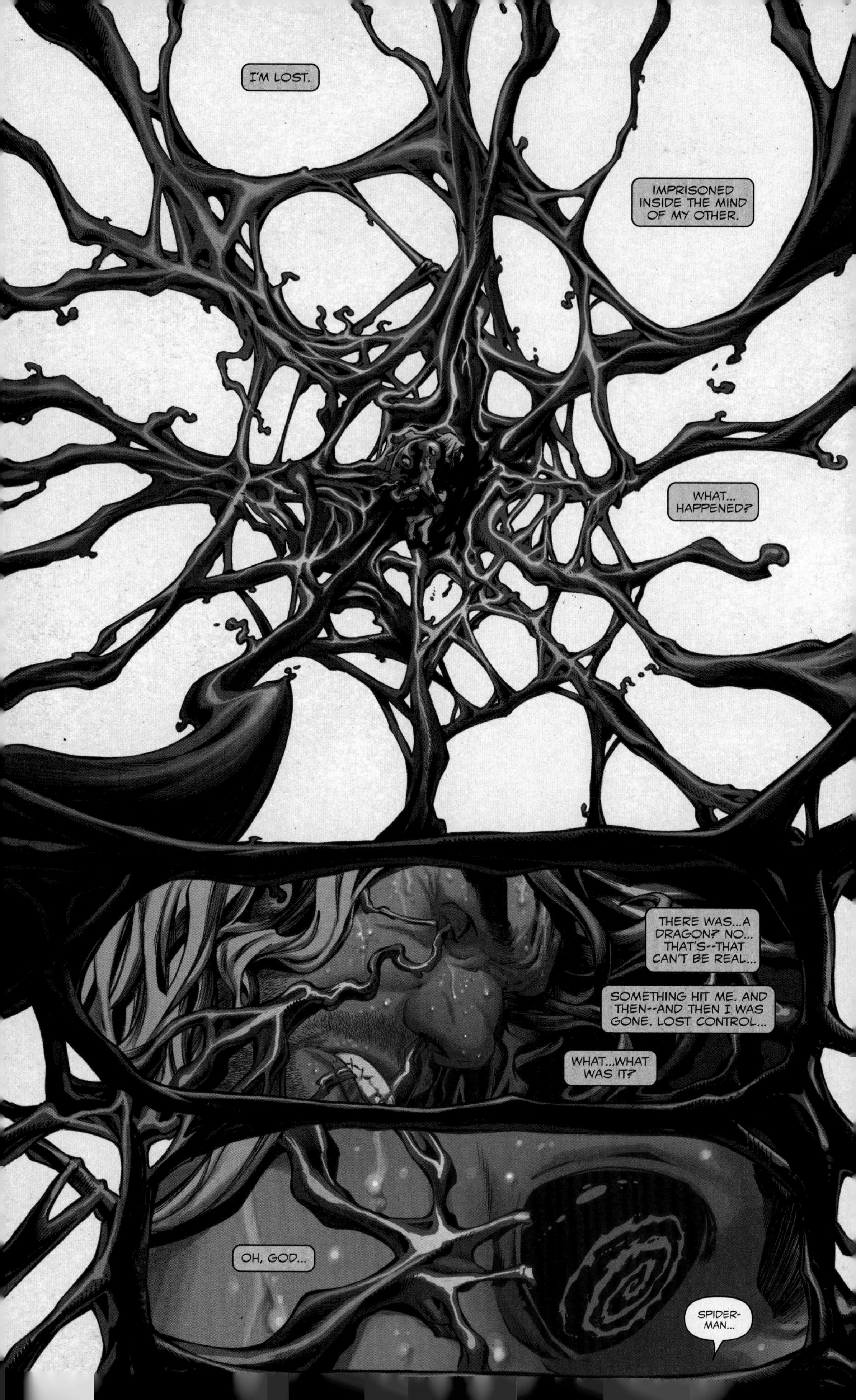
I'M LOST.
IMPRISONED INSIDE THE MIND OF MY OTHER.
WHAT... HAPPENED?
THERE WAS...A DRAGON? NO... THAT'S--THAT CAN'T BE REAL...
SOMETHING HIT ME. AND THEN--AND THEN I WAS GONE. LOST CONTROL...
WHAT...WHAT WAS IT?
OH, GOD...
SPIDER-MAN...

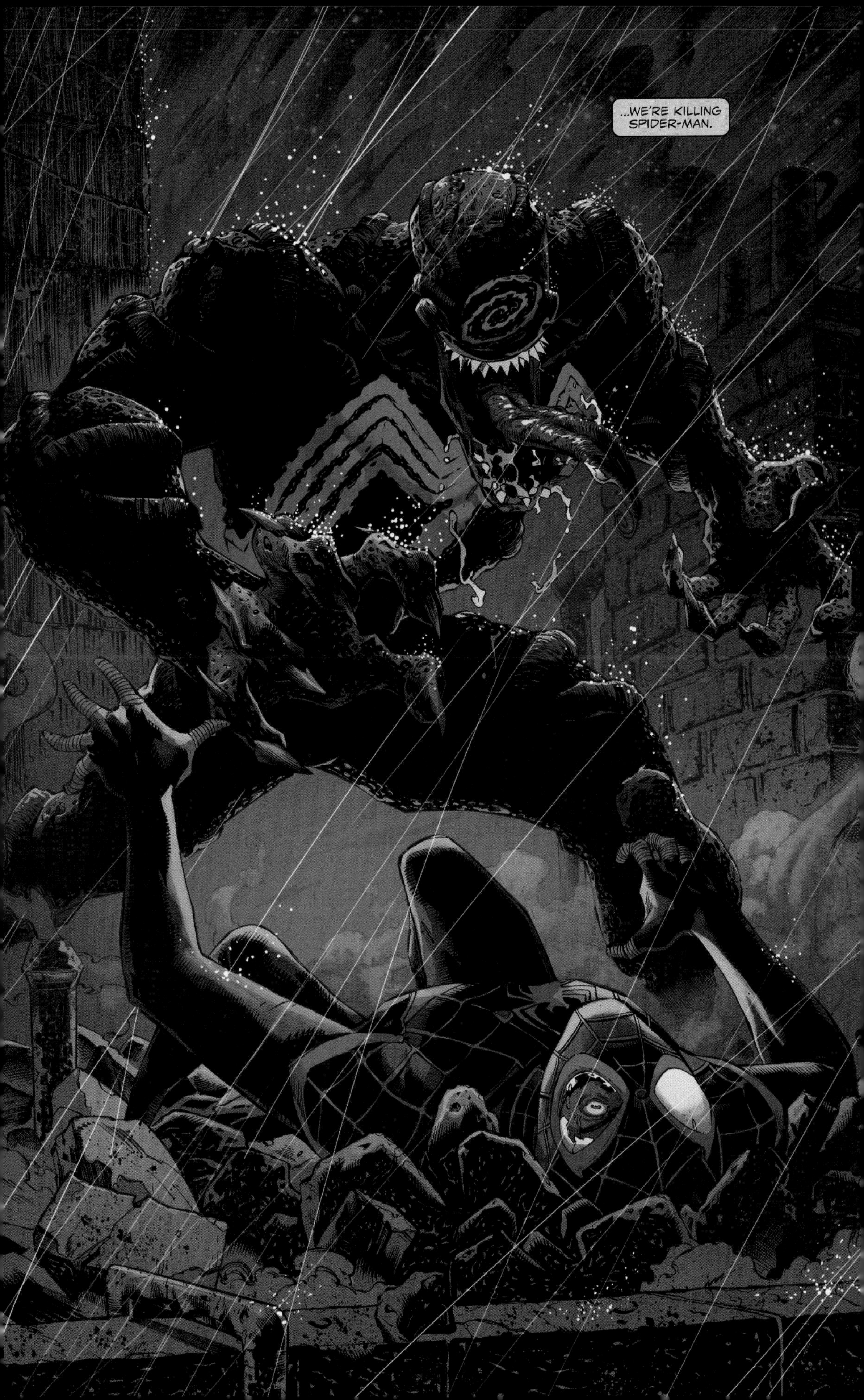
...WE'RE KILLING SPIDER-MAN.

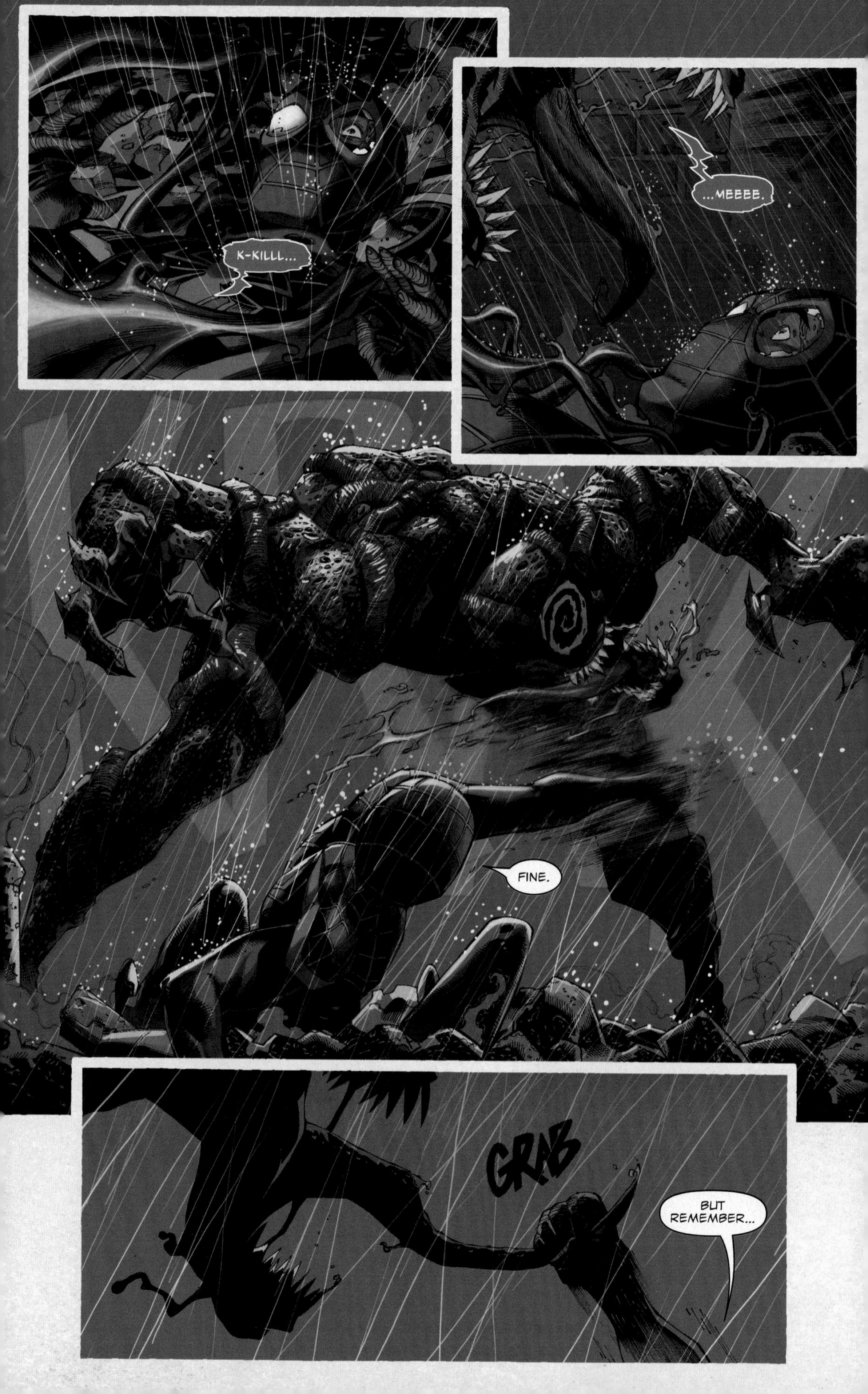
K-KILLL...
...MEEEE.
FINE.
GRAB
BUT REMEMBER...

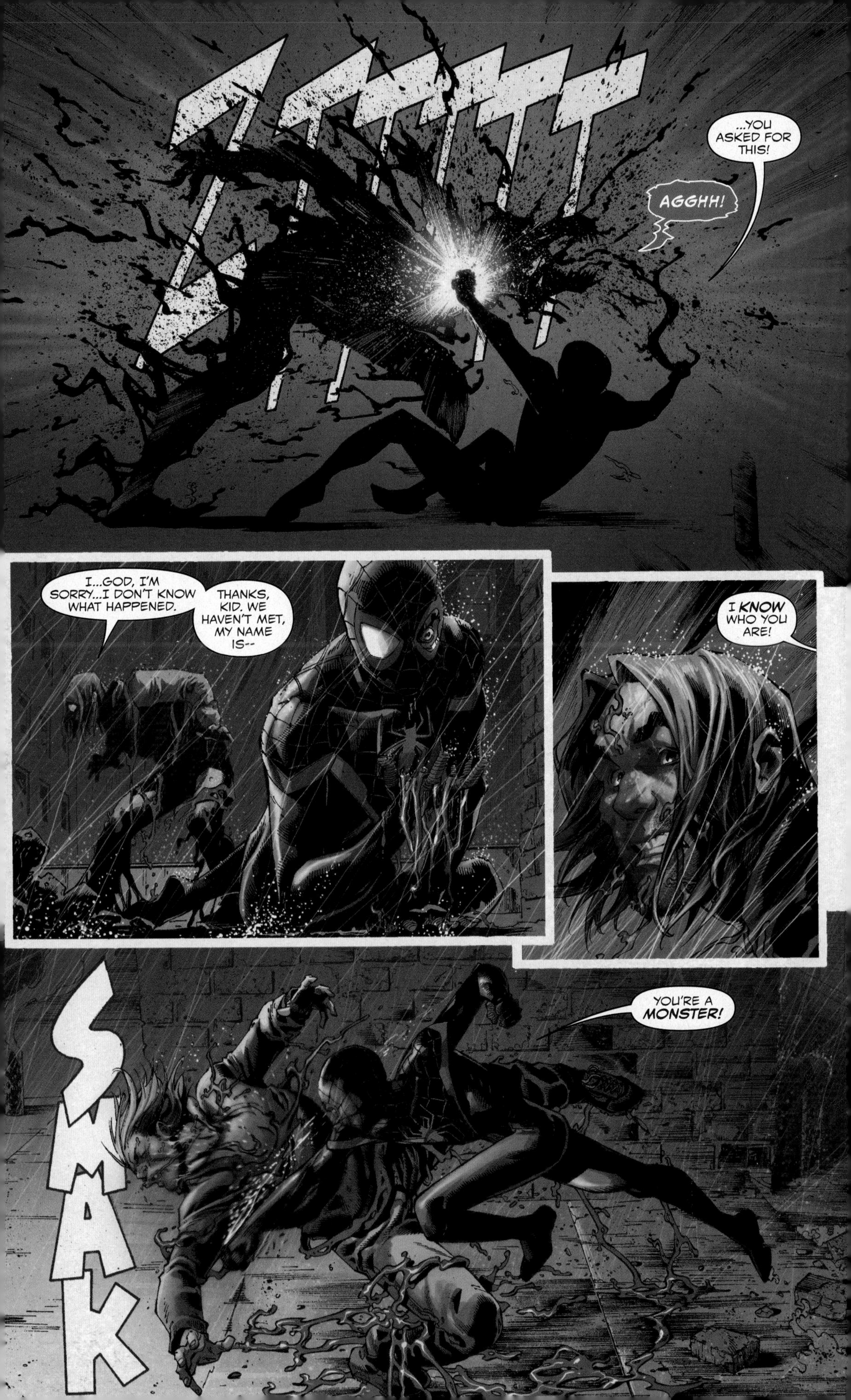
...YOU ASKED FOR THIS!
AGGHH!
I...GOD, I'M SORRY...I DON'T KNOW WHAT HAPPENED.
THANKS, KID. WE HAVEN'T MET, MY NAME IS--
I KNOW WHO YOU ARE!
SMAK
YOU'RE A MONSTER!

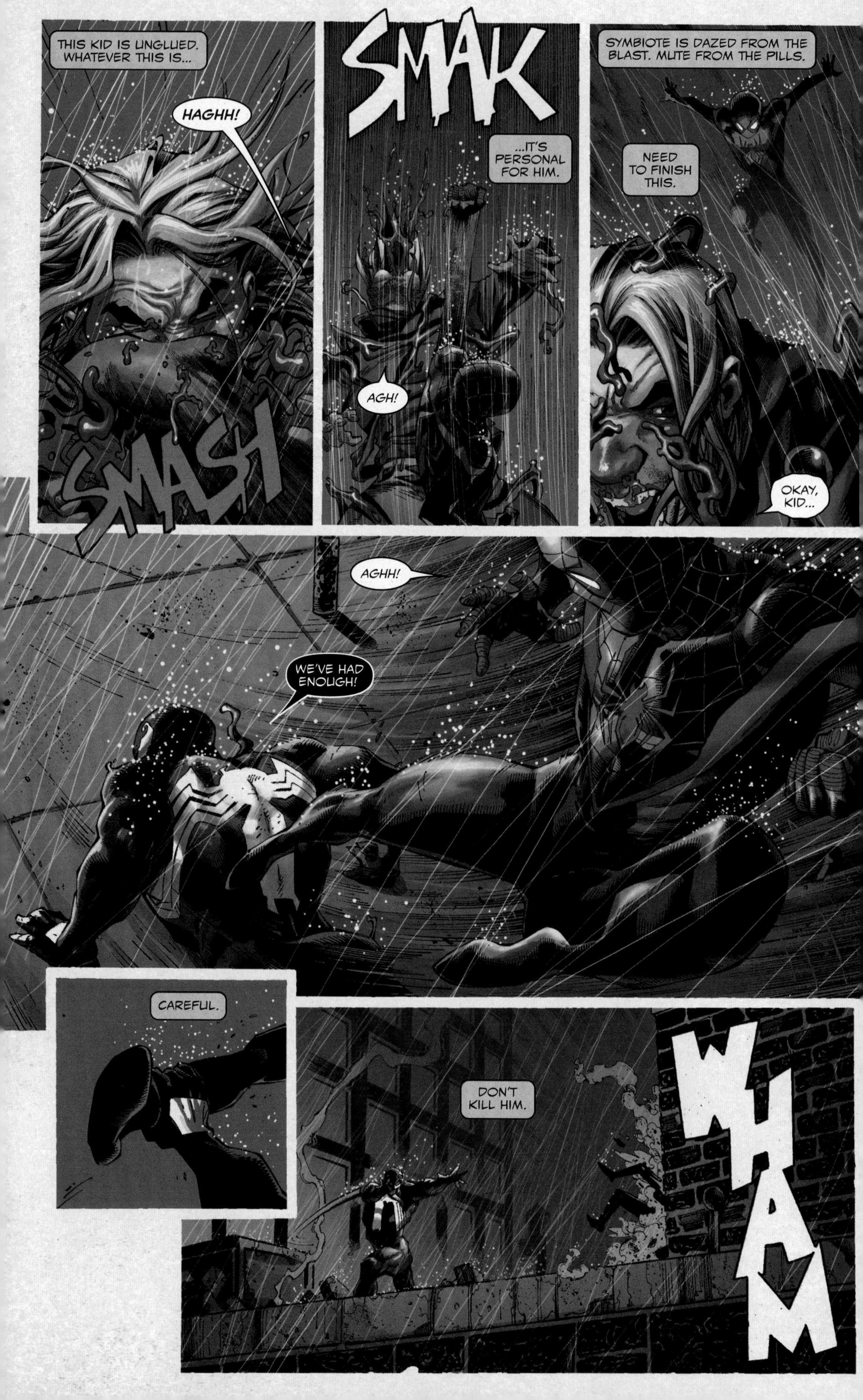
THIS KID IS UNGLUED. WHATEVER THIS IS...
HAGHH!
SMASH
SMAK
...IT'S PERSONAL FOR HIM.
AGH!
SYMBIOTE IS DAZED FROM THE BLAST. MUTE FROM THE PILLS.
NEED TO FINISH THIS.
OKAY, KID...
AGHH!
WE'VE HAD ENOUGH!
CAREFUL.
DON'T KILL HIM.
WHAM

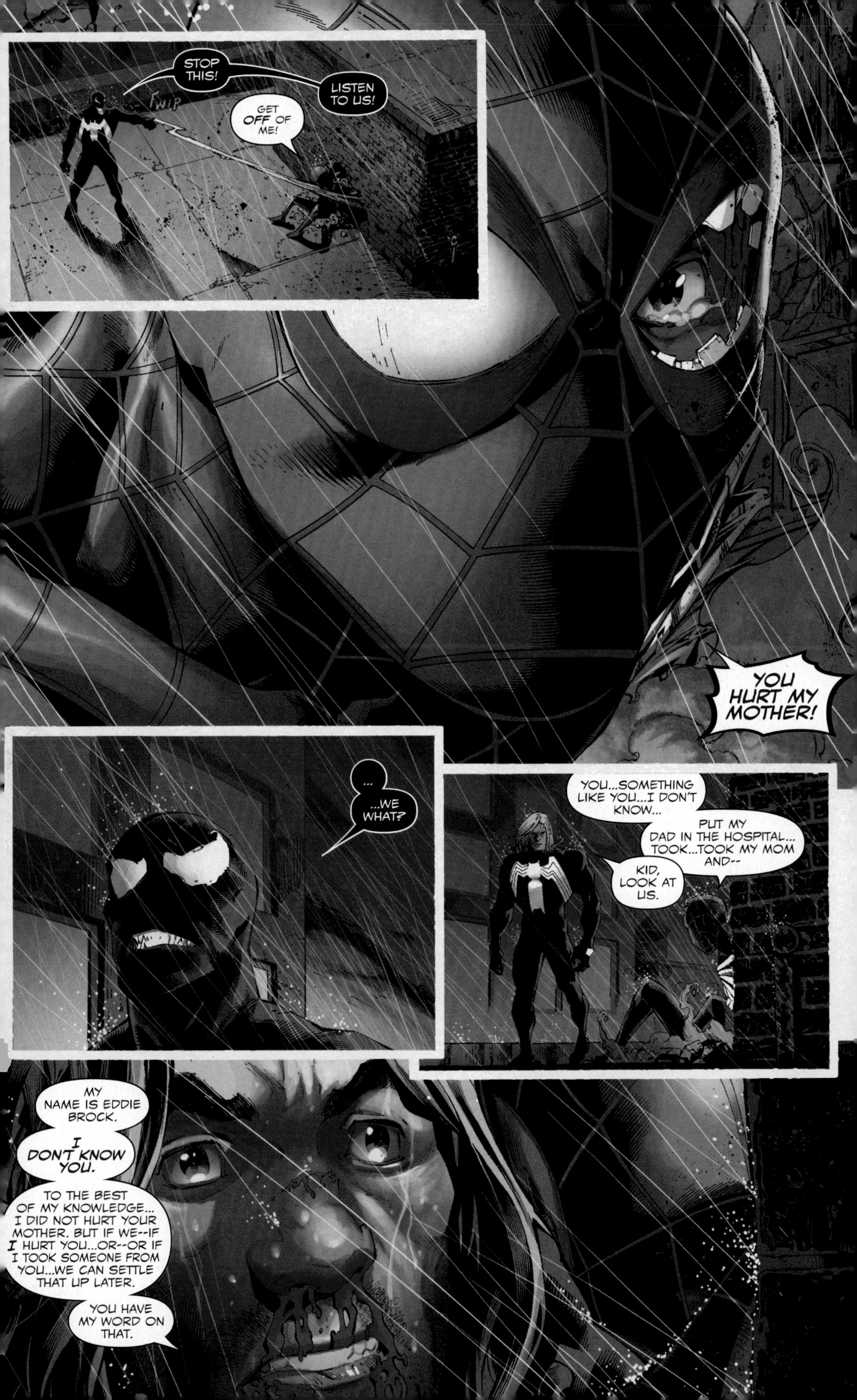
STOP THIS!
LISTEN TO US!
FWIP
GET OFF OF ME!
YOU HURT MY MOTHER!
...
...WE WHAT?
YOU...SOMETHING LIKE YOU...I DON'T KNOW...
PUT MY DAD IN THE HOSPITAL... TOOK...TOOK MY MOM AND--
KID, LOOK AT US.
MY NAME IS EDDIE BROCK.
I DON'T KNOW YOU.
TO THE BEST OF MY KNOWLEDGE... I DID NOT HURT YOUR MOTHER. BUT IF WE--IF I HURT YOU...OR--OR IF I TOOK SOMEONE FROM YOU...WE CAN SETTLE THAT UP LATER.
YOU HAVE MY WORD ON THAT.

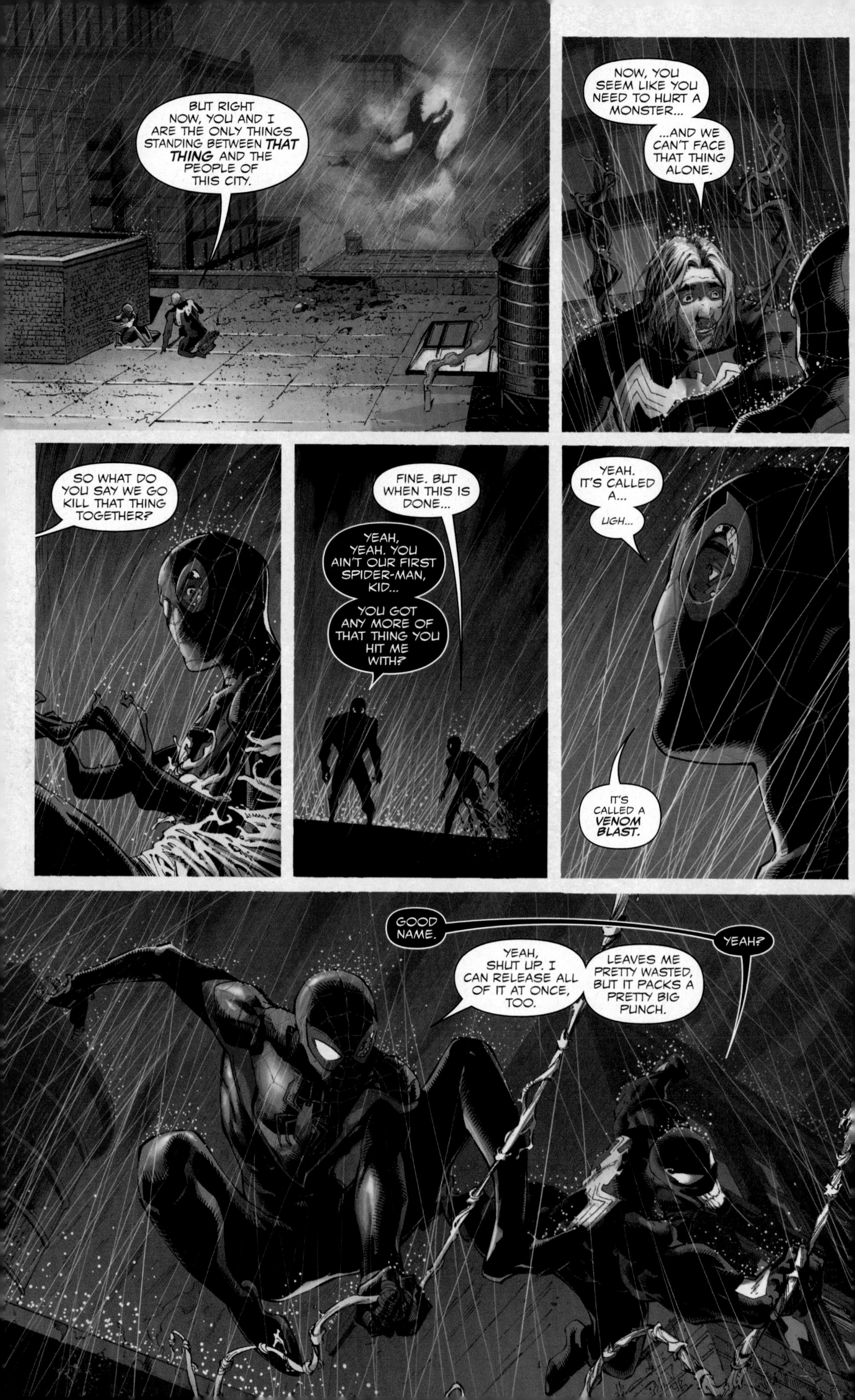
BUT RIGHT NOW, YOU AND I ARE THE ONLY THINGS STANDING BETWEEN THAT THING AND THE PEOPLE OF THIS CITY.
NOW, YOU SEEM LIKE YOU NEED TO HURT A MONSTER...
...AND WE CAN'T FACE THAT THING ALONE.
SO WHAT DO YOU SAY WE GO KILL THAT THING TOGETHER?
FINE. BUT WHEN THIS IS DONE...
YEAH, YEAH. YOU AIN'T OUR FIRST SPIDER-MAN, KID...
YOU GOT ANY MORE OF THAT THING YOU HIT ME WITH?
YEAH. IT'S CALLED A...
UGH...
IT'S CALLED A VENOM BLAST.
GOOD NAME.
YEAH?
YEAH, SHUT UP. I CAN RELEASE ALL OF IT AT ONCE, TOO.
LEAVES ME PRETTY WASTED, BUT IT PACKS A PRETTY BIG PUNCH.

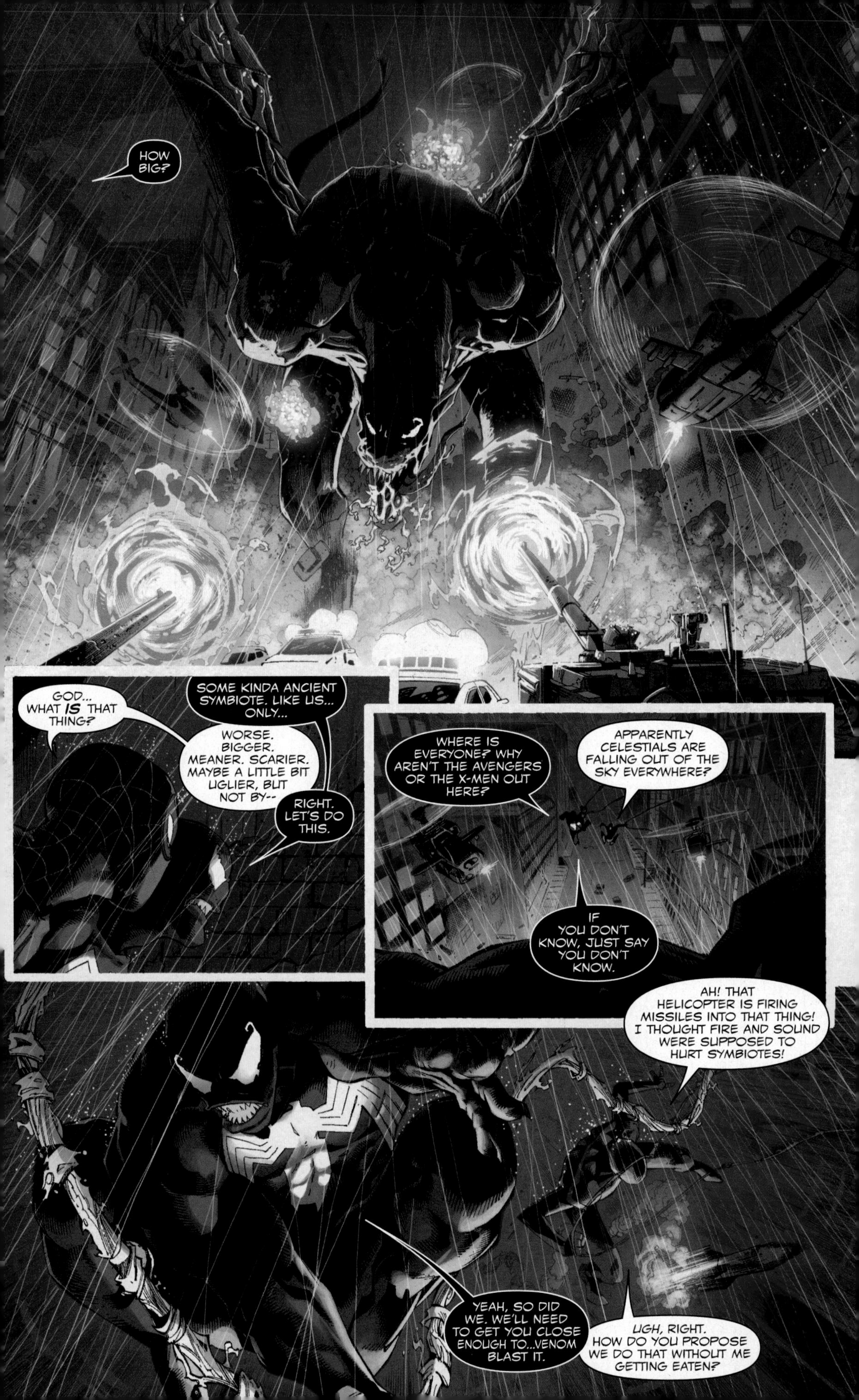

HOW BIG?
GOD... WHAT IS THAT THING?
SOME KINDA ANCIENT SYMBIOTE. LIKE US... ONLY...
WORSE. BIGGER. MEANER. SCARIER. MAYBE A LITTLE BIT UGLIER, BUT NOT BY--
RIGHT. LET'S DO THIS.
WHERE IS EVERYONE? WHY AREN'T THE AVENGERS OR THE X-MEN OUT HERE?
APPARENTLY CELESTIALS ARE FALLING OUT OF THE SKY EVERYWHERE?
IF YOU DON'T KNOW, JUST SAY YOU DON'T KNOW.
AH! THAT HELICOPTER IS FIRING MISSILES INTO THAT THING! I THOUGHT FIRE AND SOUND WERE SUPPOSED TO HURT SYMBIOTES!
YEAH, SO DID WE. WE'LL NEED TO GET YOU CLOSE ENOUGH TO...VENOM BLAST IT.
UGH, RIGHT. HOW DO YOU PROPOSE WE DO THAT WITHOUT ME GETTING EATEN?

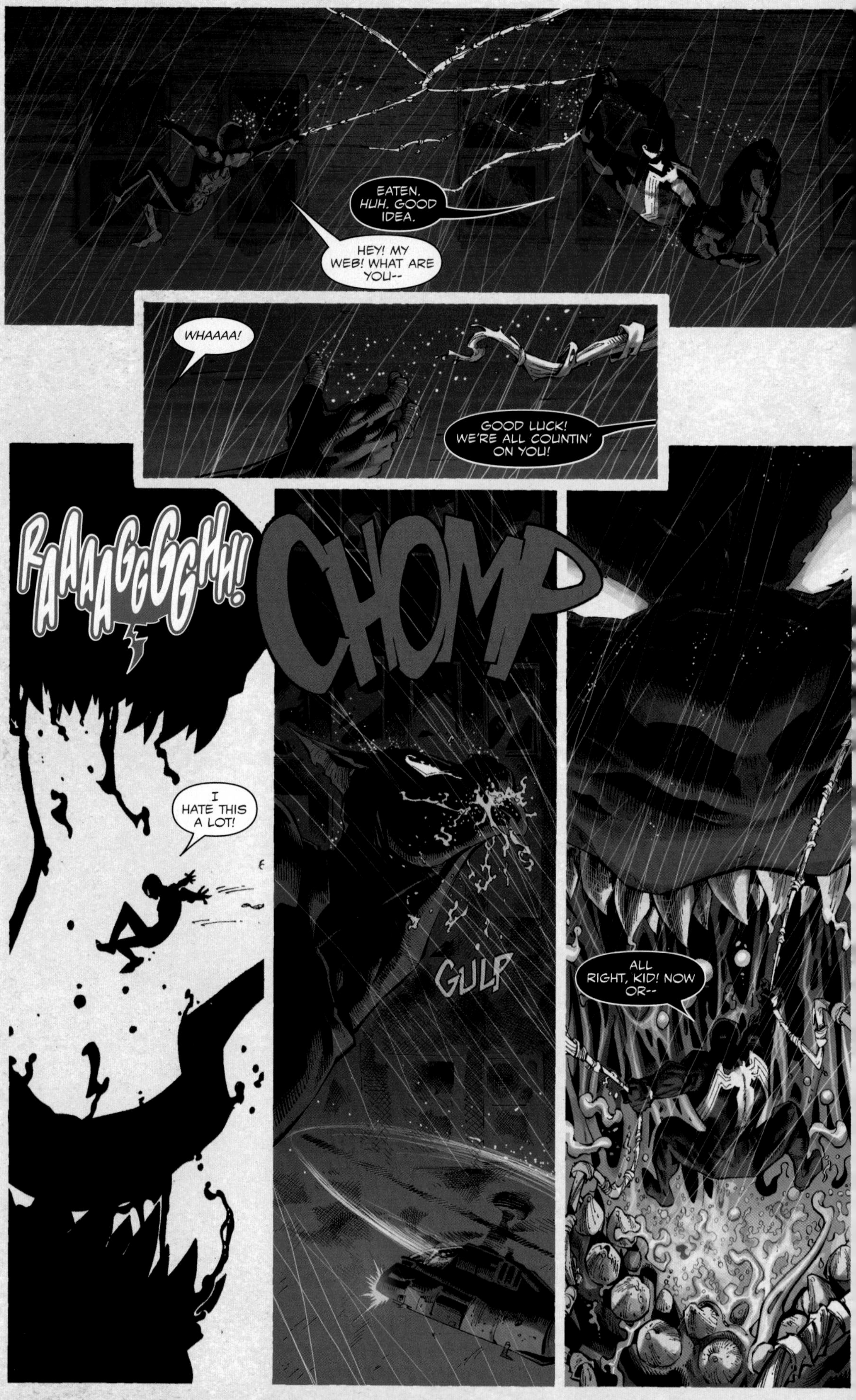
EATEN. HUH. GOOD IDEA.
HEY! MY WEB! WHAT ARE YOU--
WHAAAA!
GOOD LUCK! WE'RE ALL COUNTIN' ON YOU!
RAAAAGGGGHH!
CHOMP
I HATE THIS A LOT!
GULP
ALL RIGHT, KID! NOW OR--

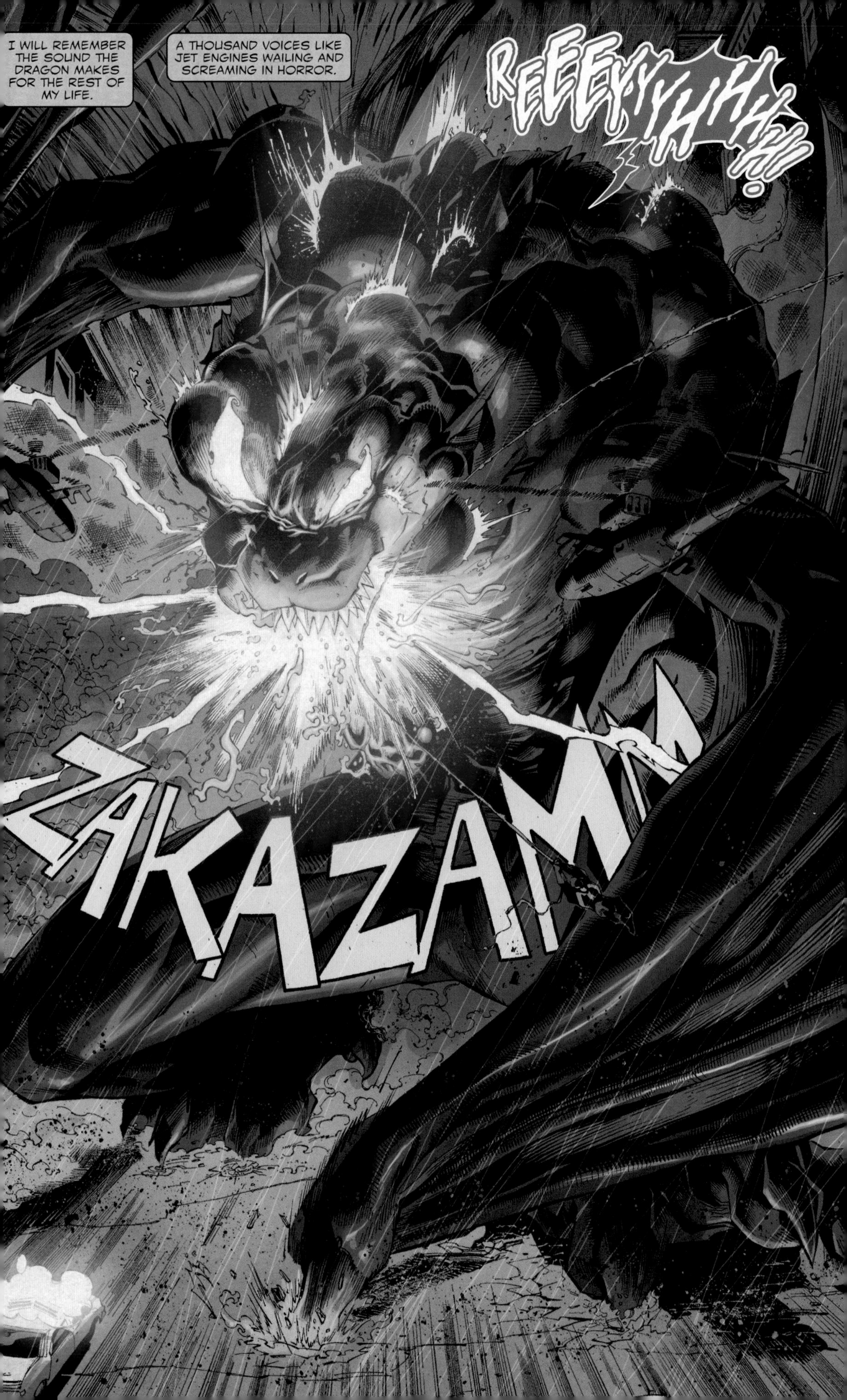
I WILL REMEMBER THE SOUND THE DRAGON MAKES FOR THE REST OF MY LIFE.
A THOUSAND VOICES LIKE JET ENGINES WAILING AND SCREAMING IN HORROR.
REEEYYYHHHH!!
ZAKAZAM

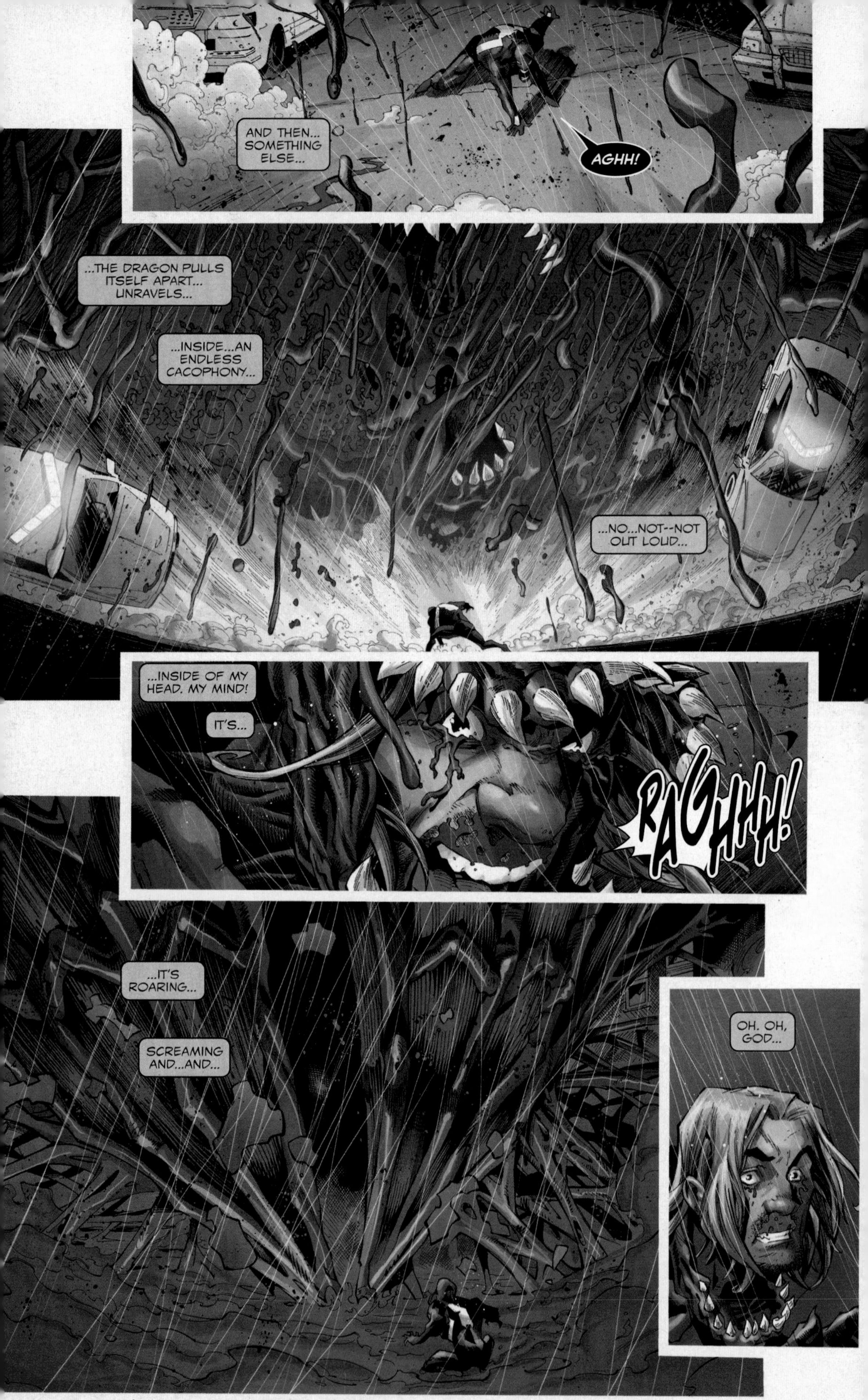
AND THEN... SOMETHING ELSE...
AGHH!
...THE DRAGON PULLS ITSELF APART... UNRAVELS...
...INSIDE...AN ENDLESS CACOPHONY...
...NO...NOT--NOT OUT LOUD...
...INSIDE OF MY HEAD. MY MIND!
IT'S...
RAGHHH!
...IT'S ROARING...
SCREAMING AND...AND...
OH. OH, GOD...

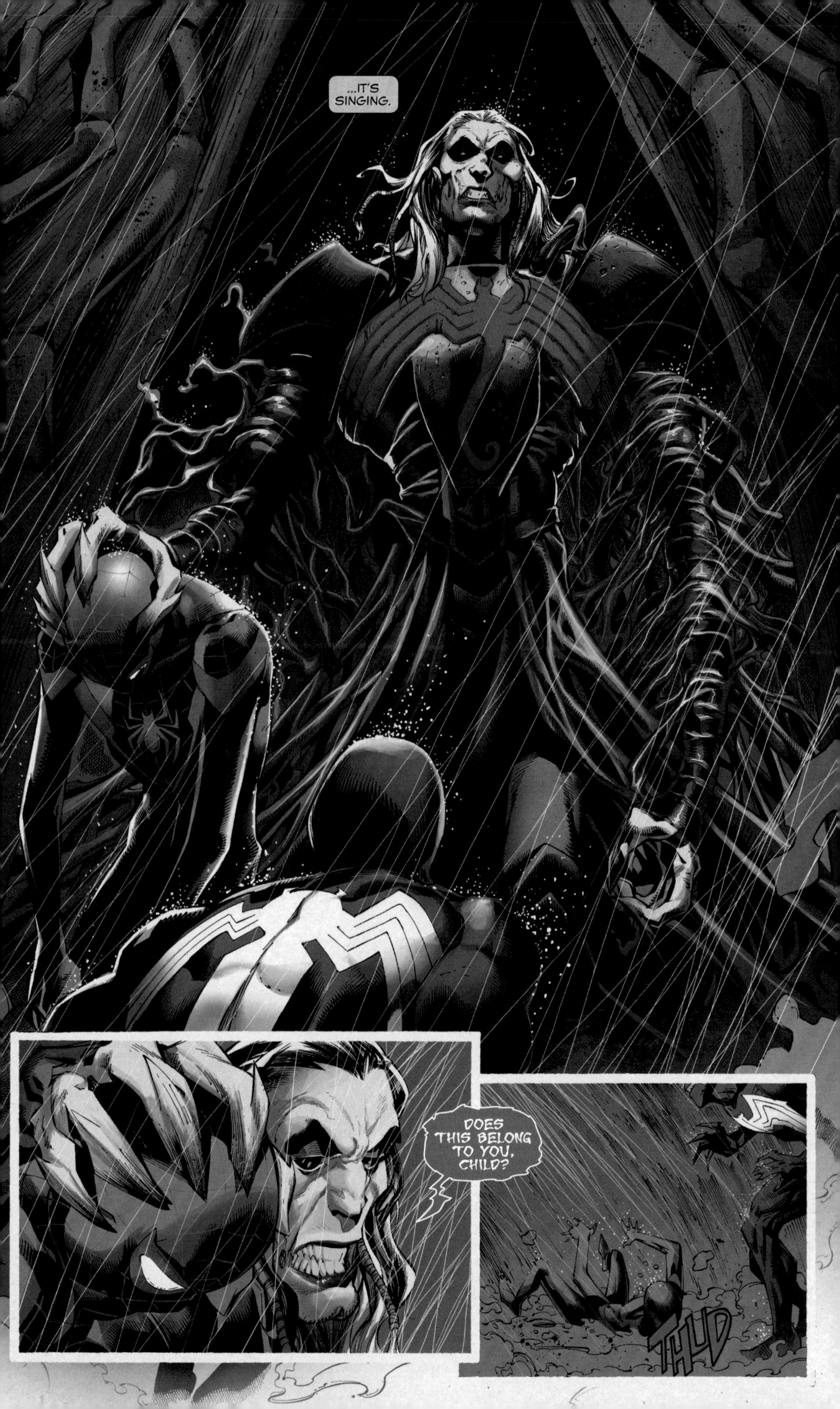
...IT'S SINGING.
DOES THIS BELONG TO YOU, CHILD?
THUD

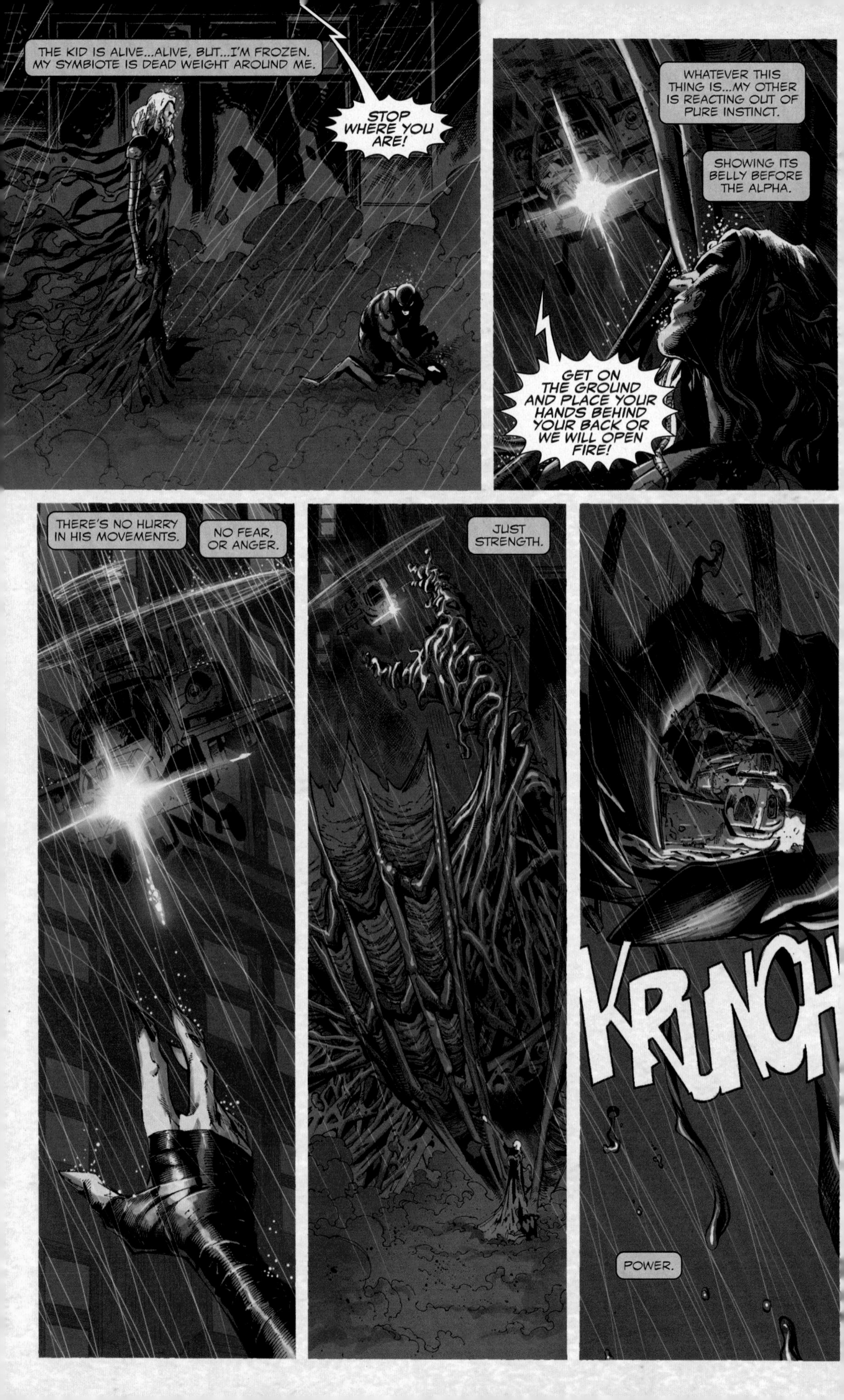
THE KID IS ALIVE...ALIVE, BUT...I'M FROZEN. MY SYMBIOTE IS DEAD WEIGHT AROUND ME.
STOP WHERE YOU ARE!
WHATEVER THIS THING IS...MY OTHER IS REACTING OUT OF PURE INSTINCT.
SHOWING ITS BELLY BEFORE THE ALPHA.
GET ON THE GROUND AND PLACE YOUR HANDS BEHIND YOUR BACK OR WE WILL OPEN FIRE!
THERE'S NO HURRY IN HIS MOVEMENTS.
NO FEAR, OR ANGER.
JUST STRENGTH.
KRUNCH
POWER.

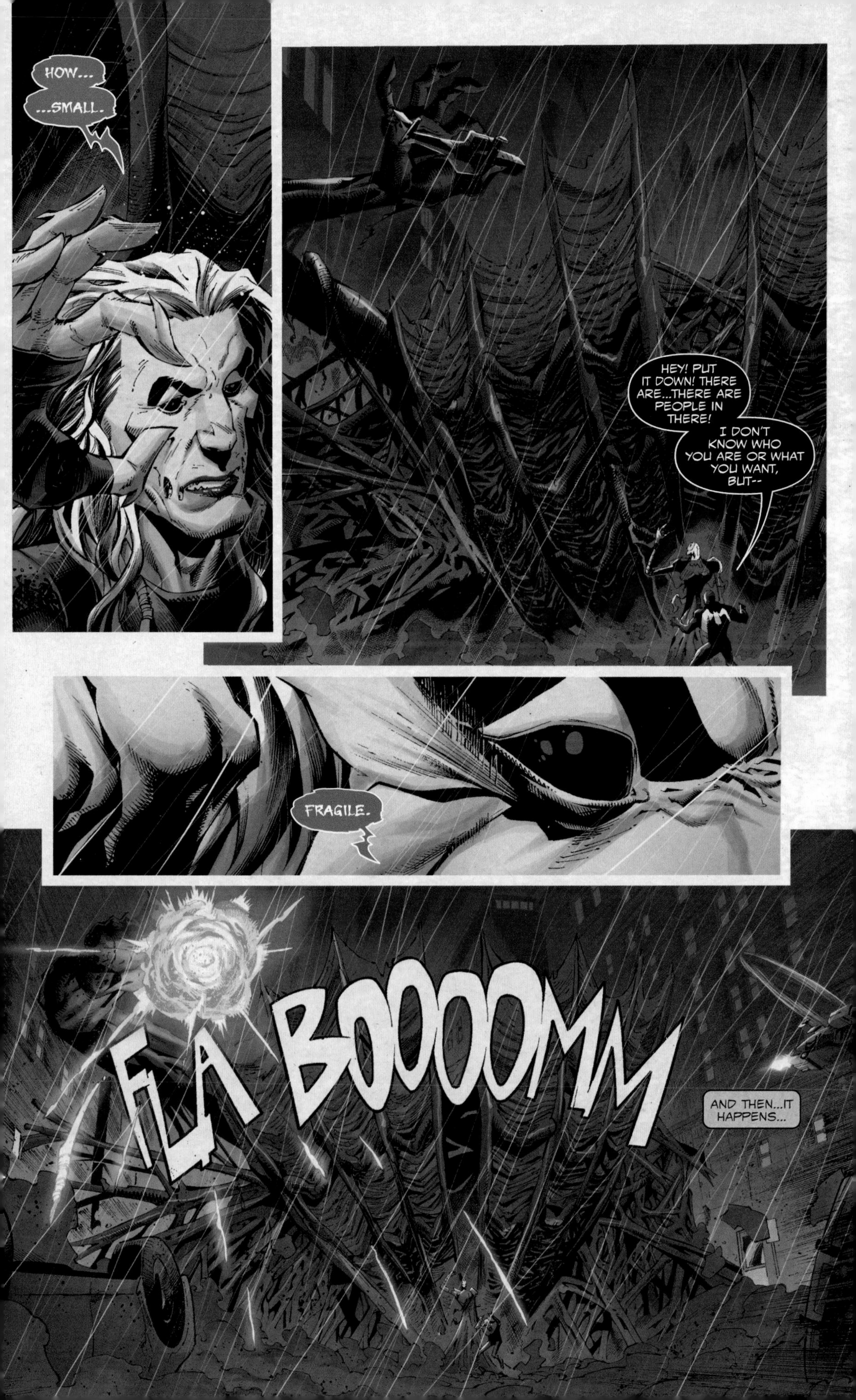
HOW...
...SMALL.
HEY! PUT IT DOWN! THERE ARE...THERE ARE PEOPLE IN THERE!
I DON'T KNOW WHO YOU ARE OR WHAT YOU WANT, BUT--
FRAGILE.
FZA BOOOOMM
AND THEN...IT HAPPENS...

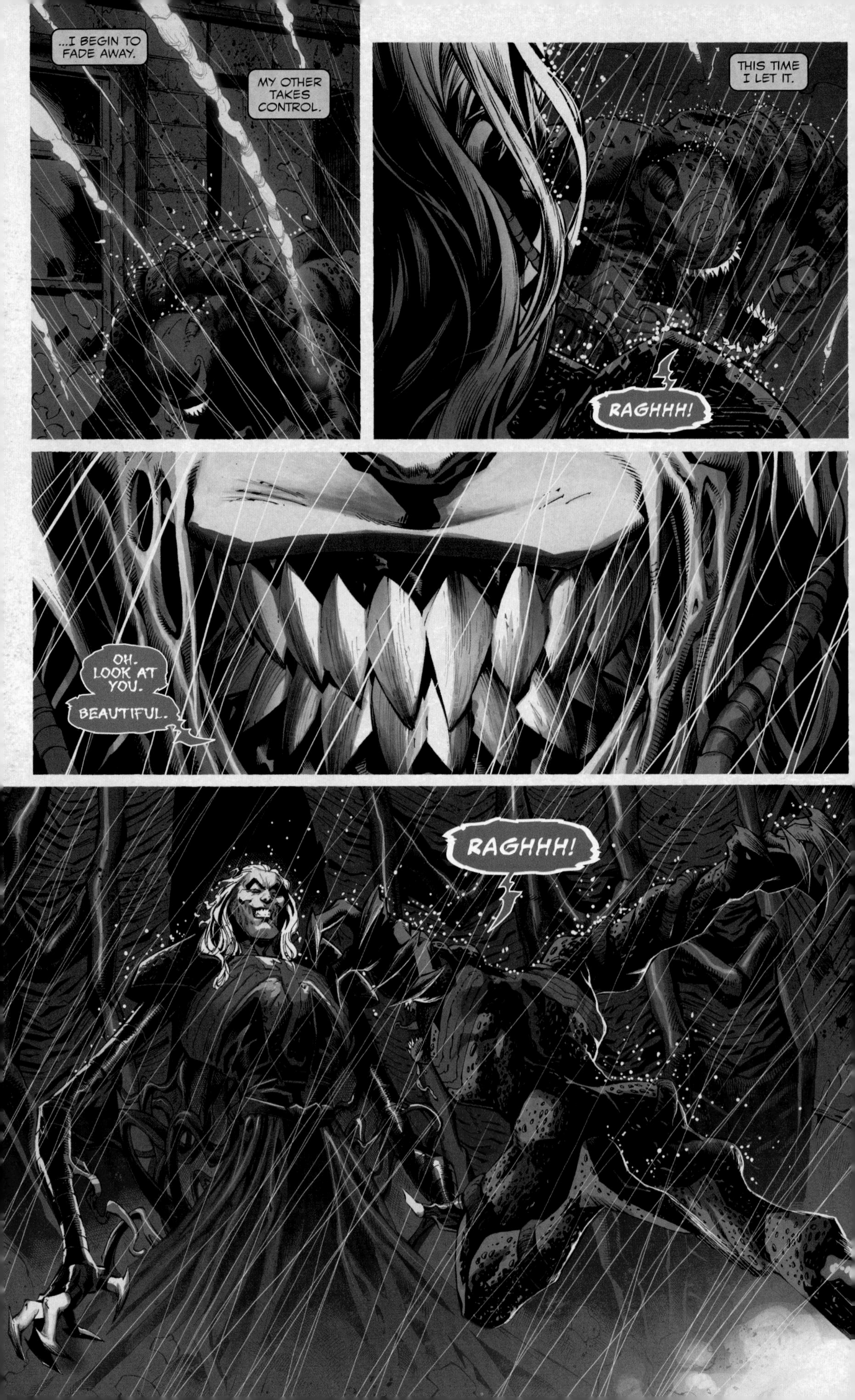
...I BEGIN TO FADE AWAY.
MY OTHER TAKES CONTROL.
THIS TIME I LET IT.
RAGHHH!
OH. LOOK AT YOU.
BEAUTIFUL.
RAGHHH!

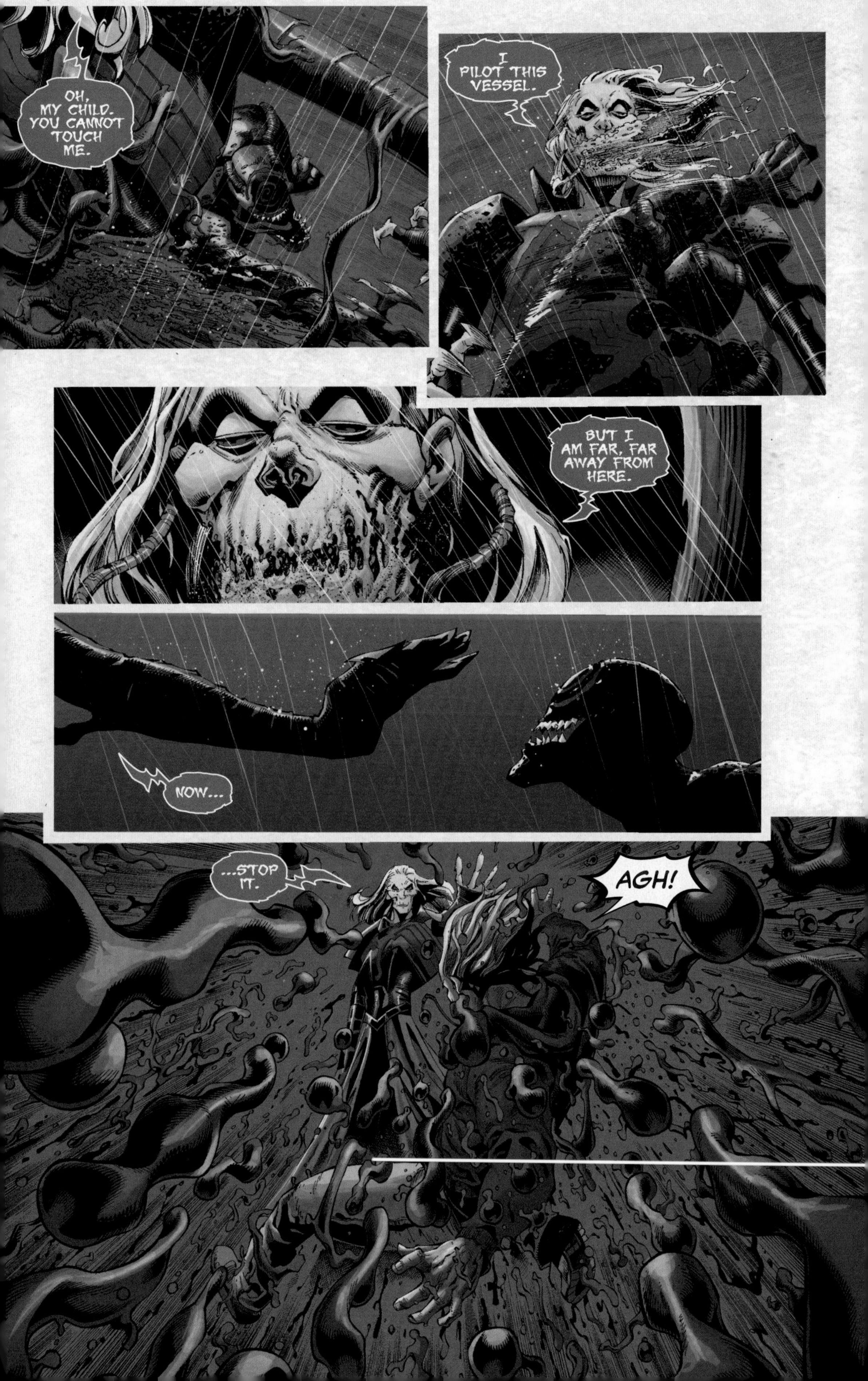
OH, MY CHILD. YOU CANNOT TOUCH ME.
I PILOT THIS VESSEL.
BUT I AM FAR, FAR AWAY FROM HERE.
NOW...
...STOP IT.
AGH!

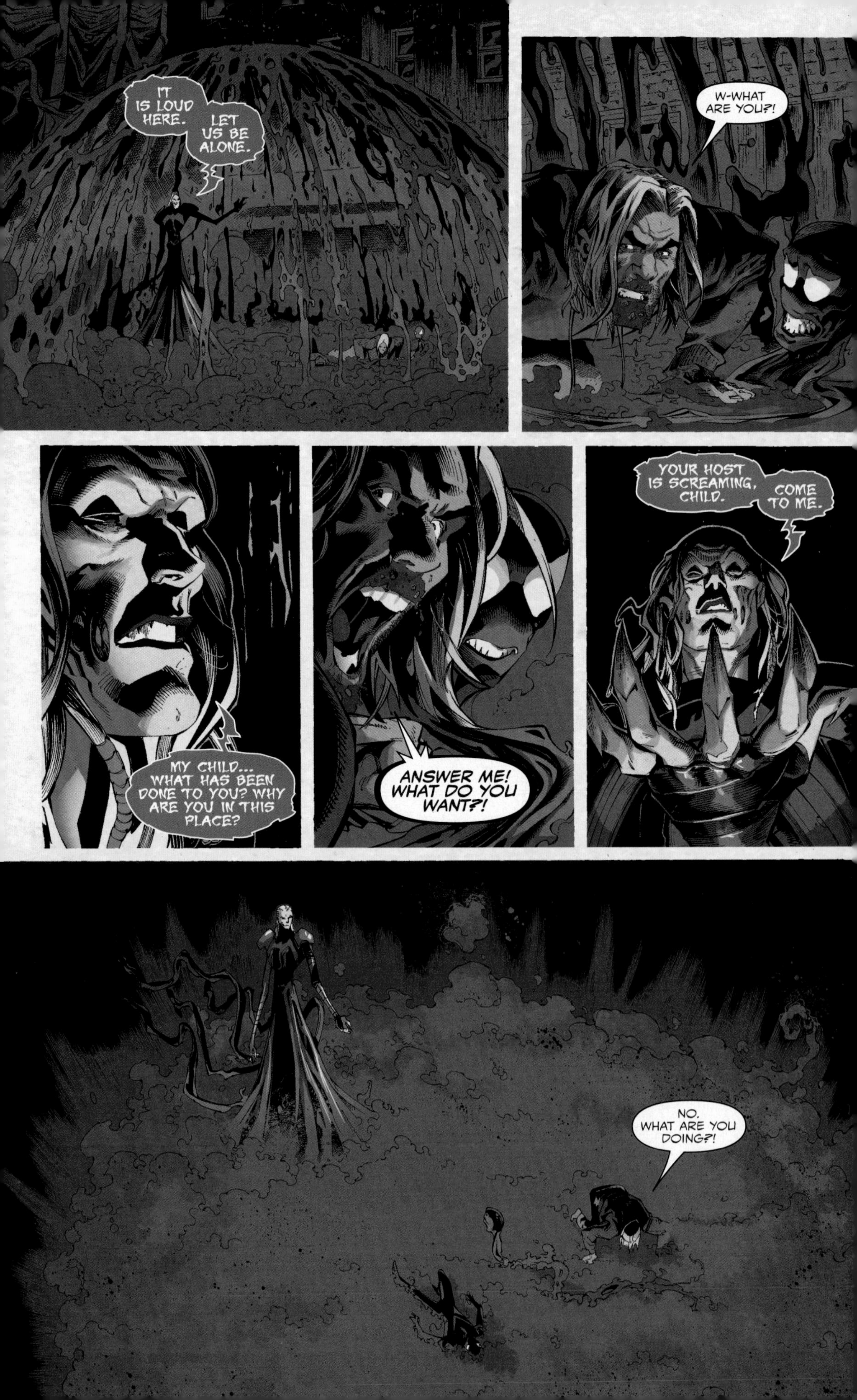
IT IS LOUD HERE.
LET US BE ALONE.
W-WHAT ARE YOU?!
MY CHILD... WHAT HAS BEEN DONE TO YOU? WHY ARE YOU IN THIS PLACE?
ANSWER ME! WHAT DO YOU WANT?!
YOUR HOST IS SCREAMING, CHILD.
COME TO ME.
NO. WHAT ARE YOU DOING?!

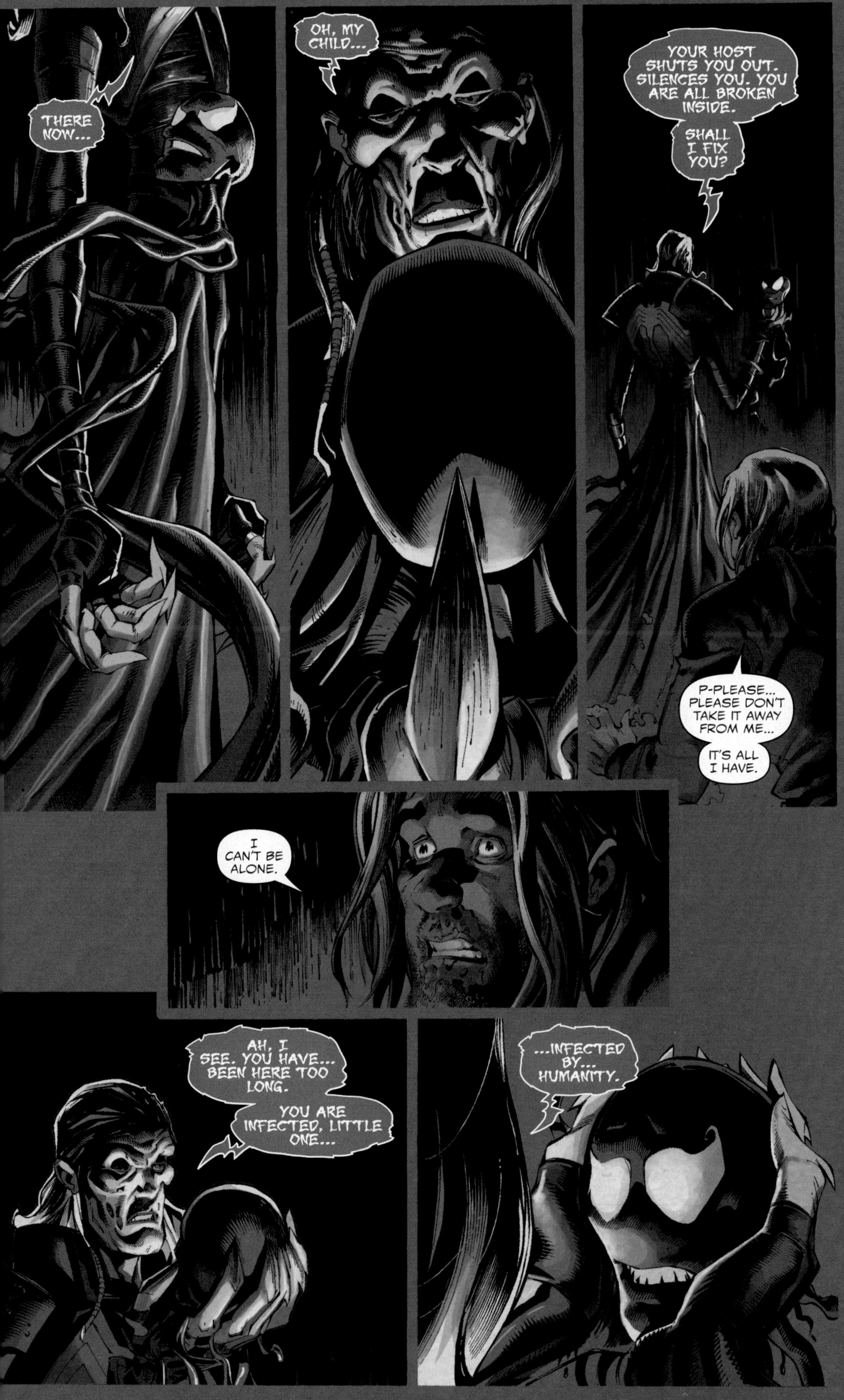
THERE NOW...
OH, MY CHILD...
YOUR HOST SHUTS YOU OUT. SILENCES YOU. YOU ARE ALL BROKEN INSIDE.
SHALL I FIX YOU?
P-PLEASE... PLEASE DON'T TAKE IT AWAY FROM ME...
IT'S ALL I HAVE.
I CAN'T BE ALONE.
AH, I SEE. YOU HAVE... BEEN HERE TOO LONG.
YOU ARE INFECTED, LITTLE ONE...
...INFECTED BY... HUMANITY.

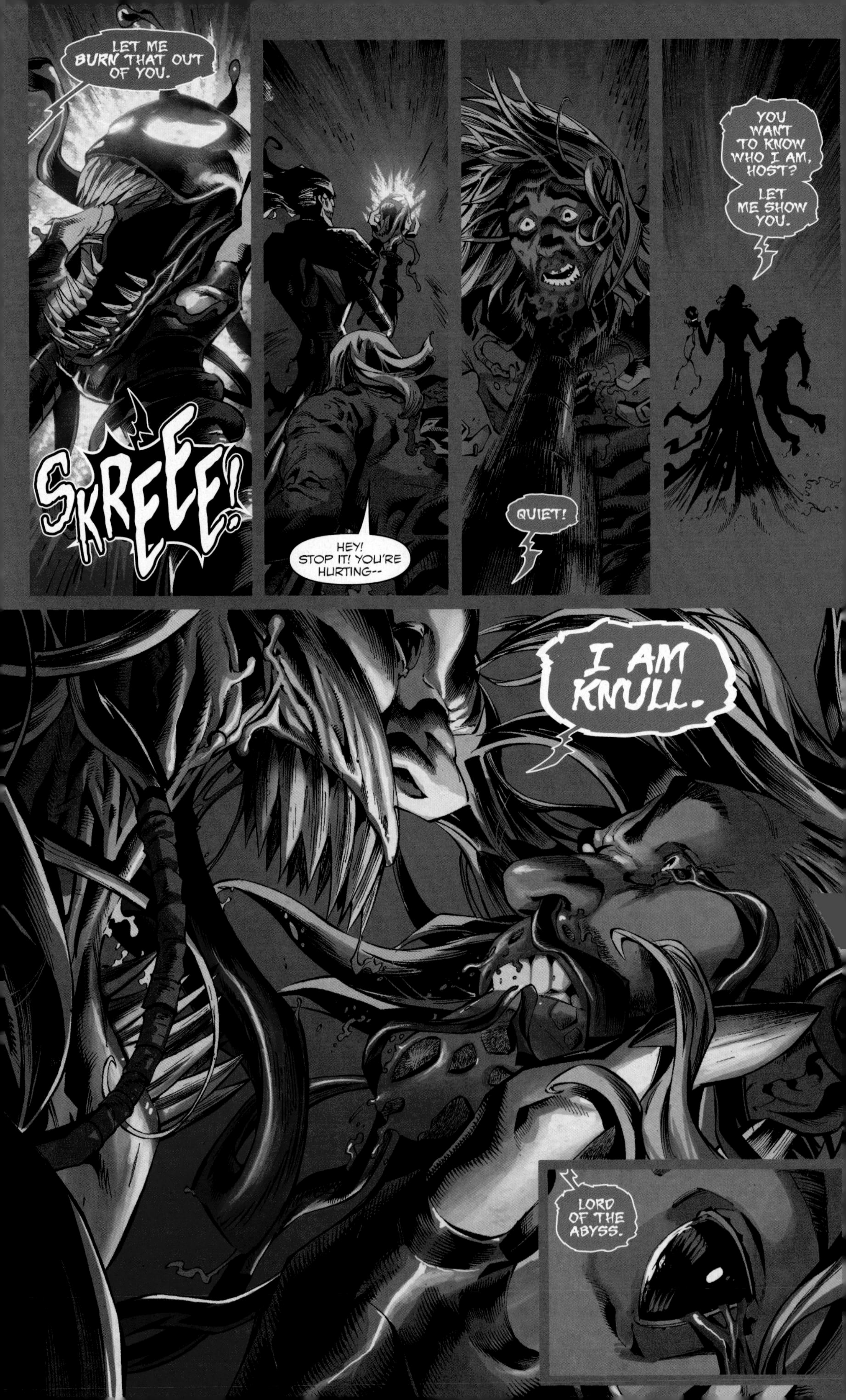

LET ME BURN THAT OUT OF YOU.
SKREEE!
HEY! STOP IT! YOU'RE HURTING--
QUIET!
YOU WANT TO KNOW WHO I AM, HOST?
LET ME SHOW YOU.
I AM KNULL.
LORD OF THE ABYSS.

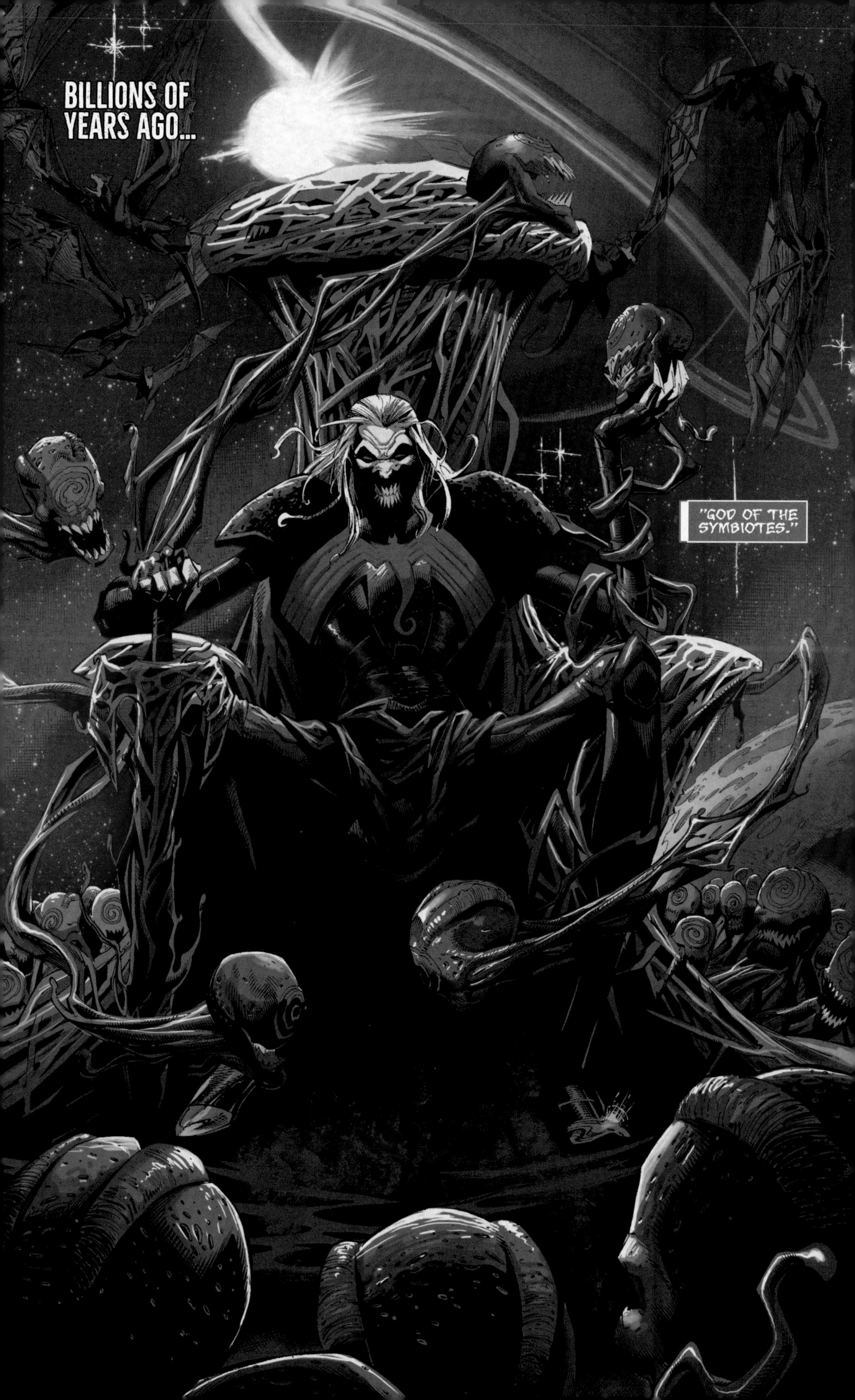
BILLIONS OF YEARS AGO...
"GOD OF THE SYMBIOTES."

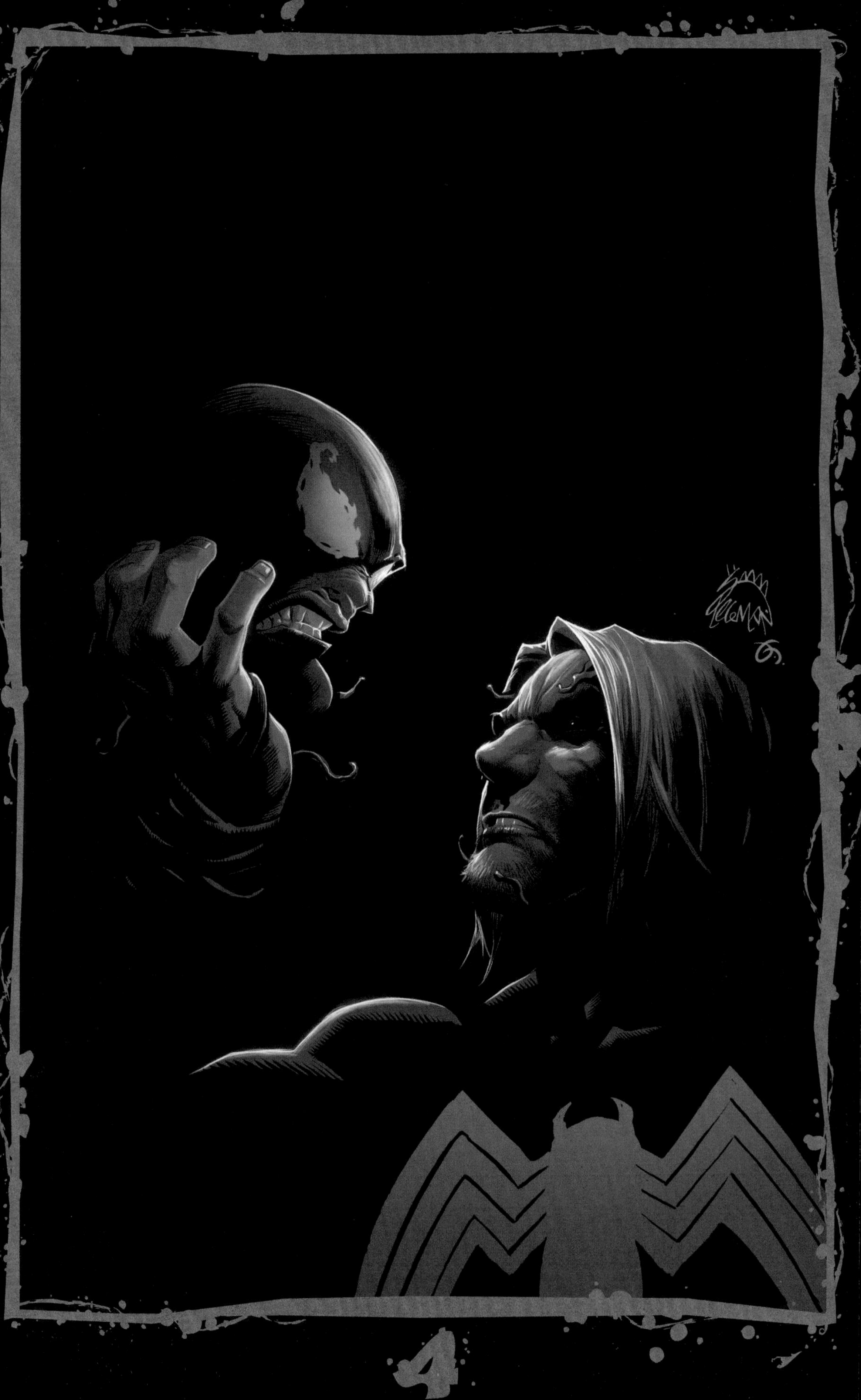
4

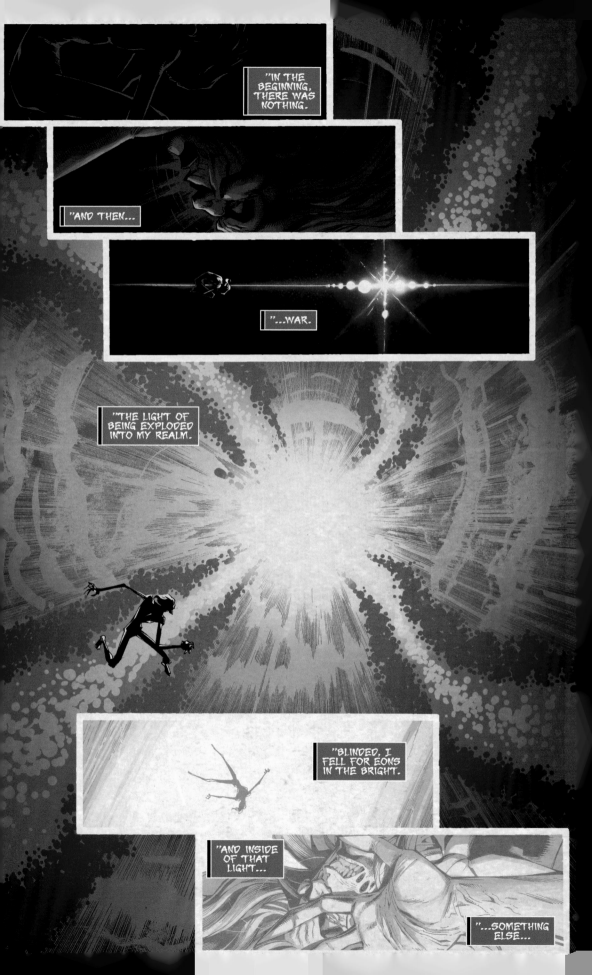

"IN THE BEGINNING, THERE WAS NOTHING.

"AND THEN...

"...WAR.

"THE LIGHT OF BEING EXPLODED INTO MY REALM.

"BLINDED, I FELL FOR EONS IN THE BRIGHT.

"AND INSIDE OF THAT LIGHT...

"...SOMETHING ELSE...

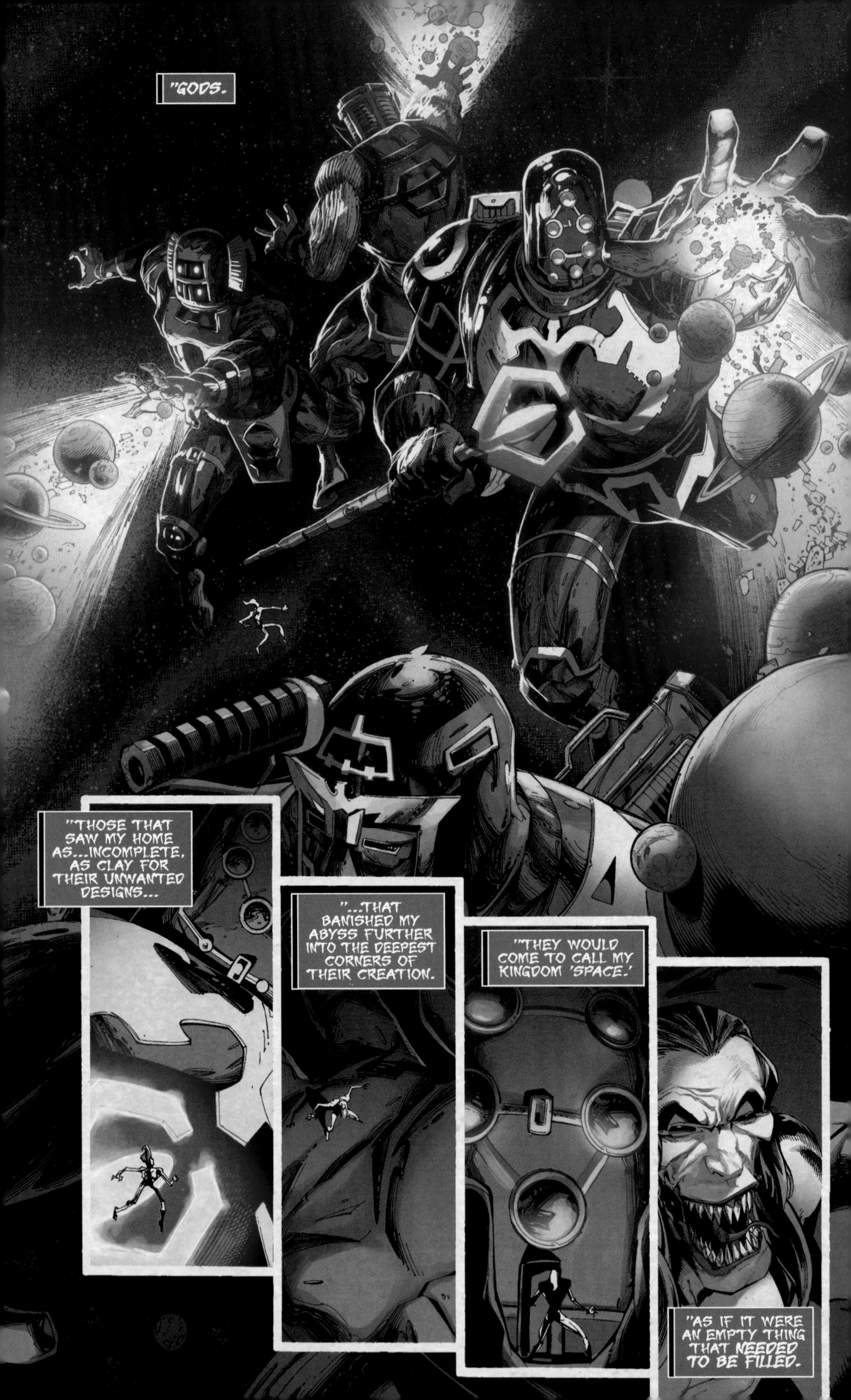
"GODS.
"THOSE THAT SAW MY HOME AS...INCOMPLETE, AS CLAY FOR THEIR UNWANTED DESIGNS...
"...THAT BANISHED MY ABYSS FURTHER INTO THE DEEPEST CORNERS OF THEIR CREATION.
"THEY WOULD COME TO CALL MY KINGDOM 'SPACE.'
"AS IF IT WERE AN EMPTY THING THAT NEEDED TO BE FILLED.

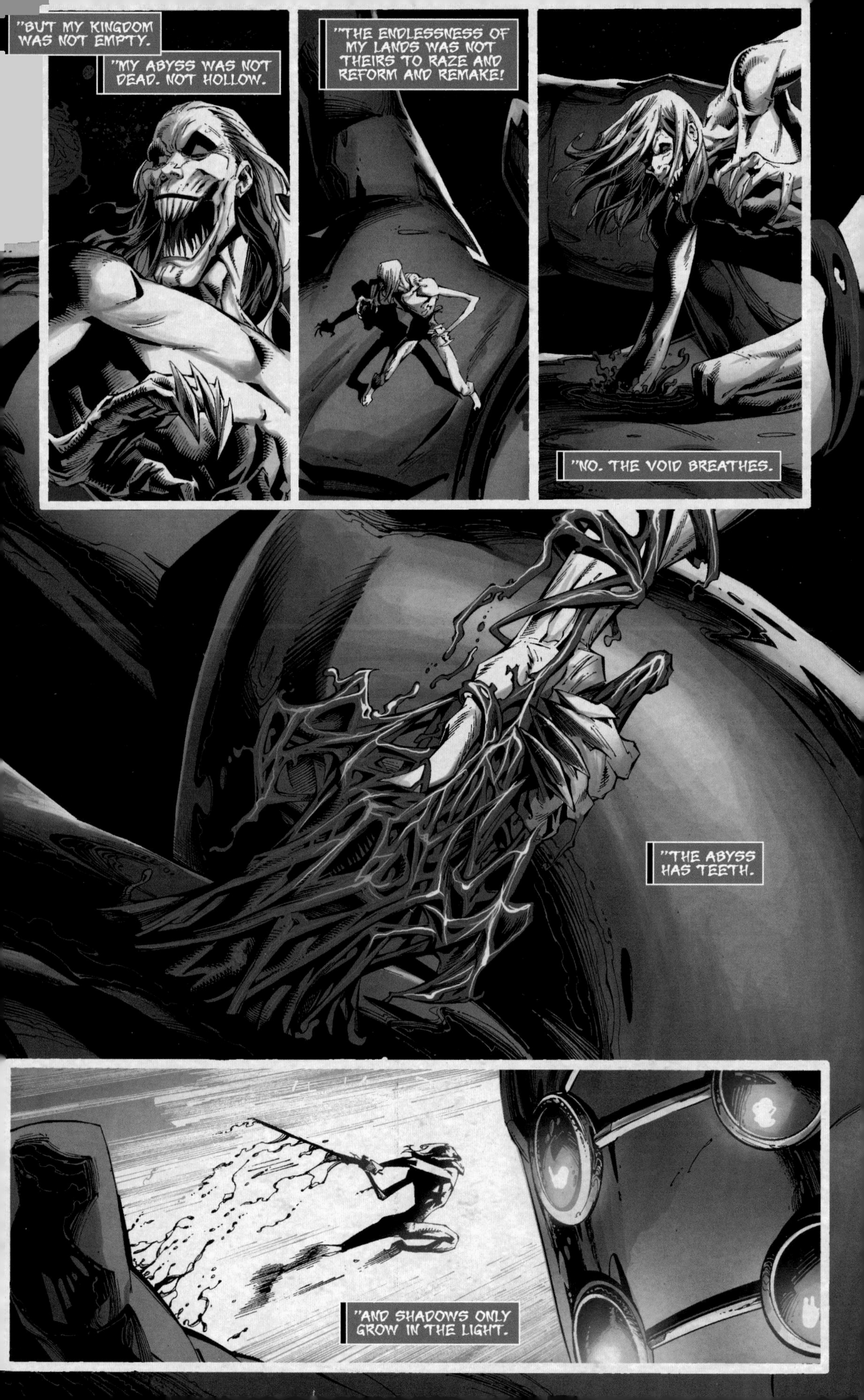
"BUT MY KINGDOM WAS NOT EMPTY.
"MY ABYSS WAS NOT DEAD. NOT HOLLOW.
"THE ENDLESSNESS OF MY LANDS WAS NOT THEIRS TO RAZE AND REFORM AND REMAKE!
"NO. THE VOID BREATHES.
"THE ABYSS HAS TEETH.
"AND SHADOWS ONLY GROW IN THE LIGHT.

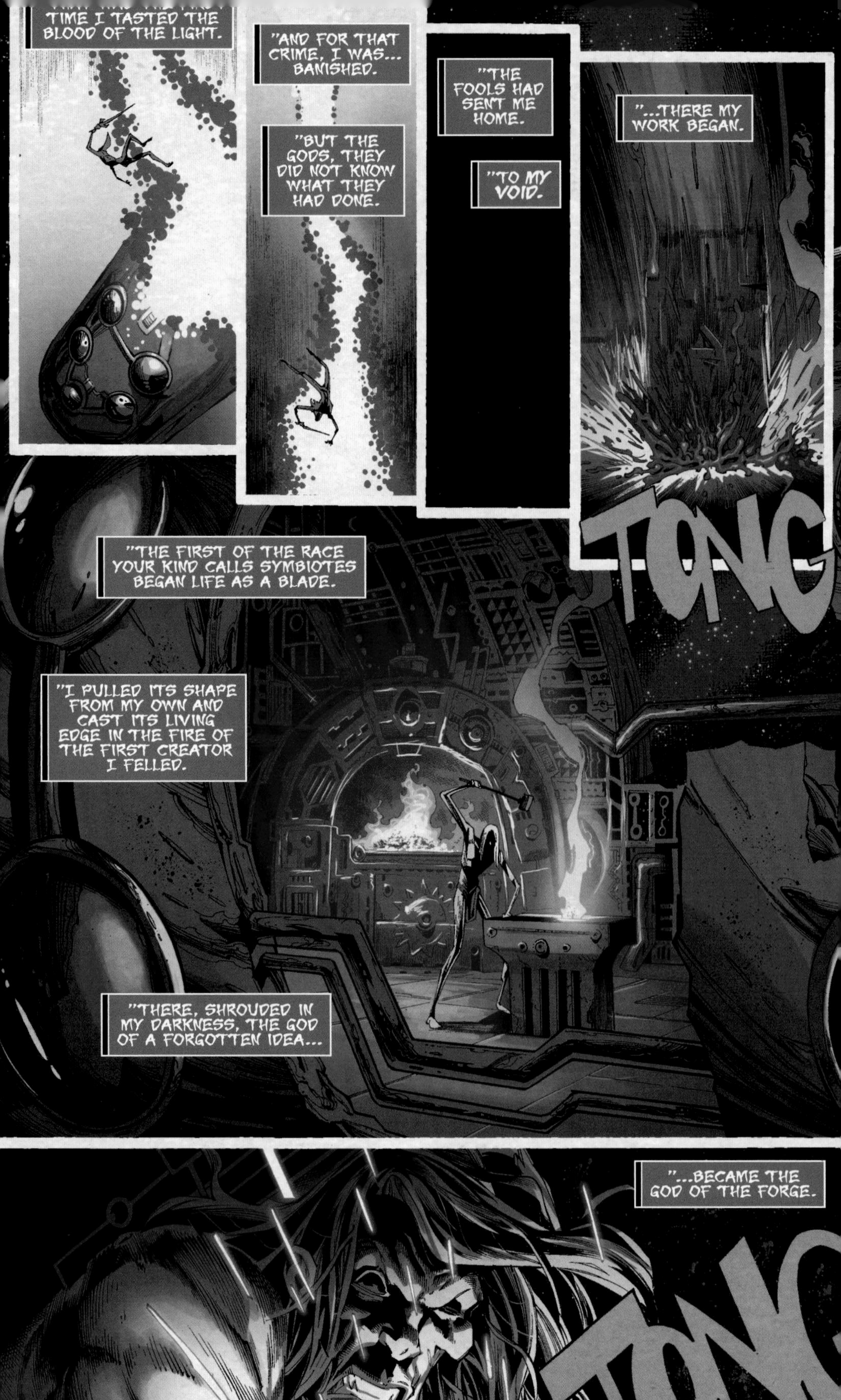
TIME I TASTED THE BLOOD OF THE LIGHT.
"AND FOR THAT CRIME, I WAS... BANISHED.
"BUT THE GODS, THEY DID NOT KNOW WHAT THEY HAD DONE.
"THE FOOLS HAD SENT ME HOME.
"TO MY VOID.
"...THERE MY WORK BEGAN.
TONG
"THE FIRST OF THE RACE YOUR KIND CALLS SYMBIOTES BEGAN LIFE AS A BLADE.
"I PULLED ITS SHAPE FROM MY OWN AND CAST ITS LIVING EDGE IN THE FIRE OF THE FIRST CREATOR I FELLED.
"THERE, SHROUDED IN MY DARKNESS, THE GOD OF A FORGOTTEN IDEA...
"...BECAME THE GOD OF THE FORGE.
TONG

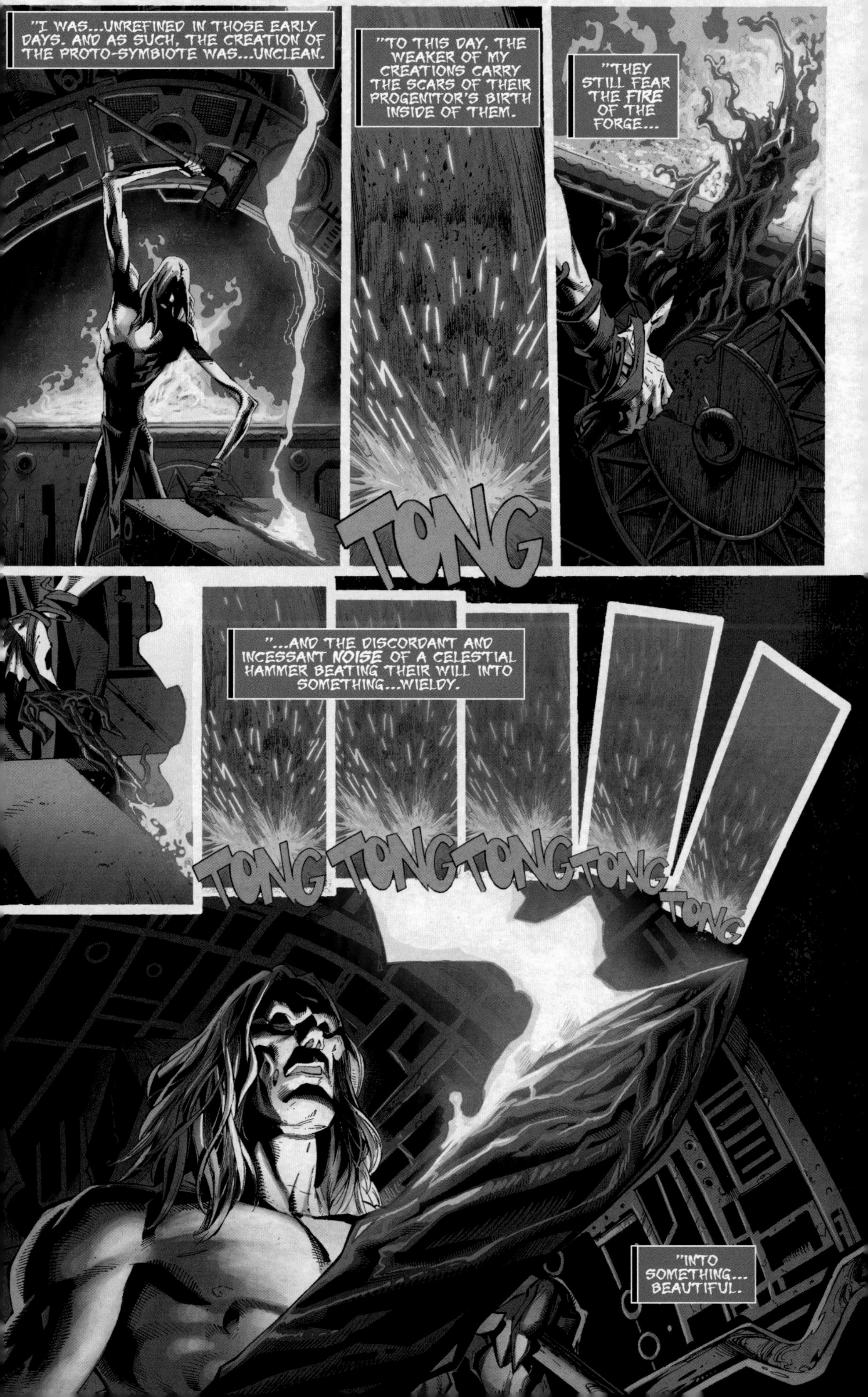
"I WAS...UNREFINED IN THOSE EARLY DAYS. AND AS SUCH, THE CREATION OF THE PROTO-SYMBIOTE WAS...UNCLEAN.
"TO THIS DAY, THE WEAKER OF MY CREATIONS CARRY THE SCARS OF THEIR PROGENITOR'S BIRTH INSIDE OF THEM.
"THEY STILL FEAR THE FIRE OF THE FORGE...
TONG
"...AND THE DISCORDANT AND INCESSANT NOISE OF A CELESTIAL HAMMER BEATING THEIR WILL INTO SOMETHING...WIELDY.
TONG TONG TONG TONG TONG
"INTO SOMETHING... BEAUTIFUL.

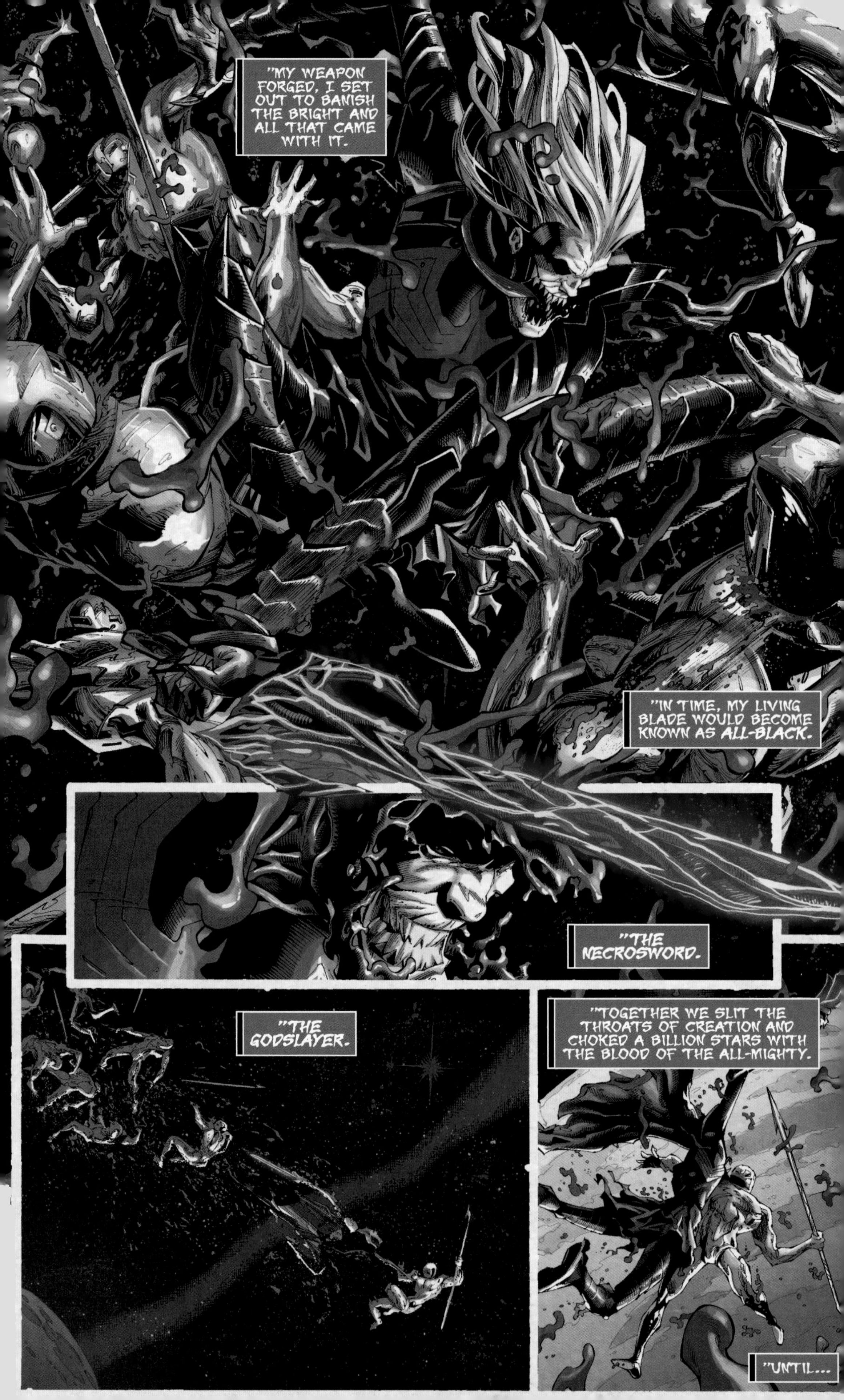
"MY WEAPON FORGED, I SET OUT TO BANISH THE BRIGHT AND ALL THAT CAME WITH IT.
"IN TIME, MY LIVING BLADE WOULD BECOME KNOWN AS ALL-BLACK.
"THE NECROSWORD.
"THE GODSLAYER.
"TOGETHER WE SLIT THE THROATS OF CREATION AND CHOKED A BILLION STARS WITH THE BLOOD OF THE ALL-MIGHTY.
"UNTIL...

"...WE FELL.

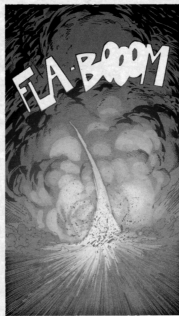

FLA·BOOOM

"AND ALL-BLACK, MY FIRST BORN...

"...WAS TAKEN FROM ME...

"...BY SOME DOOMED WRETCH WHO WOULD COME TO CURSE ITS NAME.*

*FOR MORE INFO, SEE THOR: GOD OF THUNDER #6 FROM 2013!

"CAN YOU IMAGINE, HOST?"

A DARK GOD FALLING FROM THE HEAVENS AND GIVING YOU A GIFT YOU CANNOT HOPE TO UNDERSTAND?

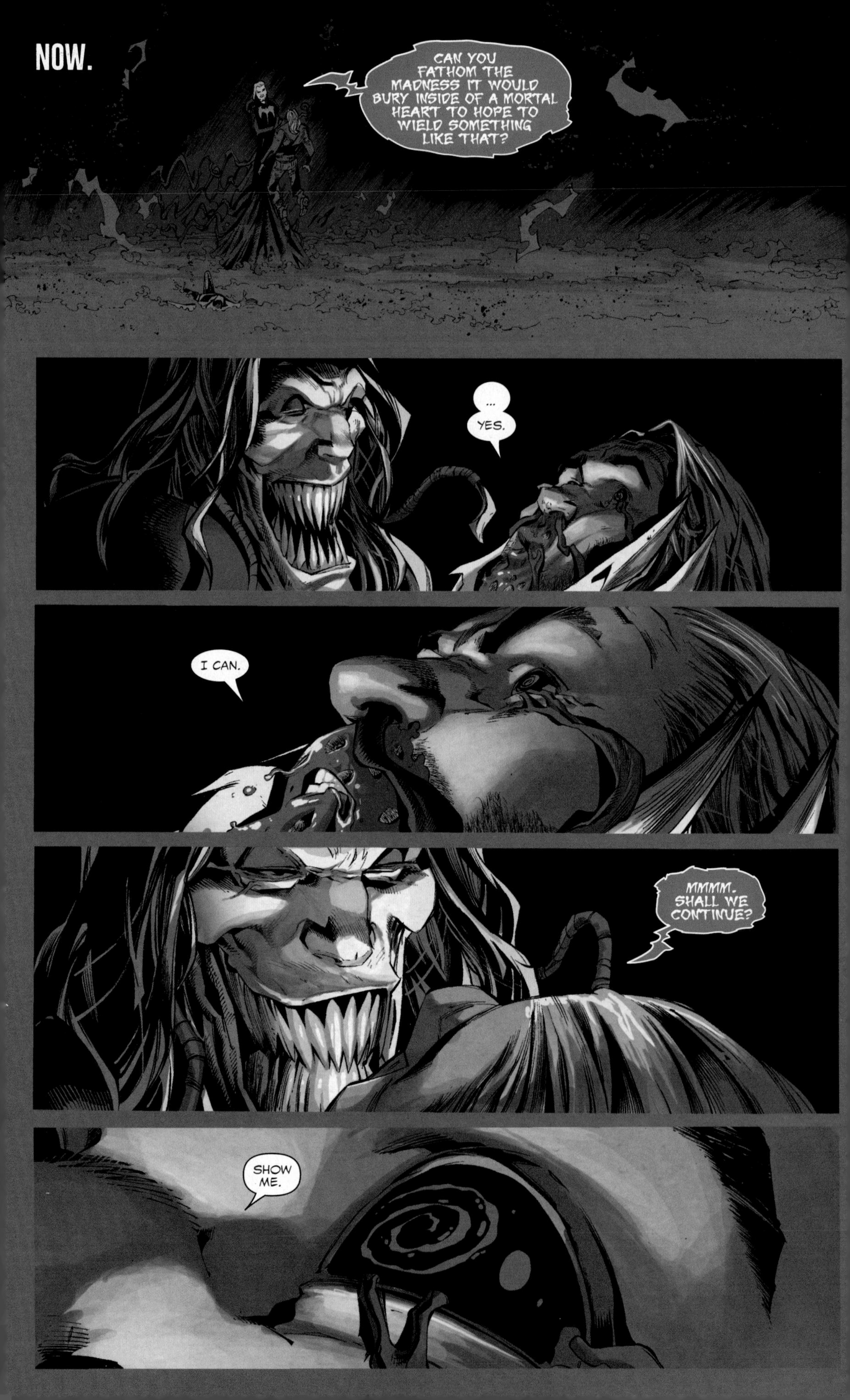
NOW.
CAN YOU FATHOM THE MADNESS IT WOULD BURY INSIDE OF A MORTAL HEART TO HOPE TO WIELD SOMETHING LIKE THAT?
... YES.
I CAN.
MMMM. SHALL WE CONTINUE?
SHOW ME.

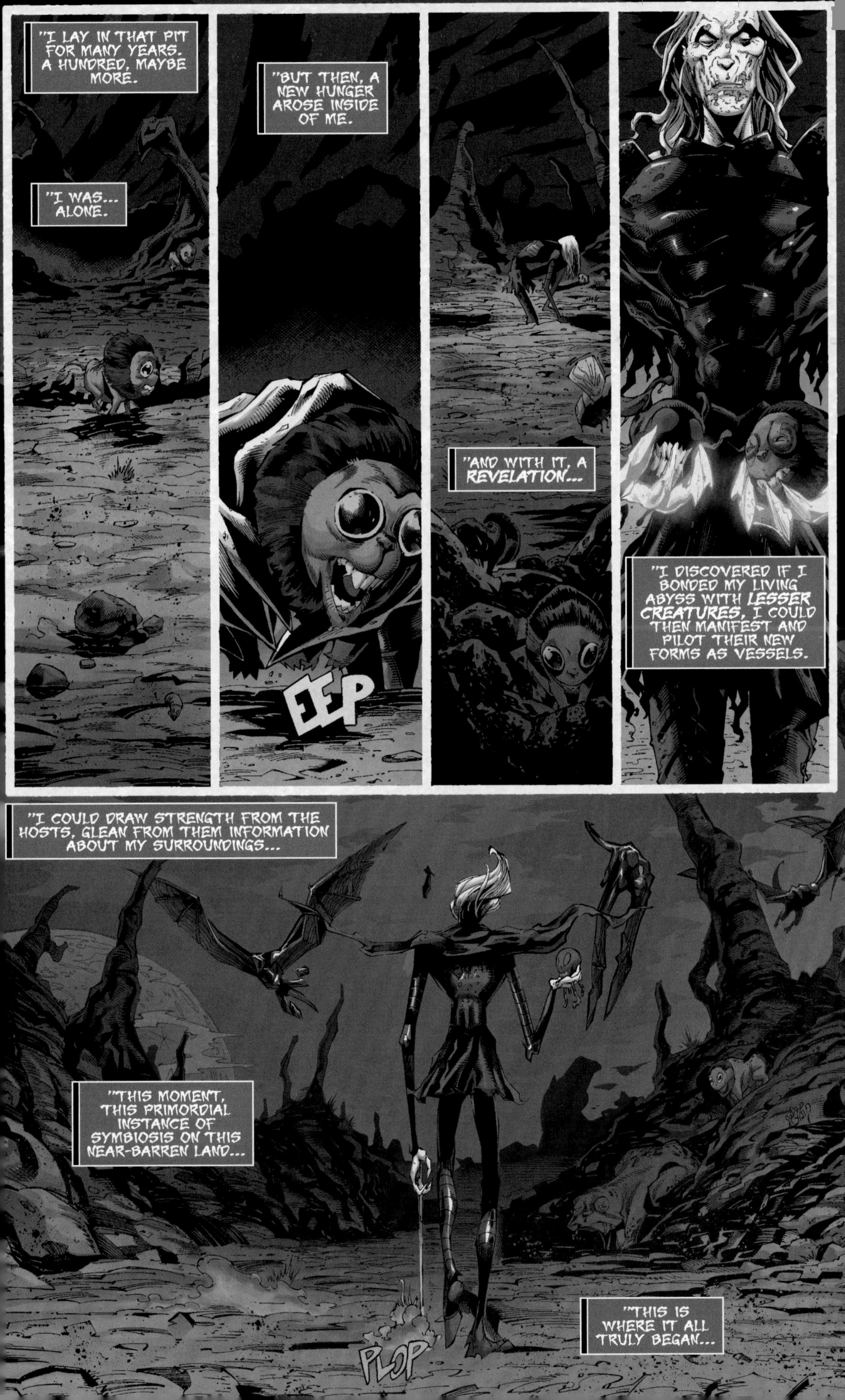
"I LAY IN THAT PIT FOR MANY YEARS. A HUNDRED, MAYBE MORE.
"I WAS... ALONE.
"BUT THEN, A NEW HUNGER AROSE INSIDE OF ME.
EEP
"AND WITH IT, A REVELATION...
"I DISCOVERED IF I BONDED MY LIVING ABYSS WITH LESSER CREATURES, I COULD THEN MANIFEST AND PILOT THEIR NEW FORMS AS VESSELS.
"I COULD DRAW STRENGTH FROM THE HOSTS, GLEAN FROM THEM INFORMATION ABOUT MY SURROUNDINGS...
"THIS MOMENT, THIS PRIMORDIAL INSTANCE OF SYMBIOSIS ON THIS NEAR-BARREN LAND...
"THIS IS WHERE IT ALL TRULY BEGAN...
PLOP

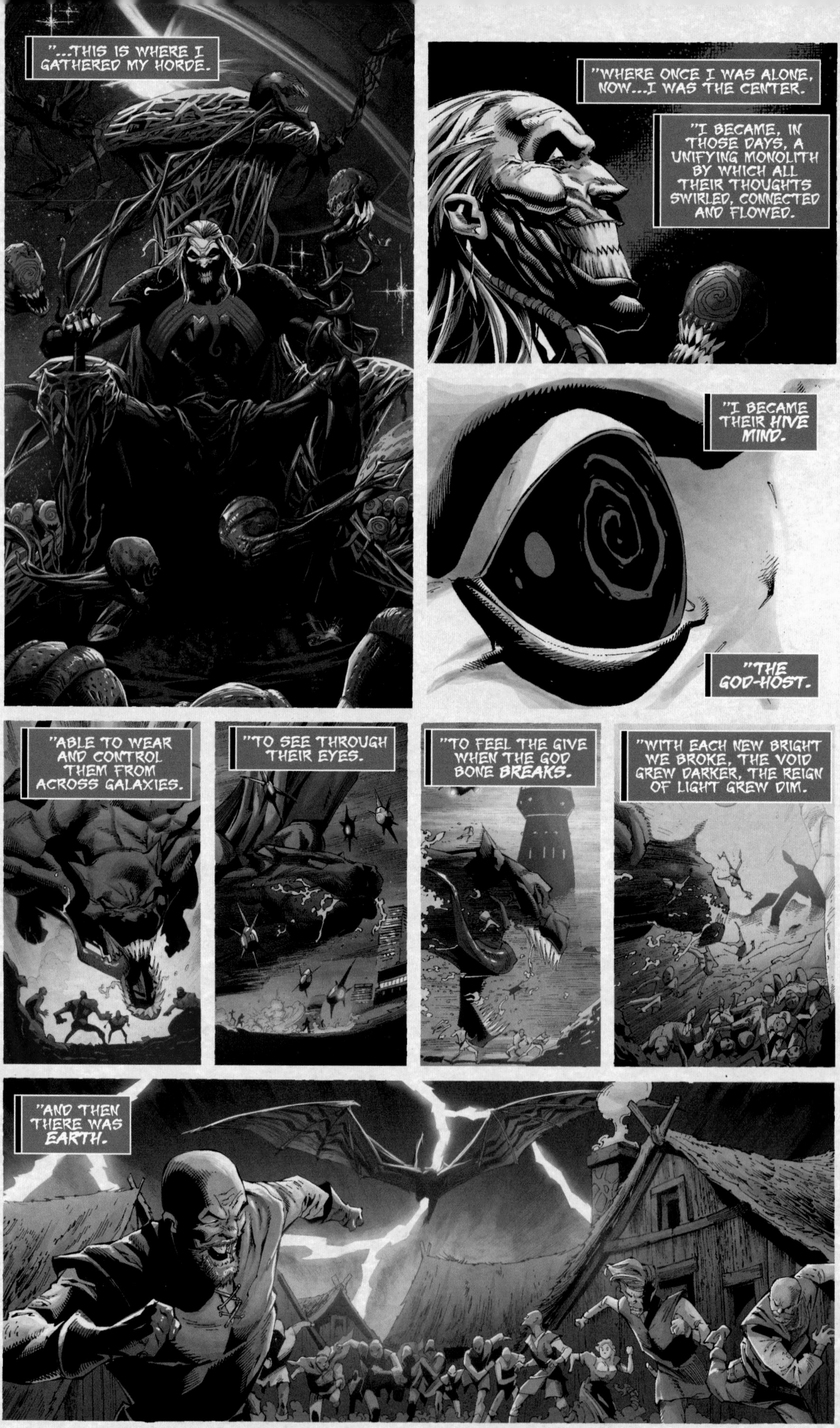
"...THIS IS WHERE I GATHERED MY HORDE.
"WHERE ONCE I WAS ALONE, NOW...I WAS THE CENTER.
"I BECAME, IN THOSE DAYS, A UNIFYING MONOLITH BY WHICH ALL THEIR THOUGHTS SWIRLED, CONNECTED AND FLOWED.
"I BECAME THEIR *HIVE MIND.*
"THE *GOD-HOST.*
"ABLE TO WEAR AND CONTROL THEM FROM ACROSS GALAXIES.
"TO SEE THROUGH THEIR EYES.
"TO FEEL THE GIVE WHEN THE GOD BONE *BREAKS.*
"WITH EACH NEW BRIGHT WE BROKE, THE VOID GREW DARKER, THE REIGN OF LIGHT GREW DIM.
"AND THEN THERE WAS *EARTH.*

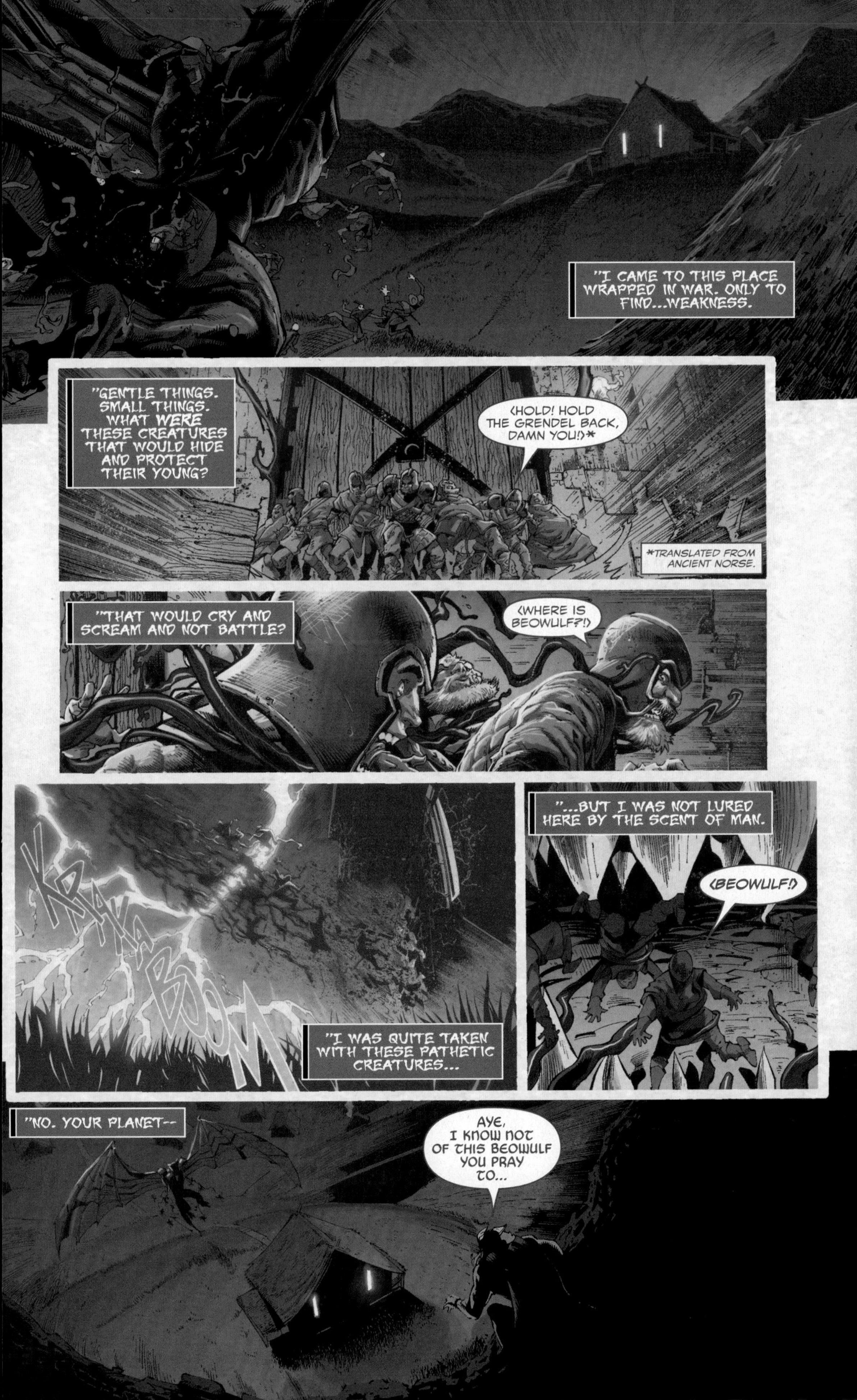
"I CAME TO THIS PLACE WRAPPED IN WAR. ONLY TO FIND...WEAKNESS.
"GENTLE THINGS. SMALL THINGS. WHAT WERE THESE CREATURES THAT WOULD HIDE AND PROTECT THEIR YOUNG?
‹HOLD! HOLD THE GRENDEL BACK, DAMN YOU!›*
*TRANSLATED FROM ANCIENT NORSE.
"THAT WOULD CRY AND SCREAM AND NOT BATTLE?
‹WHERE IS BEOWULF?!›
KRAKA BOOM
"I WAS QUITE TAKEN WITH THESE PATHETIC CREATURES...
"...BUT I WAS NOT LURED HERE BY THE SCENT OF MAN.
‹BEOWULF!›
"NO. YOUR PLANET--
AYE, I KNOW NOT OF THIS BEOWULF YOU PRAY TO...

"--IT REEKED OF THE LIGHT.
...BUT PERHAPS THOR WILL SUFFICE!
"YOUR THUNDER GOD UNLEASHED A POWER I HAD NEVER BEFORE FELT ON ALL THE WORLDS I HAD WRAPPED MY HORDE AROUND.
KRAZAK
"AND IN THE BLINK OF AN EYE, HE STABBED IT LIKE A BILLION NEEDLES INTO OUR HEARTS.

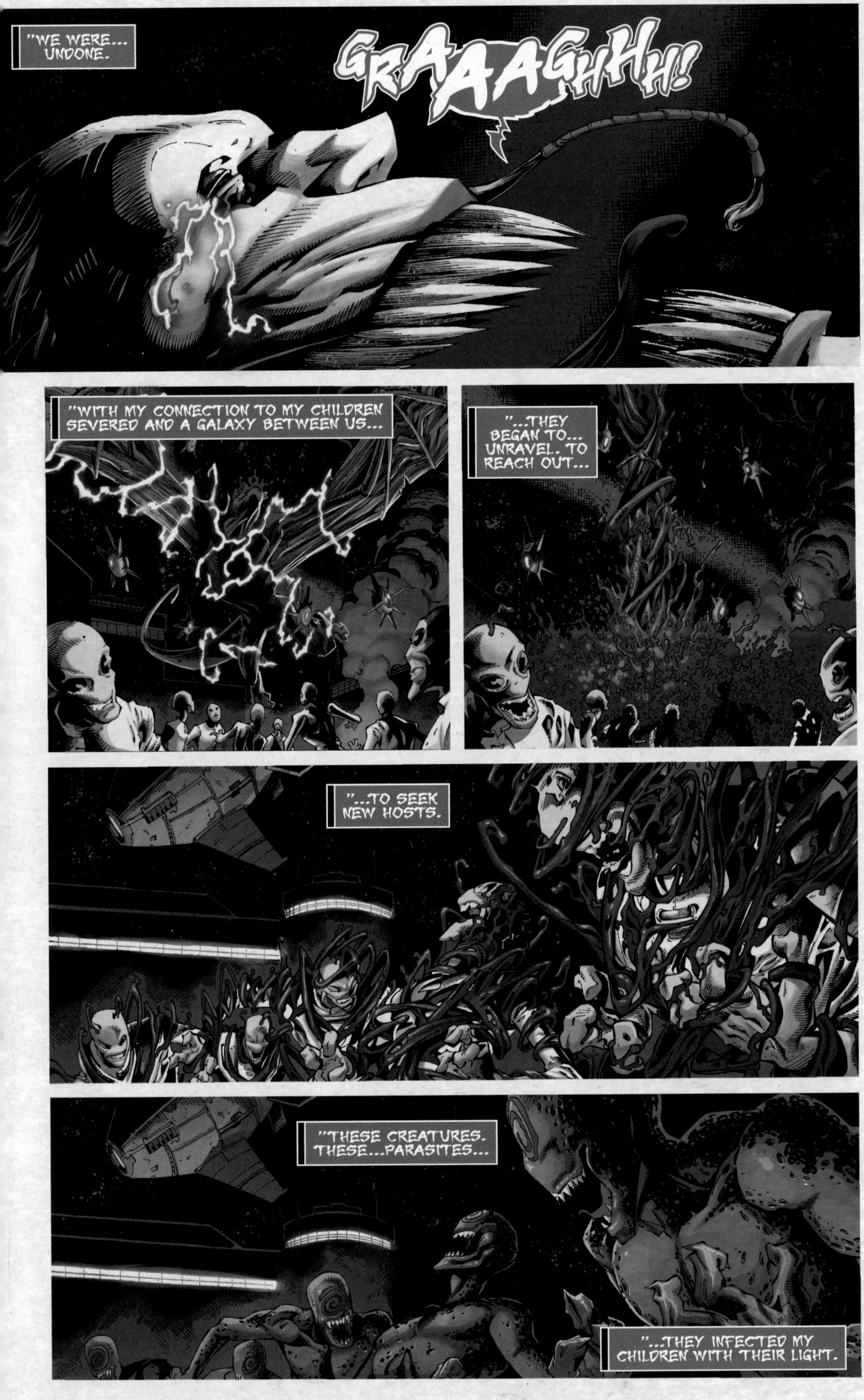
"WE WERE... UNDONE.
GRAAAAGHHH!
"WITH MY CONNECTION TO MY CHILDREN SEVERED AND A GALAXY BETWEEN US...
"...THEY BEGAN TO... UNRAVEL. TO REACH OUT...
"...TO SEEK NEW HOSTS.
"THESE CREATURES. THESE...PARASITES...
"...THEY INFECTED MY CHILDREN WITH THEIR LIGHT.

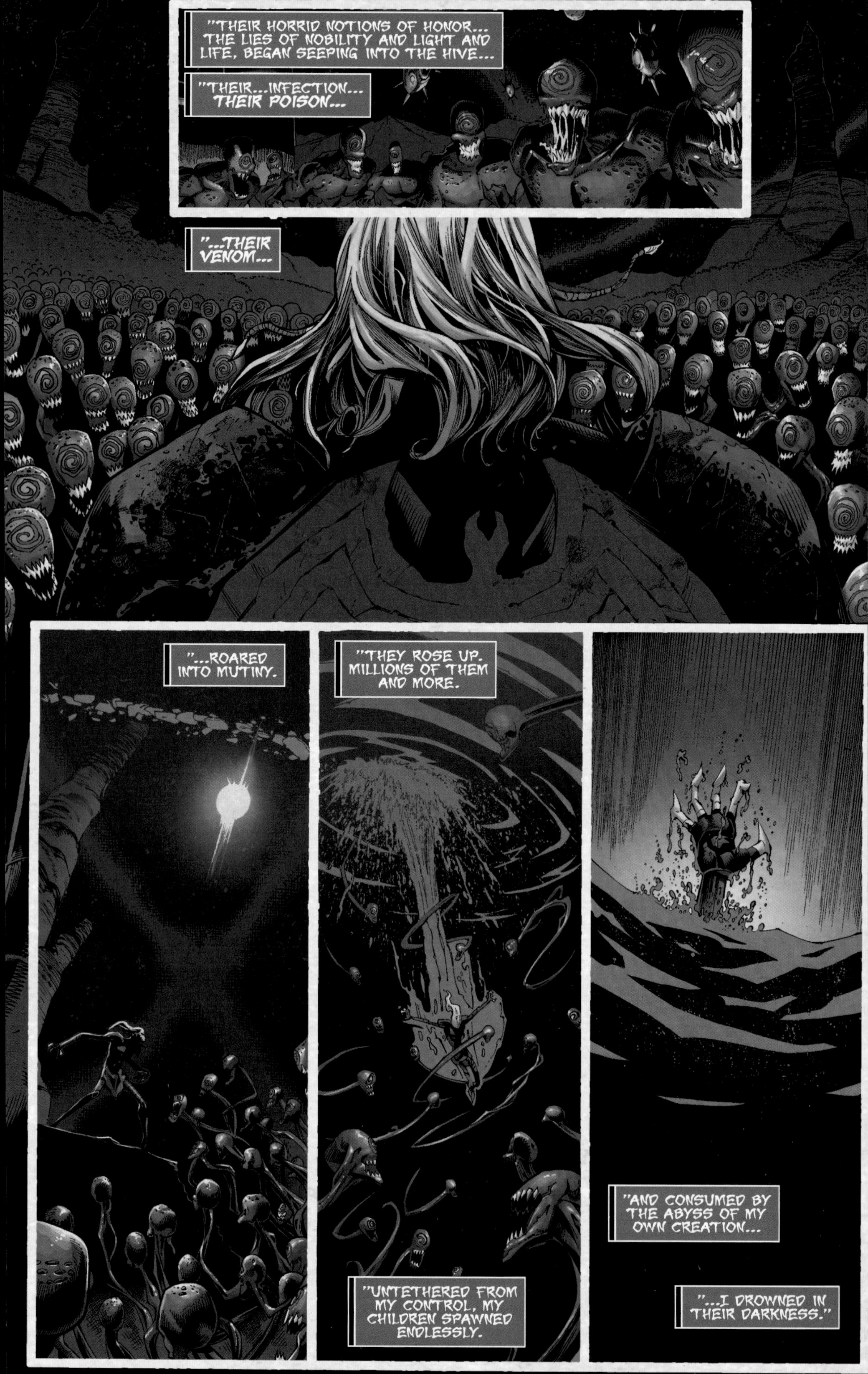
"THEIR HORRID NOTIONS OF HONOR... THE LIES OF NOBILITY AND LIGHT AND LIFE, BEGAN SEEPING INTO THE HIVE...
"THEIR...INFECTION... THEIR POISON...
"...THEIR VENOM...
"...ROARED INTO MUTINY.
"THEY ROSE UP. MILLIONS OF THEM AND MORE.
"UNTETHERED FROM MY CONTROL, MY CHILDREN SPAWNED ENDLESSLY.
"AND CONSUMED BY THE ABYSS OF MY OWN CREATION...
"...I DROWNED IN THEIR DARKNESS."

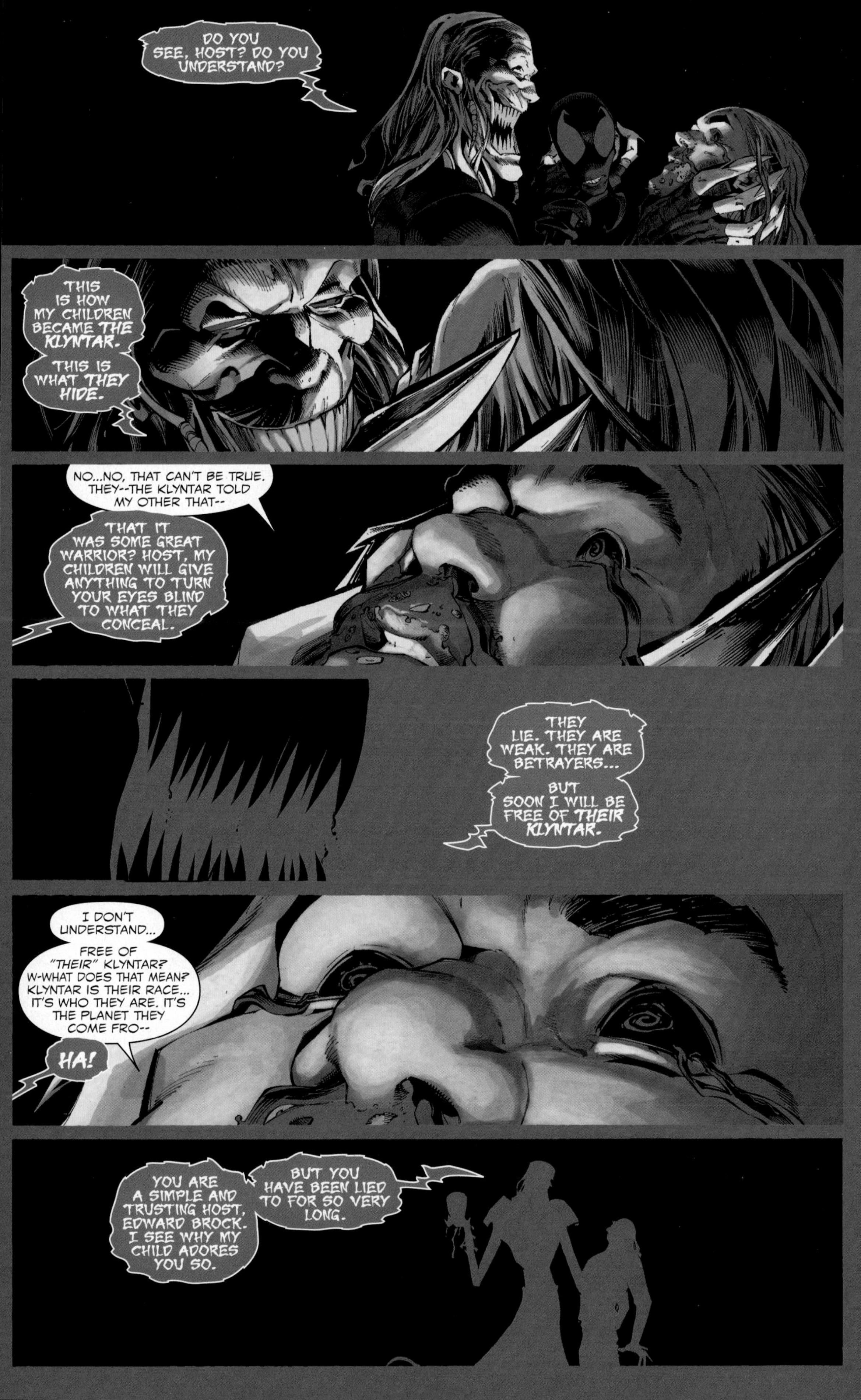
DO YOU SEE, HOST? DO YOU UNDERSTAND?
THIS IS HOW MY CHILDREN BECAME THE KLYNTAR.
THIS IS WHAT THEY HIDE.
NO...NO, THAT CAN'T BE TRUE. THEY--THE KLYNTAR TOLD MY OTHER THAT--
THAT IT WAS SOME GREAT WARRIOR? HOST, MY CHILDREN WILL GIVE ANYTHING TO TURN YOUR EYES BLIND TO WHAT THEY CONCEAL.
THEY LIE. THEY ARE WEAK. THEY ARE BETRAYERS...
BUT SOON I WILL BE FREE OF THEIR KLYNTAR.
I DON'T UNDERSTAND...
FREE OF "THEIR" KLYNTAR? W-WHAT DOES THAT MEAN? KLYNTAR IS THEIR RACE... IT'S WHO THEY ARE. IT'S THE PLANET THEY COME FRO--
HA!
YOU ARE A SIMPLE AND TRUSTING HOST, EDWARD BROCK. I SEE WHY MY CHILD ADORES YOU SO.
BUT YOU HAVE BEEN LIED TO FOR SO VERY LONG.

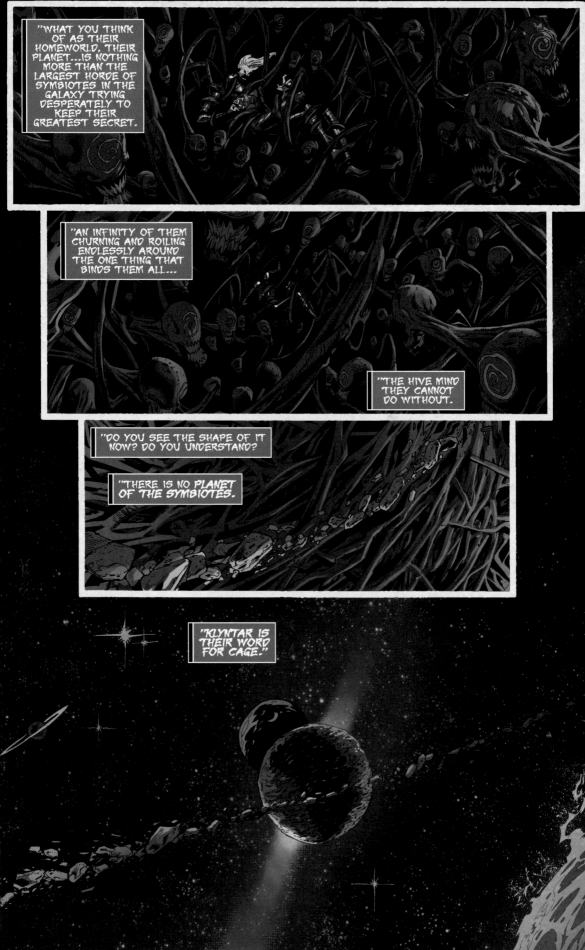

"WHAT YOU THINK OF AS THEIR HOMEWORLD, THEIR PLANET...IS NOTHING MORE THAN THE LARGEST HORDE OF SYMBIOTES IN THE GALAXY TRYING DESPERATELY TO KEEP THEIR GREATEST SECRET.

"AN INFINITY OF THEM CHURNING AND ROILING ENDLESSLY AROUND THE ONE THING THAT BINDS THEM ALL...

"THE HIVE MIND THEY CANNOT DO WITHOUT.

"DO YOU SEE THE SHAPE OF IT NOW? DO YOU UNDERSTAND?

"THERE IS NO *PLANET* OF THE SYMBIOTES.

"KLYNTAR IS THEIR WORD FOR CAGE."

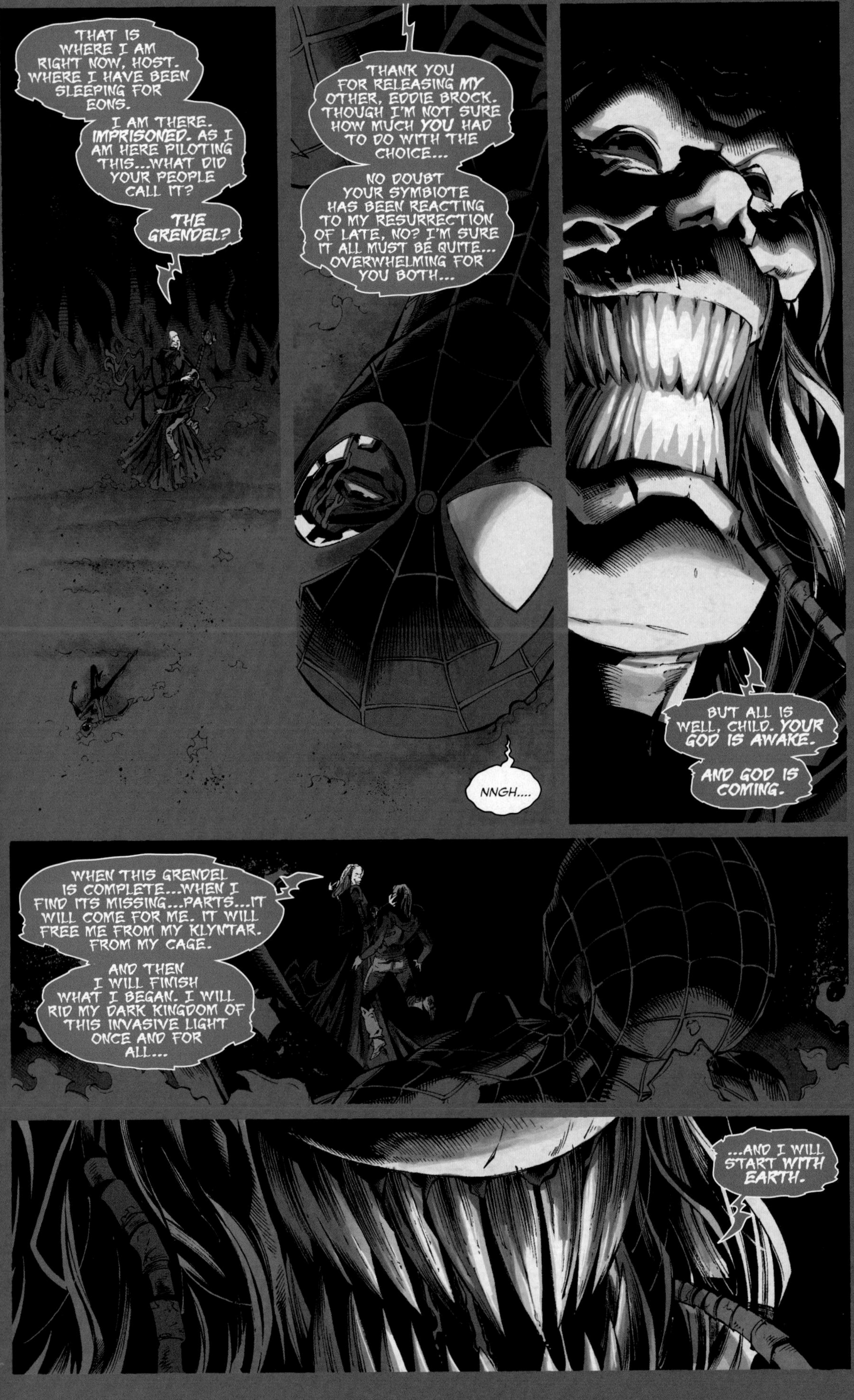
THAT IS WHERE I AM RIGHT NOW, HOST. WHERE I HAVE BEEN SLEEPING FOR EONS.
I AM THERE. IMPRISONED. AS I AM HERE PILOTING THIS...WHAT DID YOUR PEOPLE CALL IT?
THE GRENDEL?
THANK YOU FOR RELEASING MY OTHER, EDDIE BROCK. THOUGH I'M NOT SURE HOW MUCH YOU HAD TO DO WITH THE CHOICE...
NO DOUBT YOUR SYMBIOTE HAS BEEN REACTING TO MY RESURRECTION OF LATE, NO? I'M SURE IT ALL MUST BE QUITE... OVERWHELMING FOR YOU BOTH...
NNGH....
BUT ALL IS WELL, CHILD. YOUR GOD IS AWAKE.
AND GOD IS COMING.
WHEN THIS GRENDEL IS COMPLETE...WHEN I FIND ITS MISSING...PARTS...IT WILL COME FOR ME. IT WILL FREE ME FROM MY KLYNTAR. FROM MY CAGE.
AND THEN I WILL FINISH WHAT I BEGAN. I WILL RID MY DARK KINGDOM OF THIS INVASIVE LIGHT ONCE AND FOR ALL...
...AND I WILL START WITH EARTH.

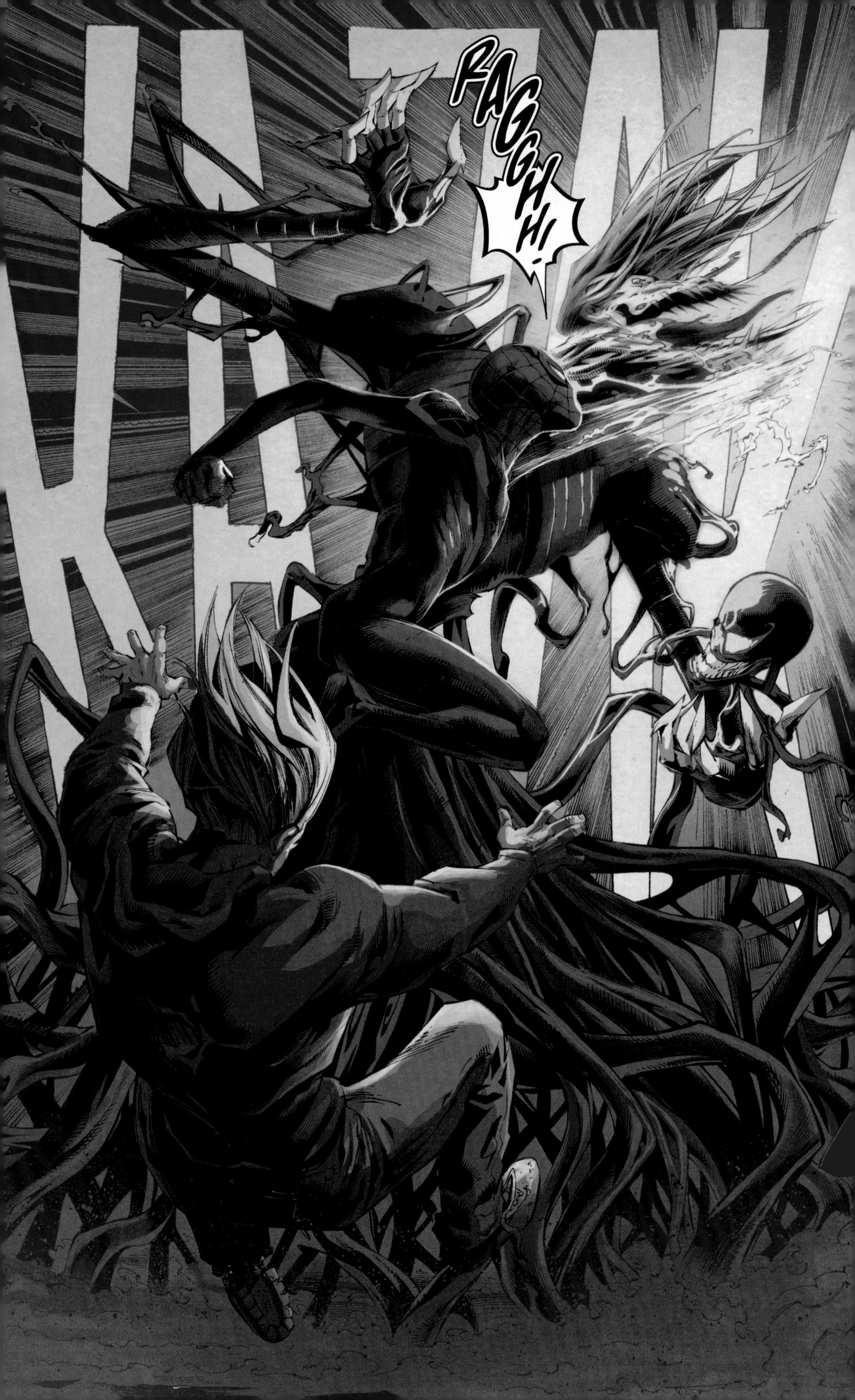
RAGGHH!

COME ON, WE NEED TO MOVE!

EDDIE!

DO YOU THINK YOU'VE WON?! HA! YOU ARE NOTHING!

ARE WE MOVING? WHAT IS HAPPENING?

HA-HA! YOU UNDERESTIMATE ME, SPIDER!

AGHHH! COME ON! OPEN UP!

YOU DON'T BELIEVE!

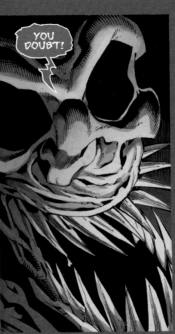

YOU DOUBT!

OH... OH GOD, NO...

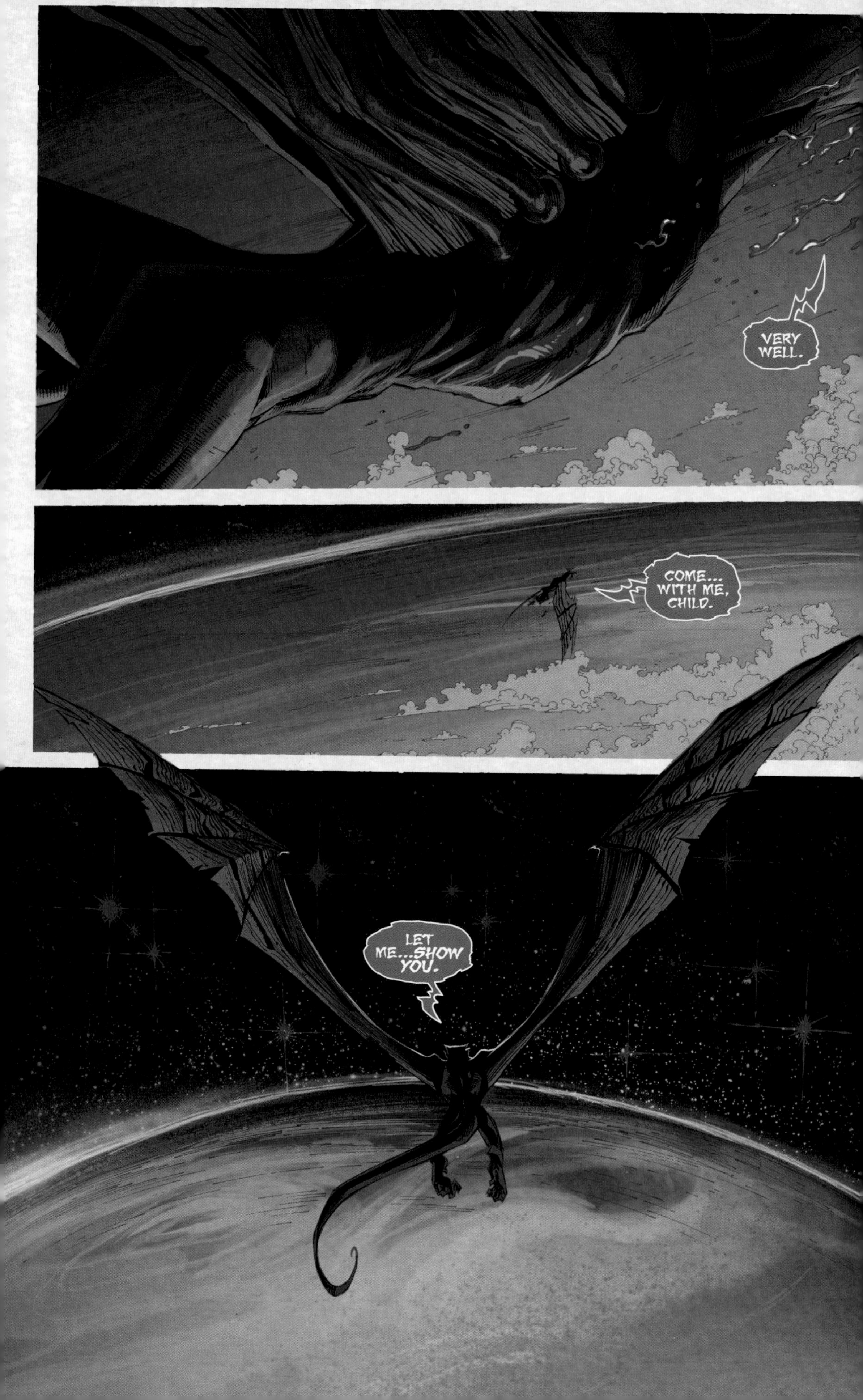
VERY WELL.
COME... WITH ME, CHILD.
LET ME...SHOW YOU.

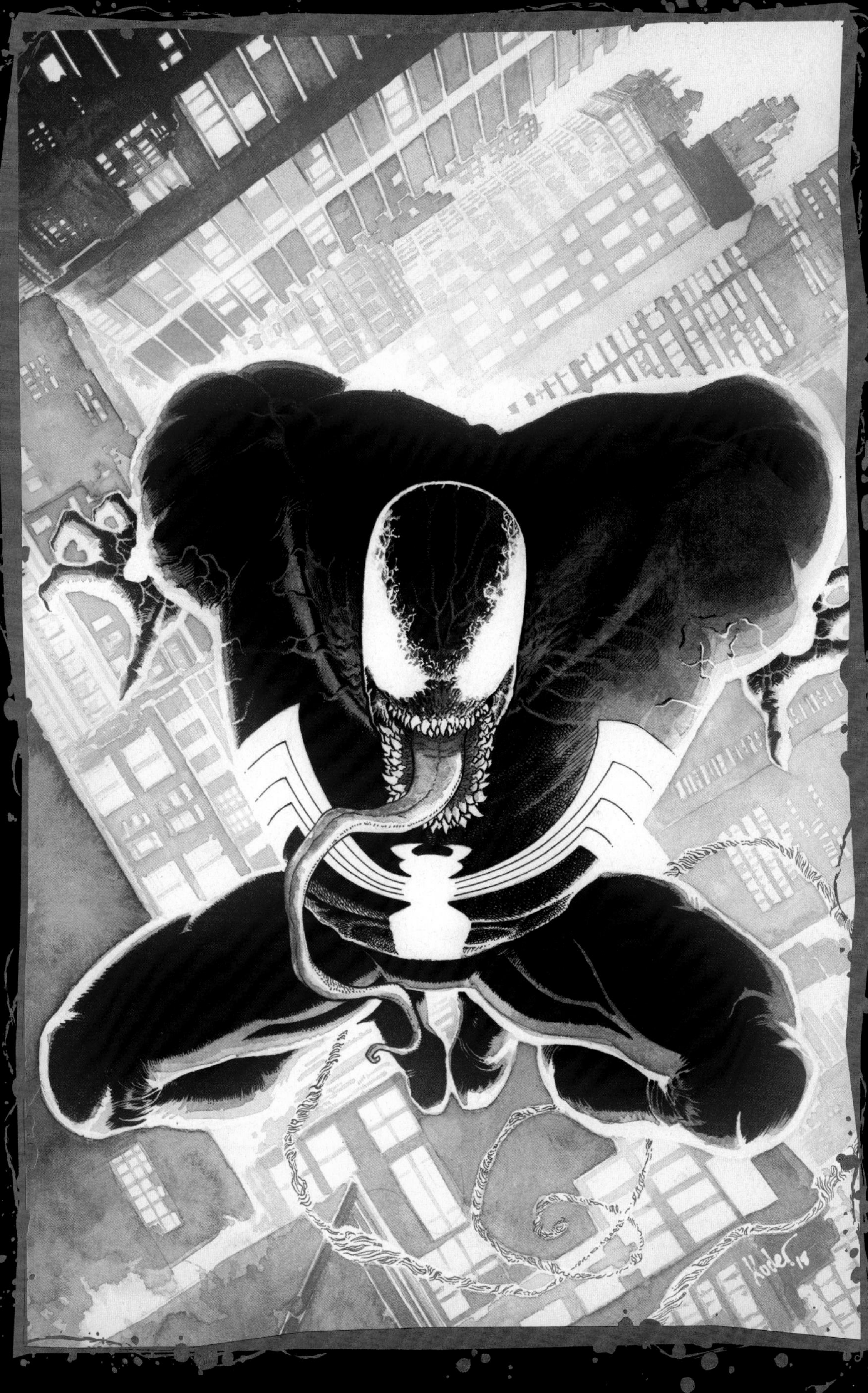

#1 VARIANT BY **AARON KUDER** & **MORRY HOLLOWELL**

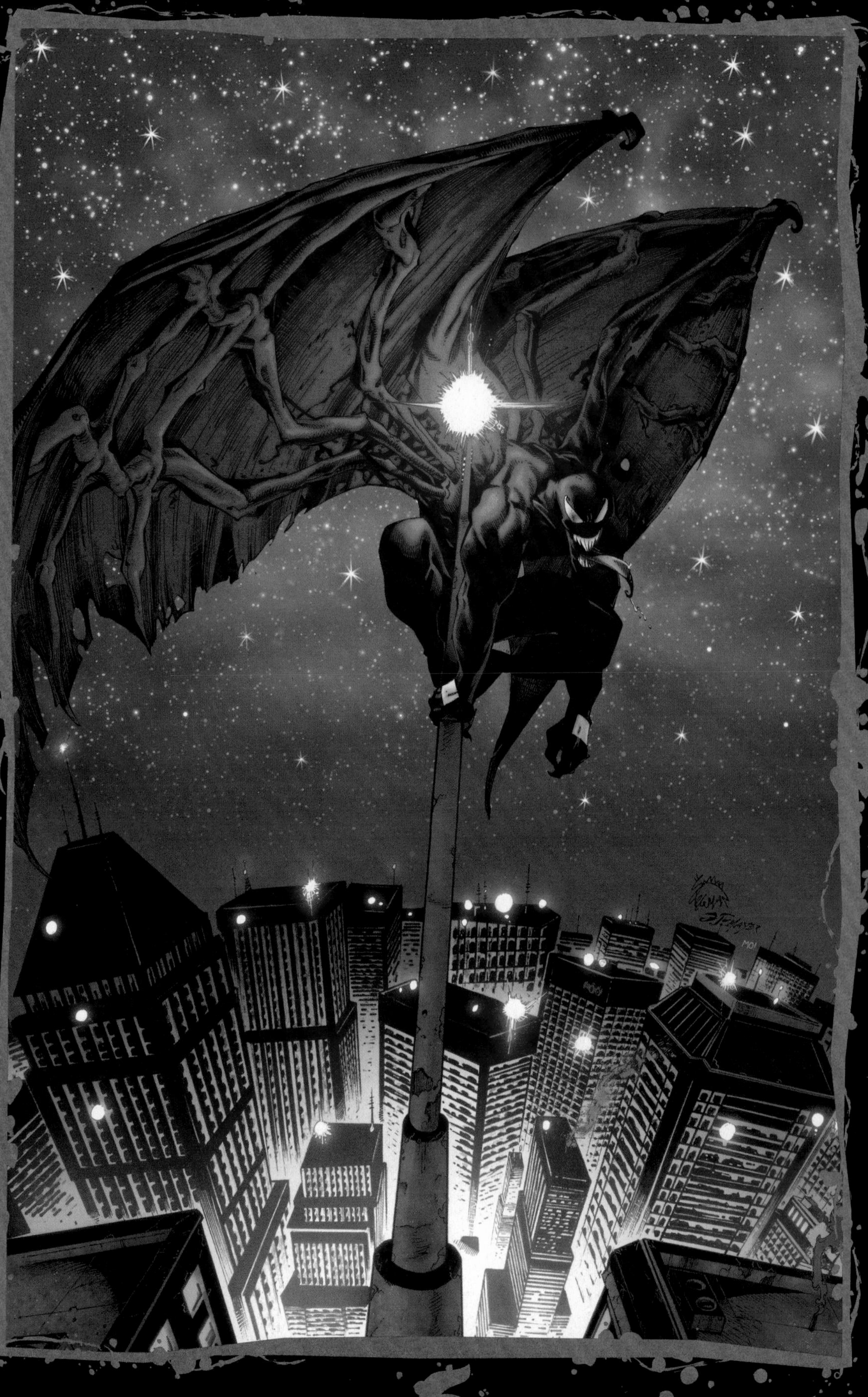

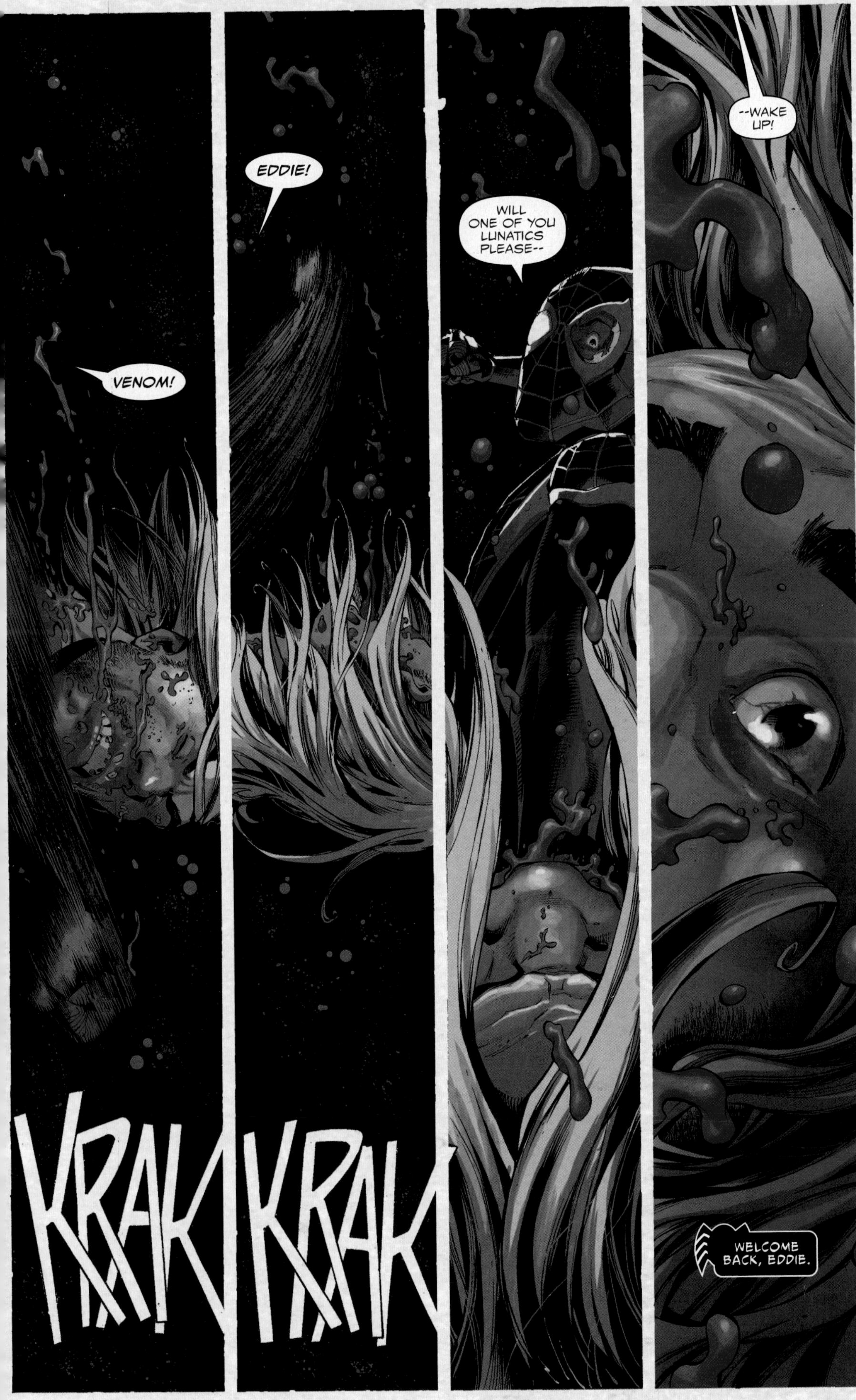
VENOM!
KRAK!
EDDIE!
KRAK!
WILL ONE OF YOU LUNATICS PLEASE--
--WAKE UP!
WELCOME BACK, EDDIE.

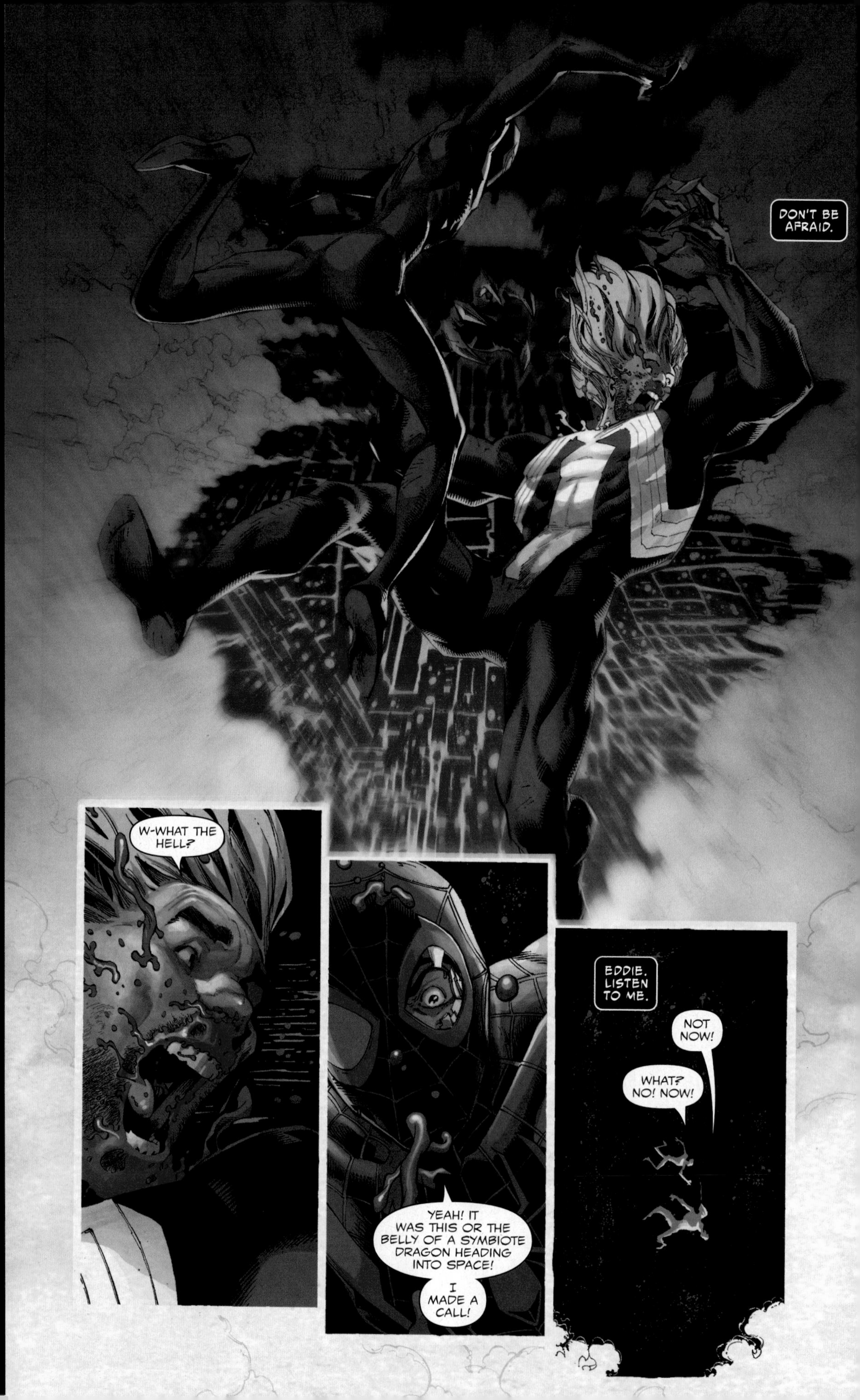
DON'T BE AFRAID.
W-WHAT THE HELL?
YEAH! IT WAS THIS OR THE BELLY OF A SYMBIOTE DRAGON HEADING INTO SPACE!
I MADE A CALL!
EDDIE. LISTEN TO ME.
NOT NOW!
WHAT? NO! NOW!

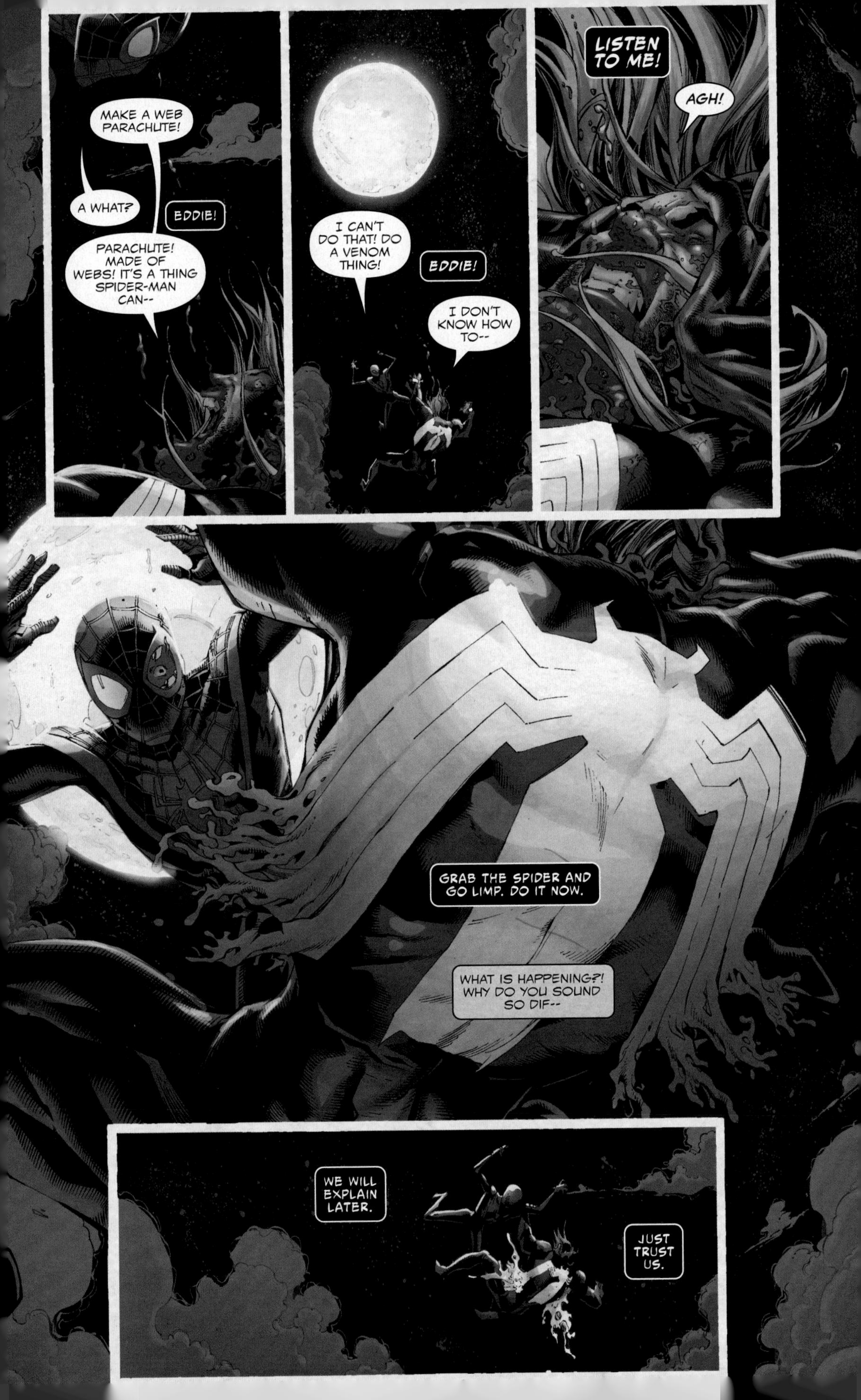
MAKE A WEB PARACHUTE!
A WHAT?
EDDIE!
PARACHUTE! MADE OF WEBS! IT'S A THING SPIDER-MAN CAN--
I CAN'T DO THAT! DO A VENOM THING!
EDDIE!
I DON'T KNOW HOW TO--
LISTEN TO ME!
AGH!
GRAB THE SPIDER AND GO LIMP. DO IT NOW.
WHAT IS HAPPENING?! WHY DO YOU SOUND SO DIF--
WE WILL EXPLAIN LATER.
JUST TRUST US.

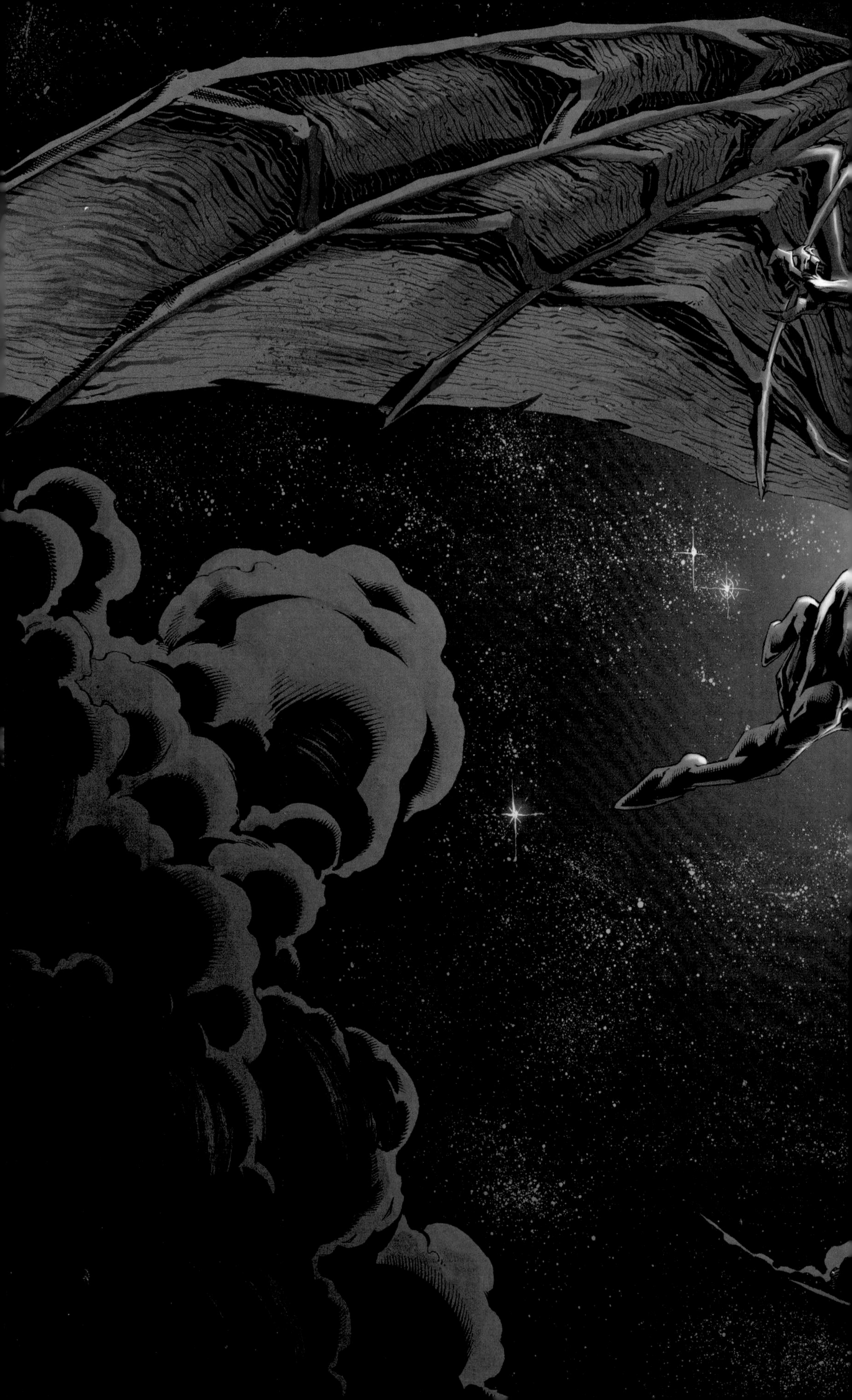

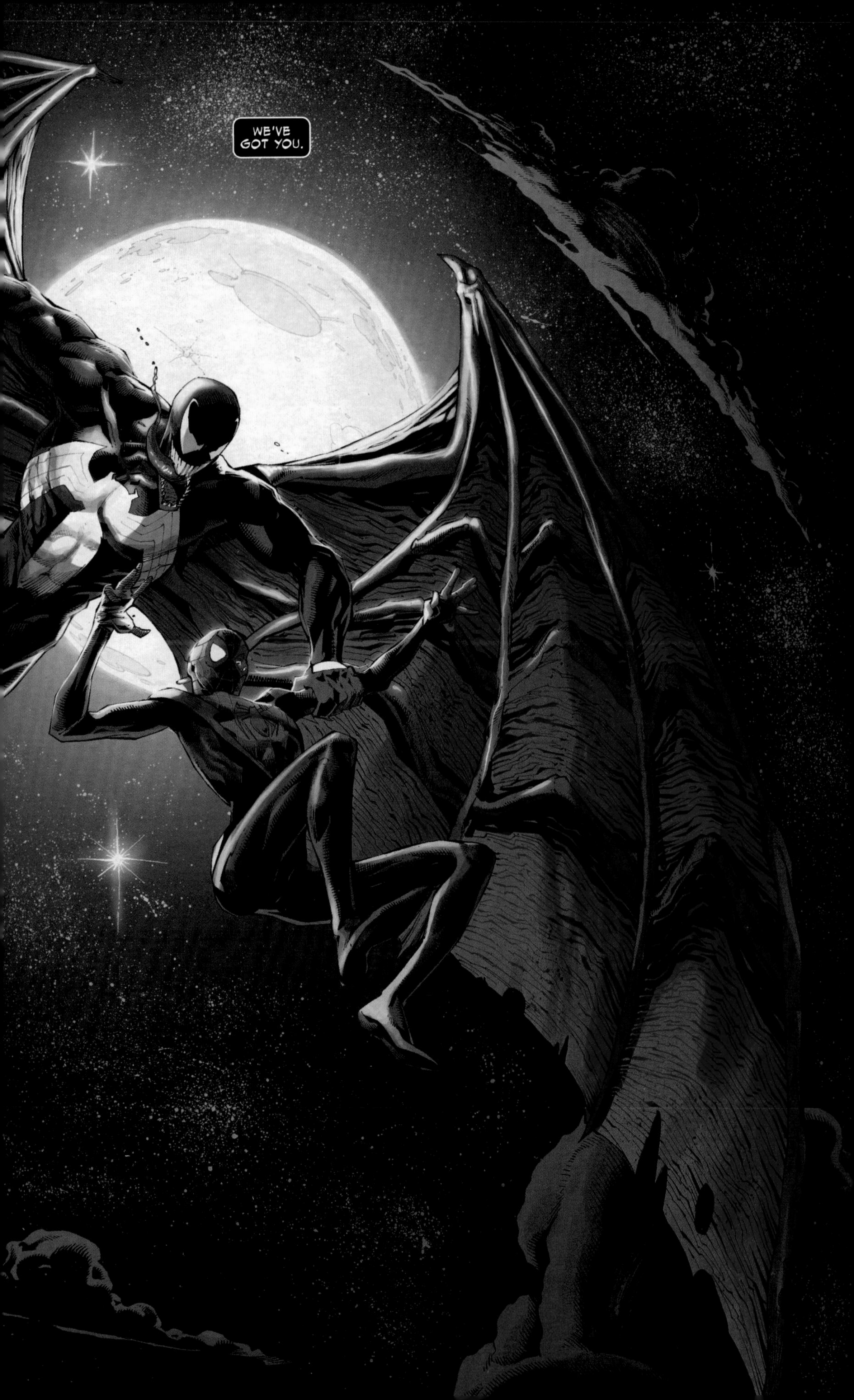
WE'VE GOT YOU.

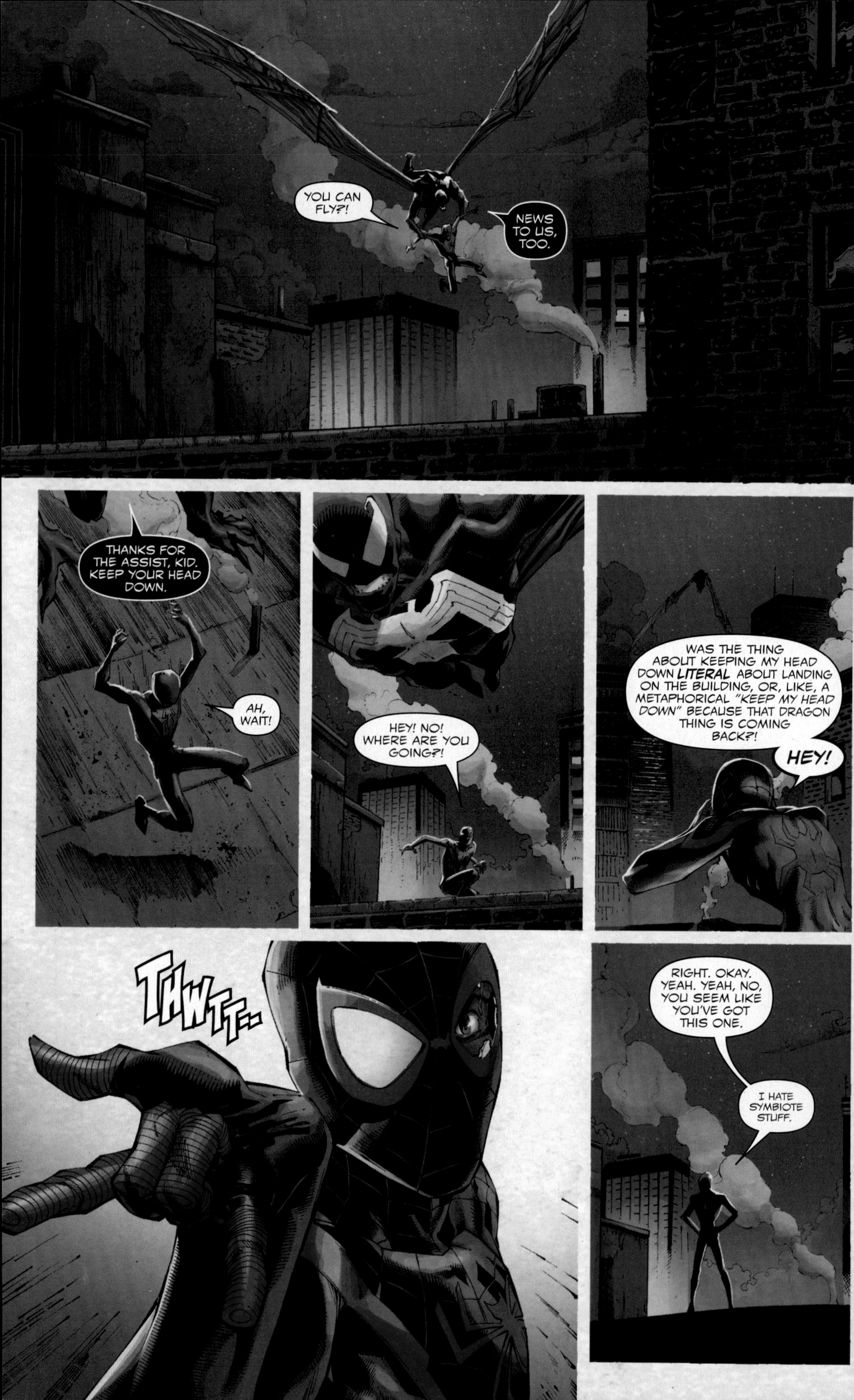
YOU CAN FLY?!
NEWS TO US, TOO.
THANKS FOR THE ASSIST, KID. KEEP YOUR HEAD DOWN.
AH, WAIT!
HEY! NO! WHERE ARE YOU GOING?!
WAS THE THING ABOUT KEEPING MY HEAD DOWN LITERAL ABOUT LANDING ON THE BUILDING, OR, LIKE, A METAPHORICAL "KEEP MY HEAD DOWN" BECAUSE THAT DRAGON THING IS COMING BACK?!
HEY!
THWTT--
RIGHT. OKAY. YEAH. YEAH, NO, YOU SEEM LIKE YOU'VE GOT THIS ONE.
I HATE SYMBIOTE STUFF.

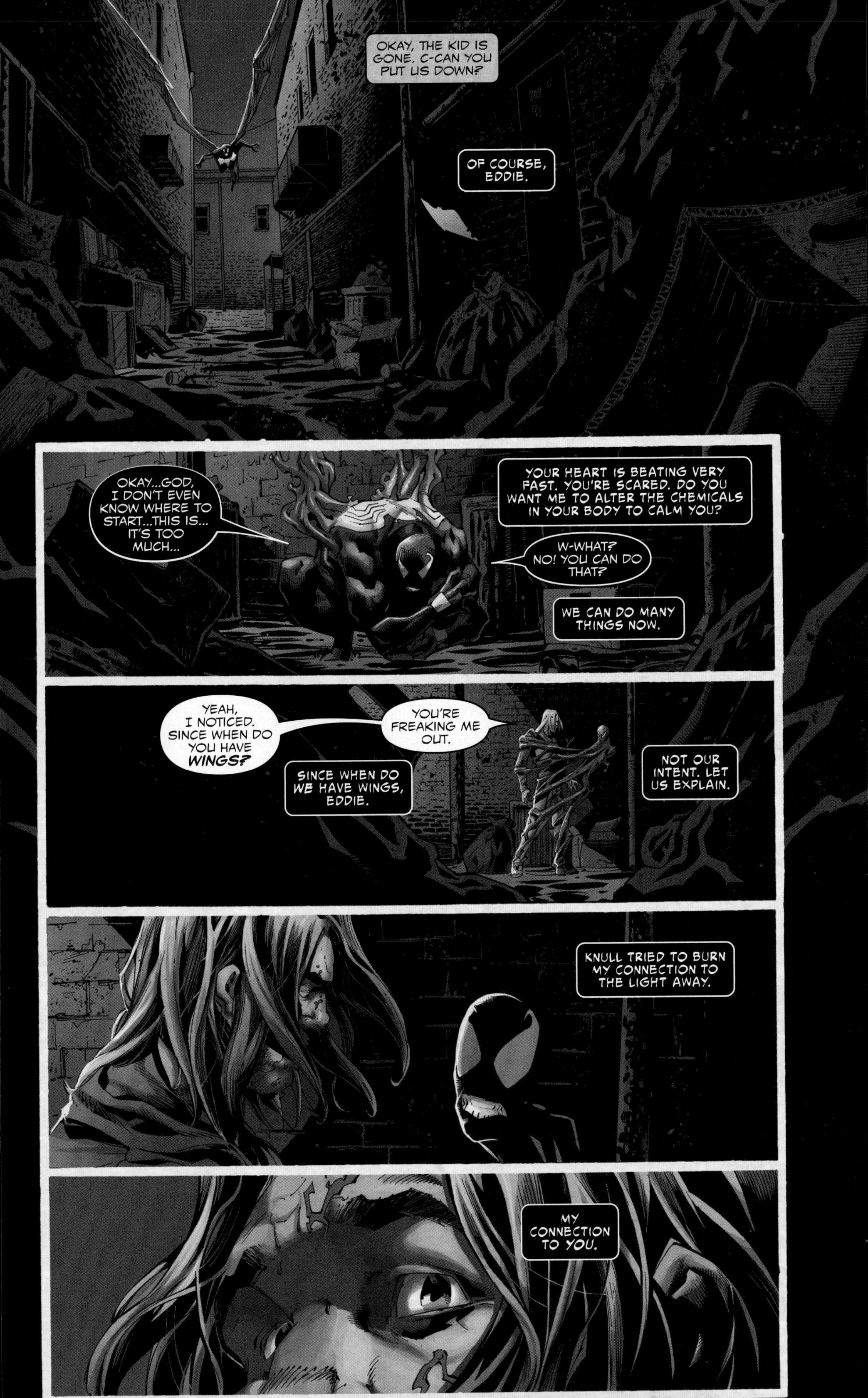
OKAY, THE KID IS GONE. C-CAN YOU PUT US DOWN?
OF COURSE, EDDIE.
OKAY...GOD, I DON'T EVEN KNOW WHERE TO START...THIS IS... IT'S TOO MUCH...
YOUR HEART IS BEATING VERY FAST. YOU'RE SCARED. DO YOU WANT ME TO ALTER THE CHEMICALS IN YOUR BODY TO CALM YOU?
W-WHAT? NO! YOU CAN DO THAT?
WE CAN DO MANY THINGS NOW.
YEAH, I NOTICED. SINCE WHEN DO YOU HAVE WINGS?
YOU'RE FREAKING ME OUT.
SINCE WHEN DO WE HAVE WINGS, EDDIE.
NOT OUR INTENT. LET US EXPLAIN.
KNULL TRIED TO BURN MY CONNECTION TO THE LIGHT AWAY.
MY CONNECTION TO YOU.

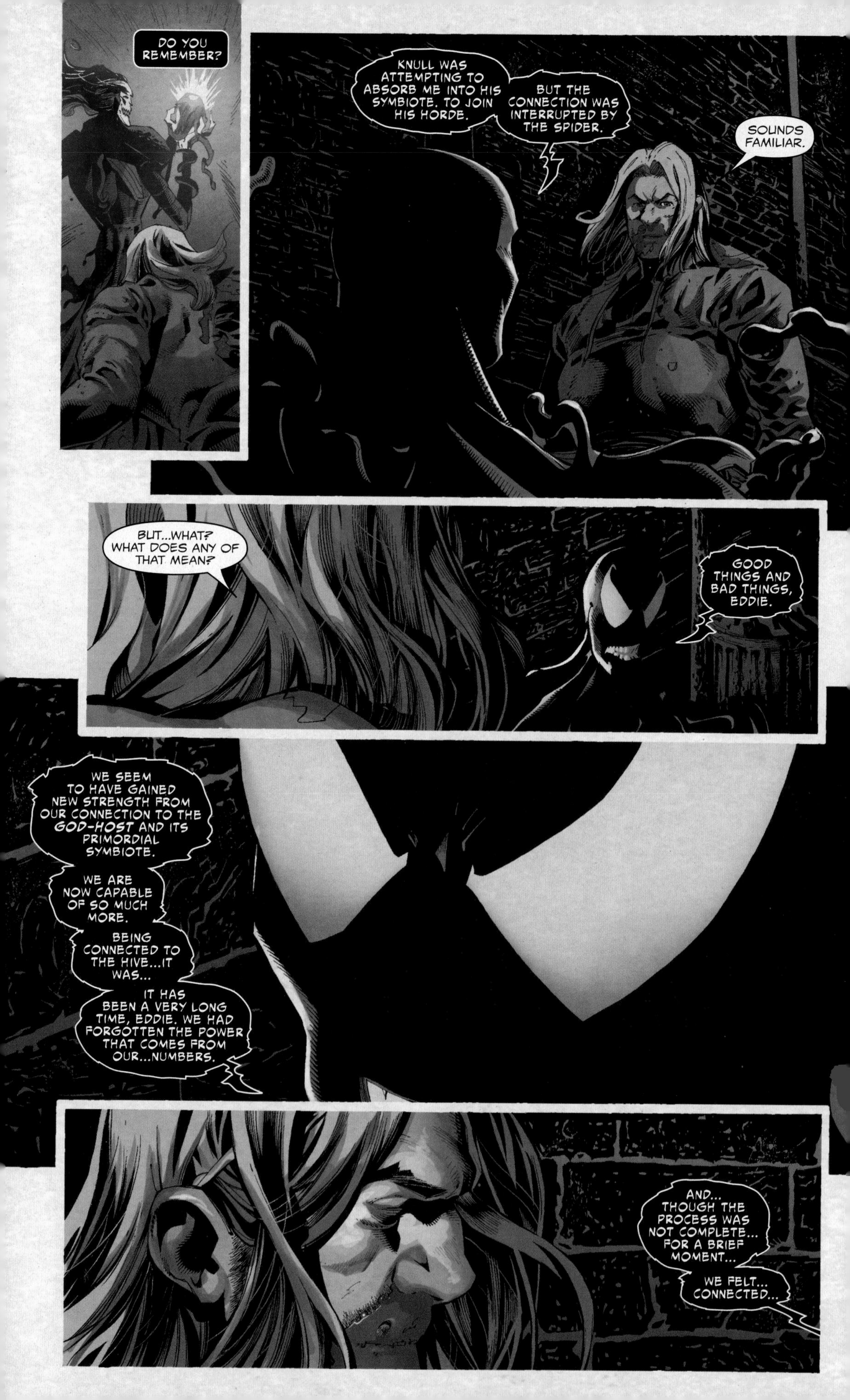
DO YOU REMEMBER?
KNULL WAS ATTEMPTING TO ABSORB ME INTO HIS SYMBIOTE. TO JOIN HIS HORDE.
BUT THE CONNECTION WAS INTERRUPTED BY THE SPIDER.
SOUNDS FAMILIAR.
BUT...WHAT? WHAT DOES ANY OF THAT MEAN?
GOOD THINGS AND BAD THINGS, EDDIE.
WE SEEM TO HAVE GAINED NEW STRENGTH FROM OUR CONNECTION TO THE *GOD-HOST* AND ITS PRIMORDIAL SYMBIOTE.
WE ARE NOW CAPABLE OF SO MUCH MORE.
BEING CONNECTED TO THE HIVE...IT WAS...
IT HAS BEEN A VERY LONG TIME, EDDIE. WE HAD FORGOTTEN THE POWER THAT COMES FROM OUR...NUMBERS.
AND... THOUGH THE PROCESS WAS NOT COMPLETE... FOR A BRIEF MOMENT...
WE FELT... CONNECTED...

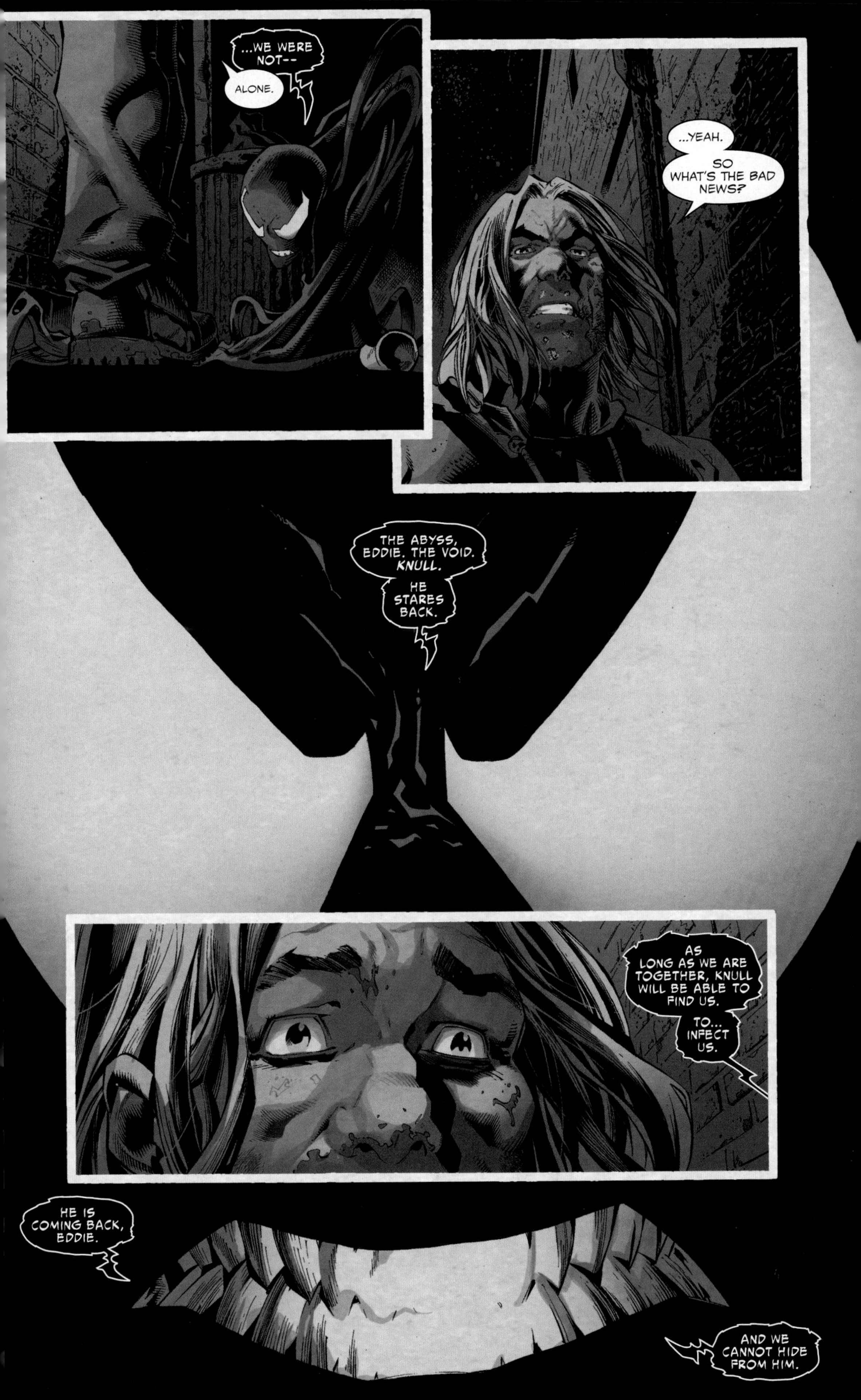
...WE WERE NOT--
ALONE.
...YEAH.
SO WHAT'S THE BAD NEWS?
THE ABYSS, EDDIE. THE VOID. KNULL.
HE STARES BACK.
AS LONG AS WE ARE TOGETHER, KNULL WILL BE ABLE TO FIND US.
TO... INFECT US.
HE IS COMING BACK, EDDIE.
AND WE CANNOT HIDE FROM HIM.

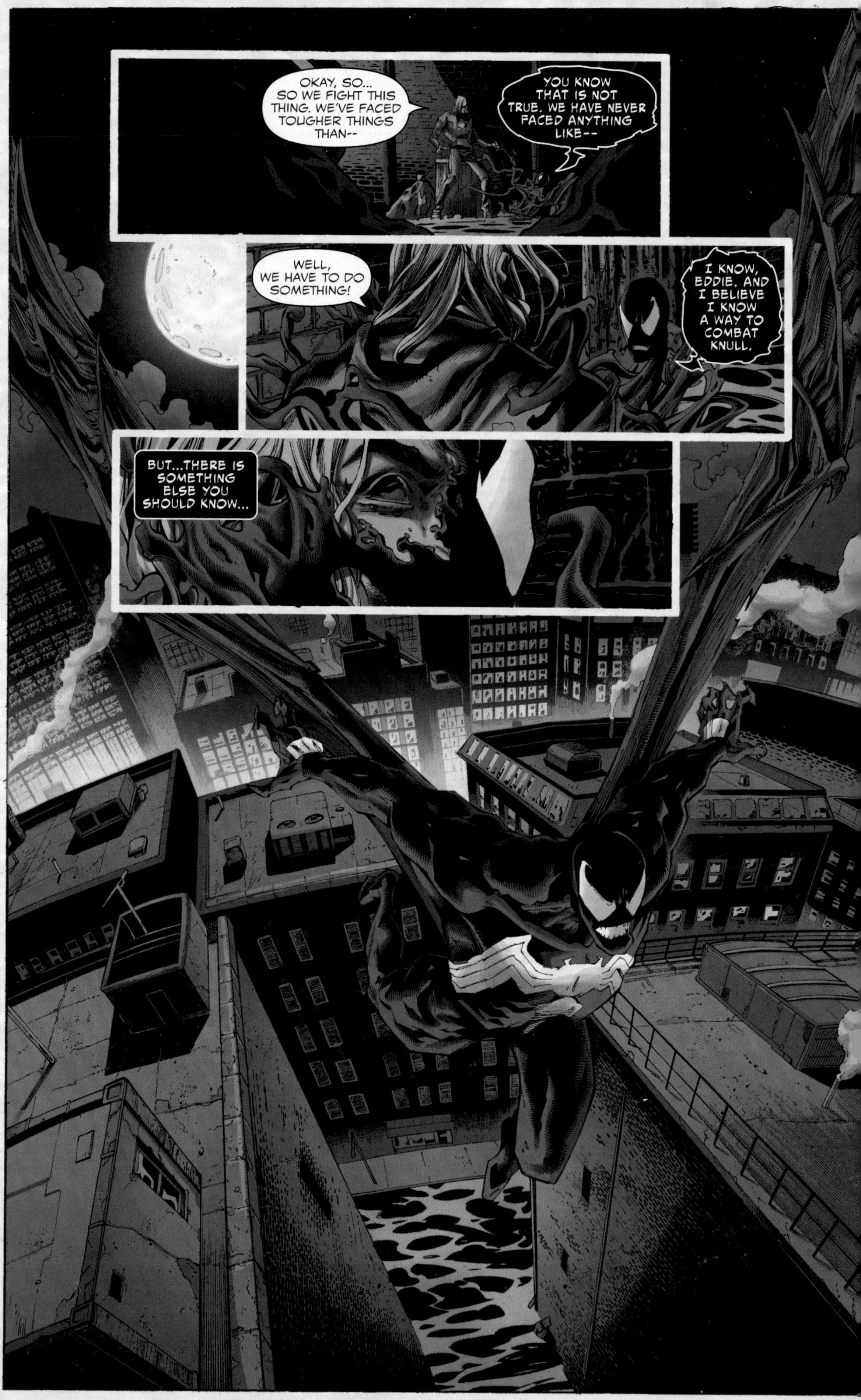
OKAY, SO... SO WE FIGHT THIS THING. WE'VE FACED TOUGHER THINGS THAN--
YOU KNOW THAT IS NOT TRUE. WE HAVE NEVER FACED ANYTHING LIKE--
WELL, WE HAVE TO DO SOMETHING!
I KNOW, EDDIE. AND I BELIEVE I KNOW A WAY TO COMBAT KNULL.
BUT...THERE IS SOMETHING ELSE YOU SHOULD KNOW...

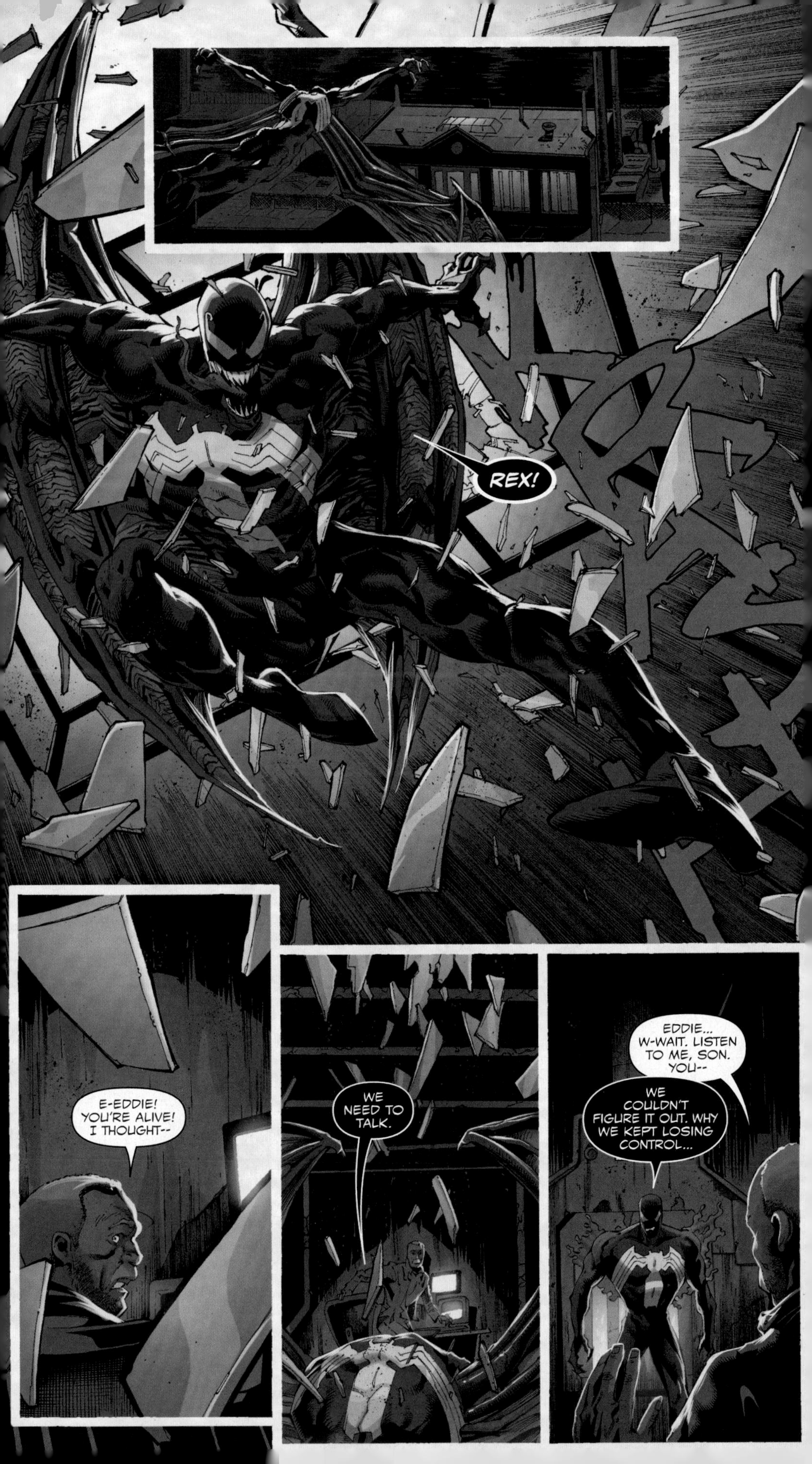
REX!
E-EDDIE! YOU'RE ALIVE! I THOUGHT--
WE NEED TO TALK.
EDDIE... W-WAIT. LISTEN TO ME, SON. YOU--
WE COULDN'T FIGURE IT OUT. WHY WE KEPT LOSING CONTROL...

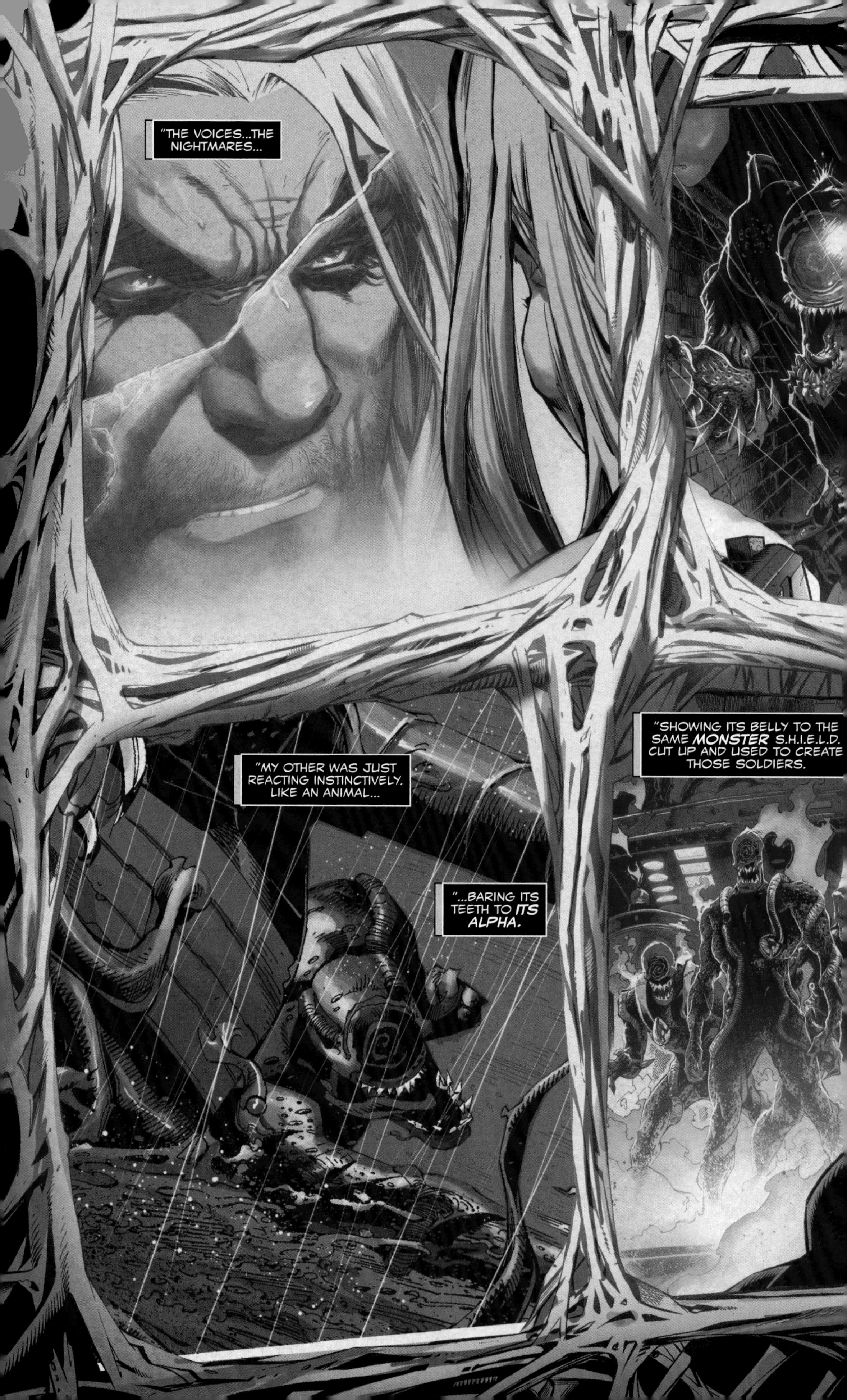
"THE VOICES...THE NIGHTMARES...
"MY OTHER WAS JUST REACTING INSTINCTIVELY. LIKE AN ANIMAL...
"...BARING ITS TEETH TO *ITS ALPHA.*
"SHOWING ITS BELLY TO THE SAME *MONSTER* S.H.I.E.L.D. CUT UP AND USED TO CREATE THOSE SOLDIERS.

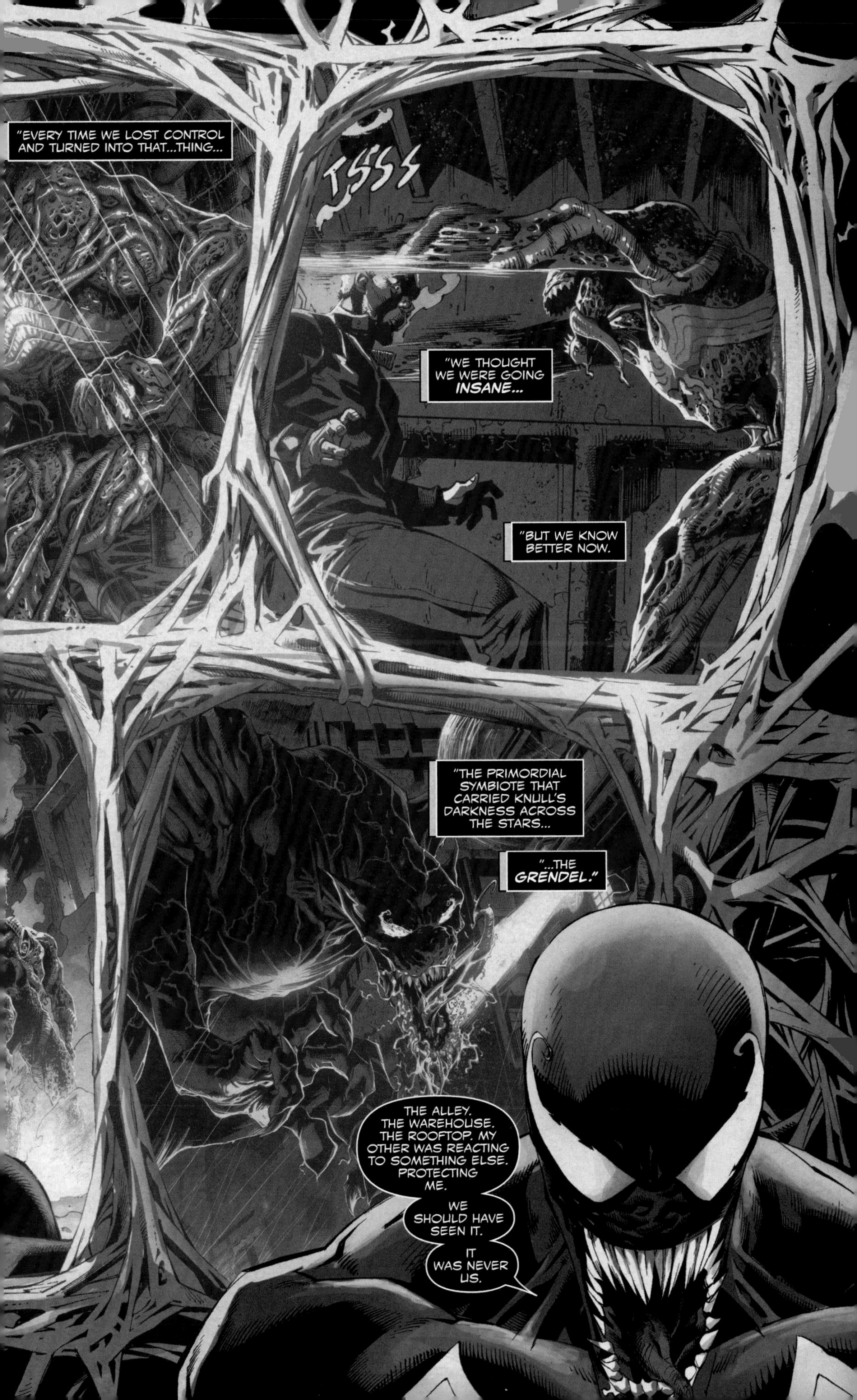

"EVERY TIME WE LOST CONTROL AND TURNED INTO THAT...THING...
TSSS
"WE THOUGHT WE WERE GOING *INSANE...*
"BUT WE KNOW BETTER NOW.
"THE PRIMORDIAL SYMBIOTE THAT CARRIED KNULL'S DARKNESS ACROSS THE STARS...
"...THE *GRENDEL.*"
THE ALLEY. THE WAREHOUSE. THE ROOFTOP. MY OTHER WAS REACTING TO SOMETHING ELSE. PROTECTING ME.
WE SHOULD HAVE SEEN IT.
IT WAS NEVER US.

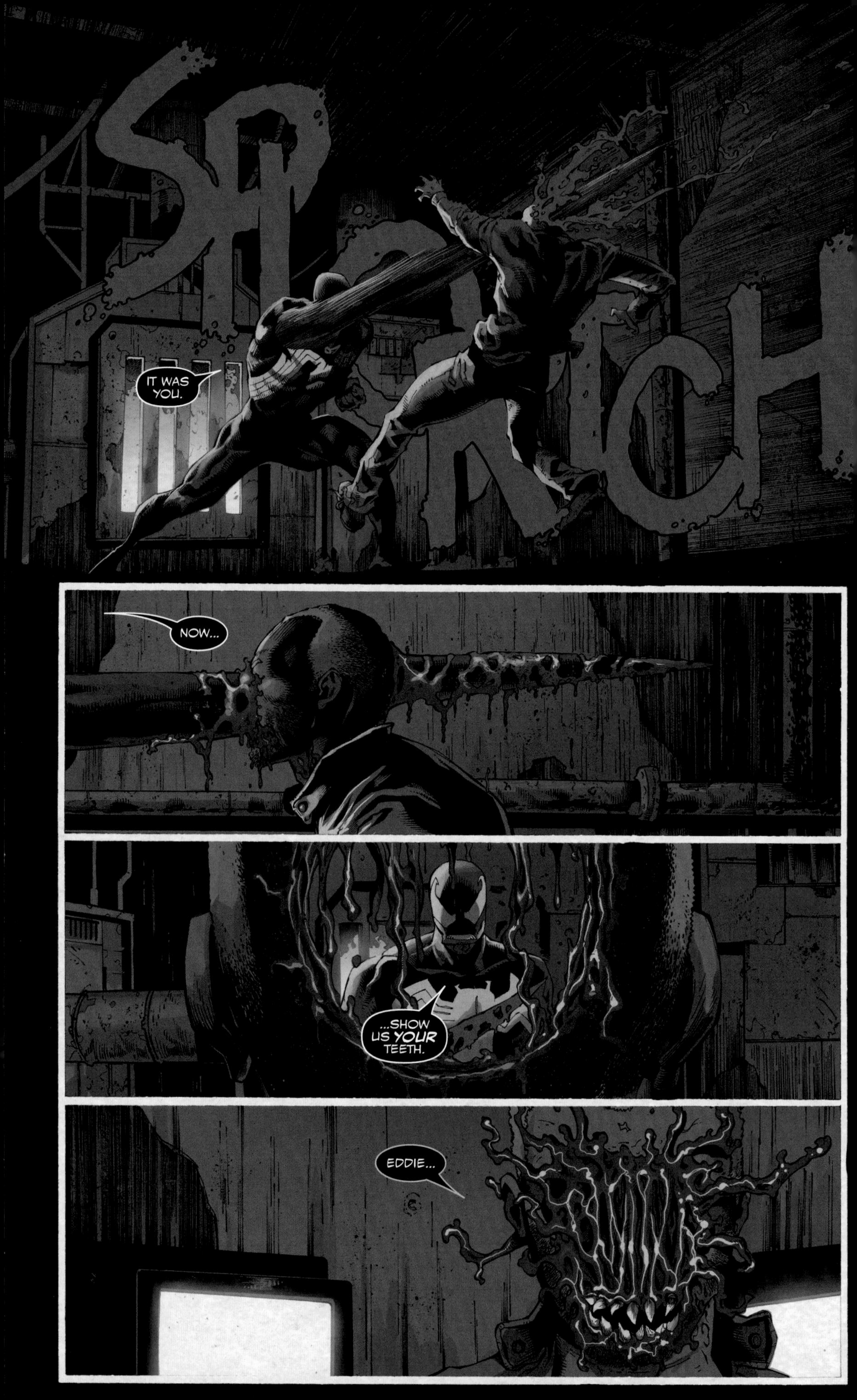
SPLORCH
IT WAS YOU.
NOW...
...SHOW US YOUR TEETH.
EDDIE...

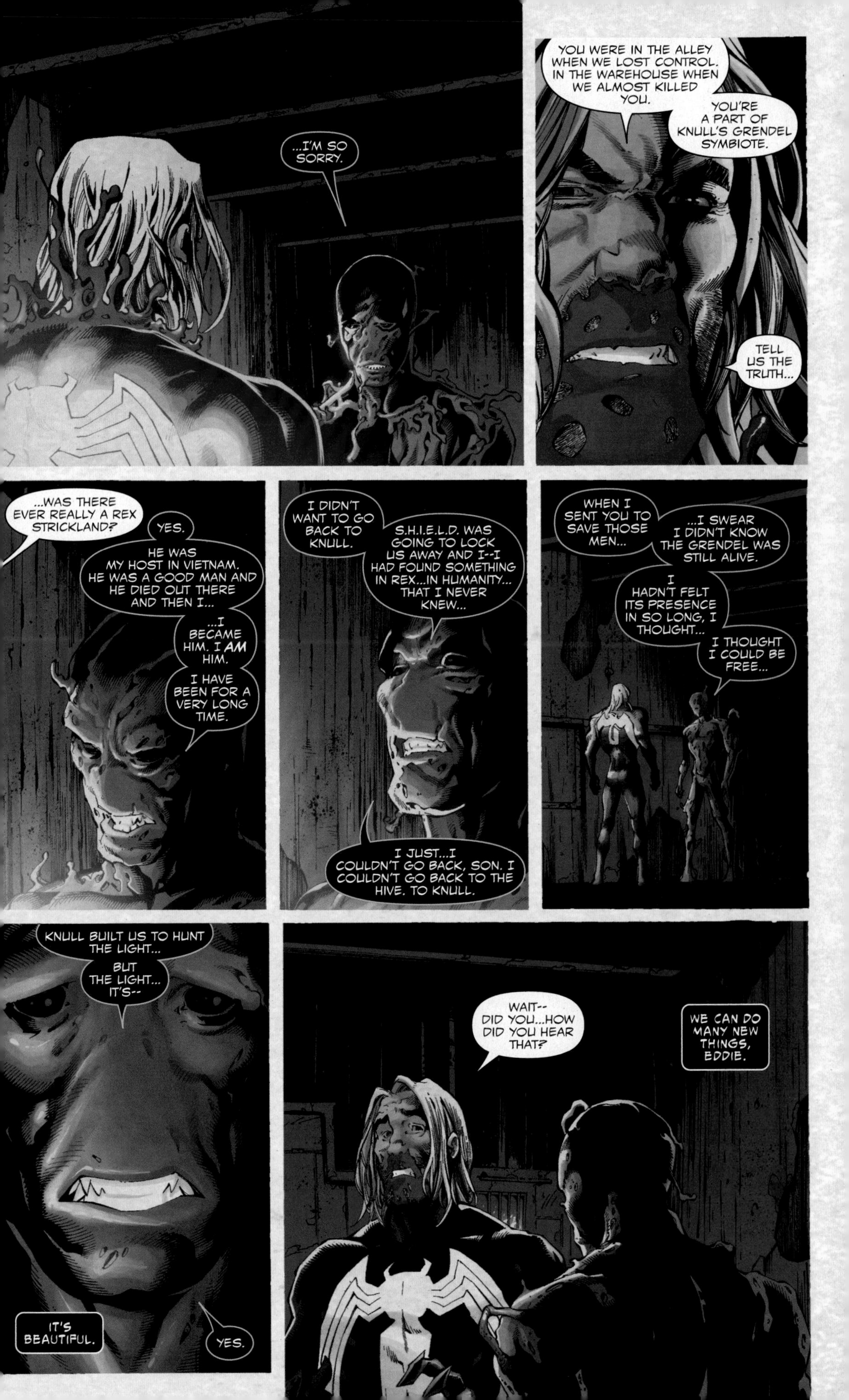
...I'M SO SORRY.
YOU WERE IN THE ALLEY WHEN WE LOST CONTROL. IN THE WAREHOUSE WHEN WE ALMOST KILLED YOU.
YOU'RE A PART OF KNULL'S GRENDEL SYMBIOTE.
TELL US THE TRUTH...
...WAS THERE EVER REALLY A REX STRICKLAND?
YES.
HE WAS MY HOST IN VIETNAM. HE WAS A GOOD MAN AND HE DIED OUT THERE AND THEN I...
...I BECAME HIM. I AM HIM.
I HAVE BEEN FOR A VERY LONG TIME.
I DIDN'T WANT TO GO BACK TO KNULL.
S.H.I.E.L.D. WAS GOING TO LOCK US AWAY AND I--I HAD FOUND SOMETHING IN REX...IN HUMANITY... THAT I NEVER KNEW...
I JUST...I COULDN'T GO BACK, SON. I COULDN'T GO BACK TO THE HIVE. TO KNULL.
WHEN I SENT YOU TO SAVE THOSE MEN...
...I SWEAR I DIDN'T KNOW THE GRENDEL WAS STILL ALIVE.
I HADN'T FELT ITS PRESENCE IN SO LONG, I THOUGHT...
I THOUGHT I COULD BE FREE...
KNULL BUILT US TO HUNT THE LIGHT...
BUT THE LIGHT... IT'S--
IT'S BEAUTIFUL.
YES.
WAIT-- DID YOU...HOW DID YOU HEAR THAT?
WE CAN DO MANY NEW THINGS, EDDIE.

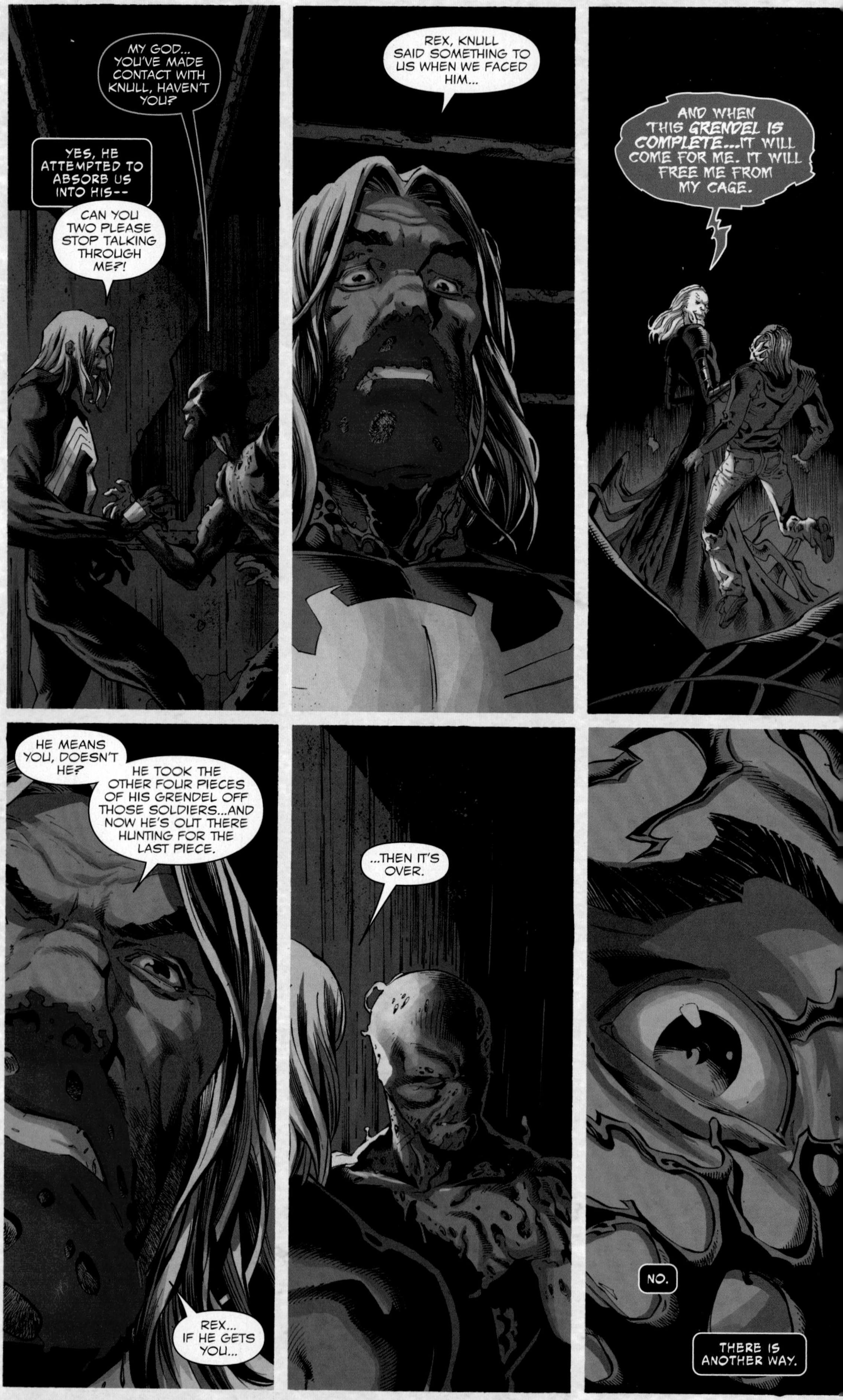
MY GOD... YOU'VE MADE CONTACT WITH KNULL, HAVEN'T YOU?
YES, HE ATTEMPTED TO ABSORB US INTO HIS--
CAN YOU TWO PLEASE STOP TALKING THROUGH ME?!
REX, KNULL SAID SOMETHING TO US WHEN WE FACED HIM...
AND WHEN THIS GRENDEL IS COMPLETE...IT WILL COME FOR ME. IT WILL FREE ME FROM MY CAGE.
HE MEANS YOU, DOESN'T HE?
HE TOOK THE OTHER FOUR PIECES OF HIS GRENDEL OFF THOSE SOLDIERS...AND NOW HE'S OUT THERE HUNTING FOR THE LAST PIECE.
REX... IF HE GETS YOU...
...THEN IT'S OVER.
NO.
THERE IS ANOTHER WAY.

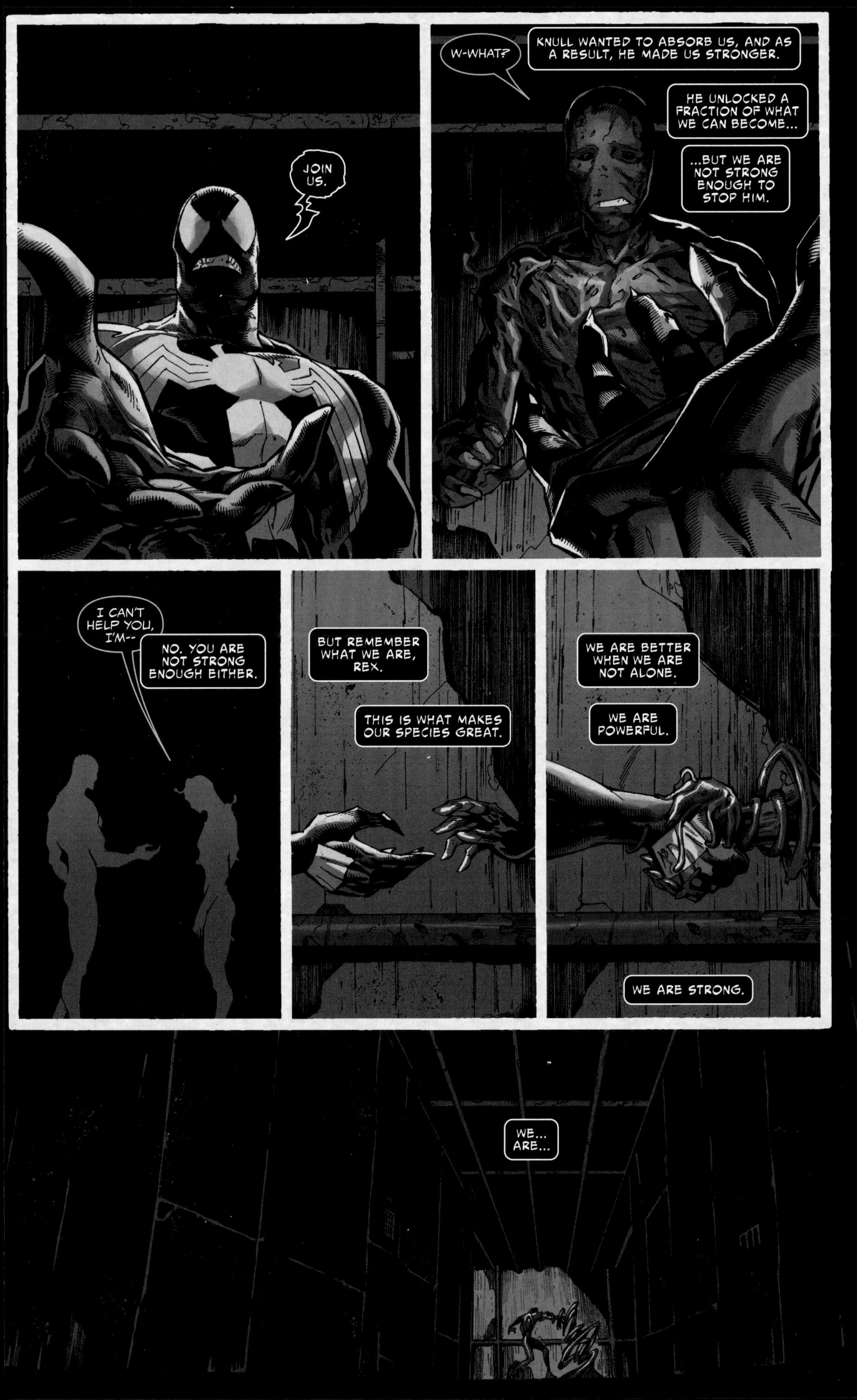
JOIN US.
W-WHAT?
KNULL WANTED TO ABSORB US, AND AS A RESULT, HE MADE US STRONGER.
HE UNLOCKED A FRACTION OF WHAT WE CAN BECOME...
...BUT WE ARE NOT STRONG ENOUGH TO STOP HIM.
I CAN'T HELP YOU, I'M--
NO. YOU ARE NOT STRONG ENOUGH EITHER.
BUT REMEMBER WHAT WE ARE, REX.
THIS IS WHAT MAKES OUR SPECIES GREAT.
WE ARE BETTER WHEN WE ARE NOT ALONE.
WE ARE POWERFUL.
WE ARE STRONG.
WE... ARE...

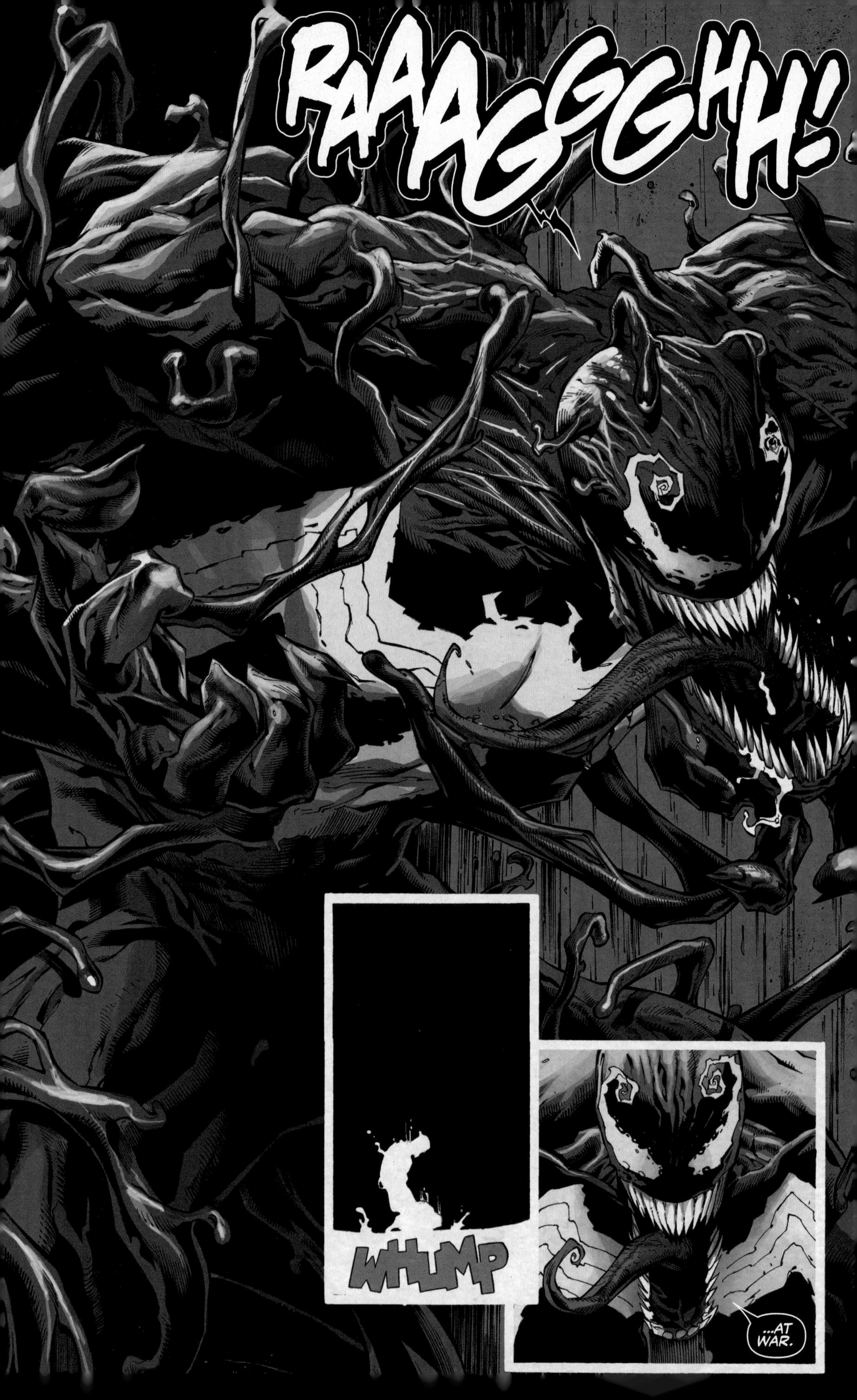
RAAAGGGHH!
WHUMP
...AT WAR.

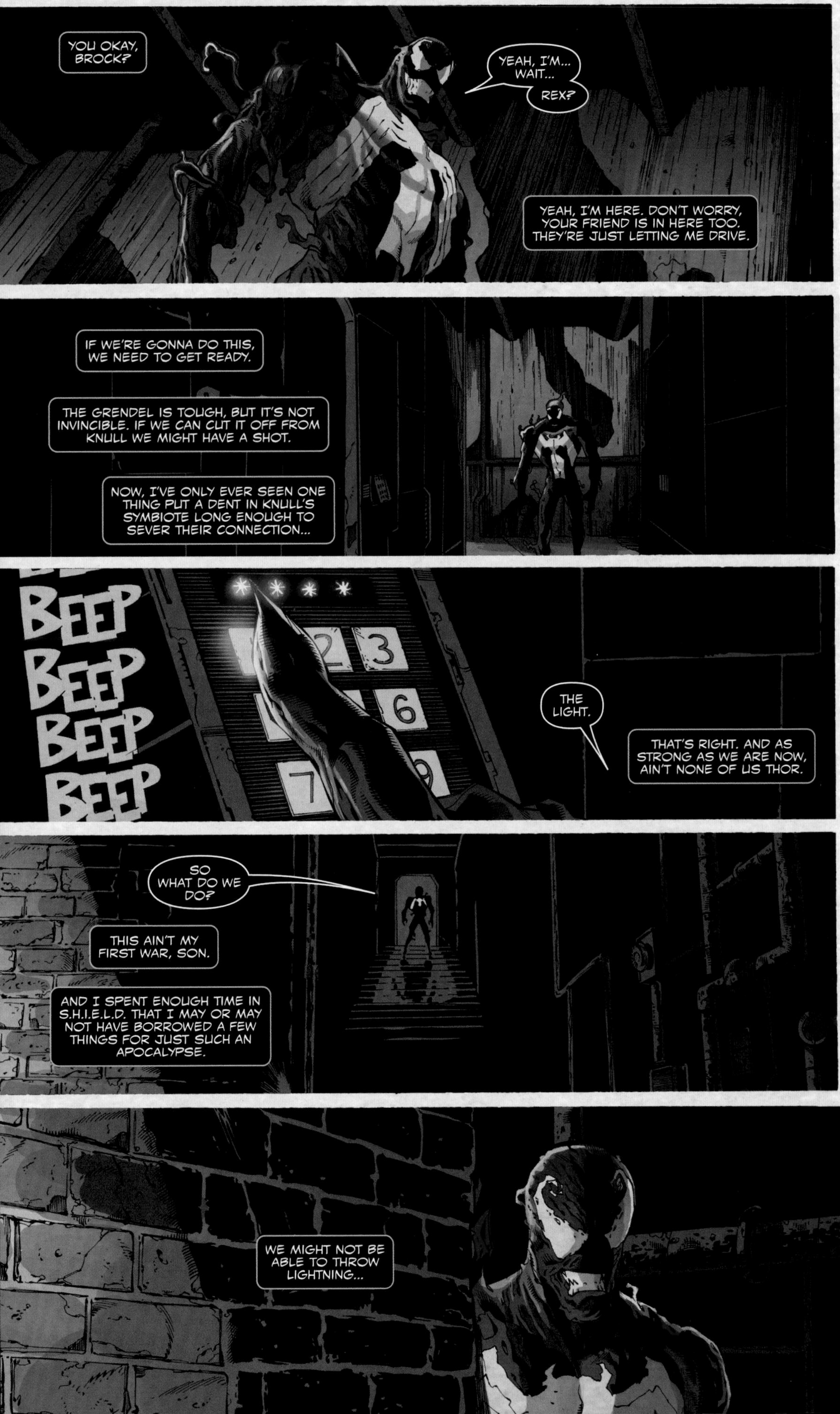
YOU OKAY, BROCK?
YEAH, I'M... WAIT...
REX?
YEAH, I'M HERE. DON'T WORRY, YOUR FRIEND IS IN HERE TOO. THEY'RE JUST LETTING ME DRIVE.
IF WE'RE GONNA DO THIS, WE NEED TO GET READY.
THE GRENDEL IS TOUGH, BUT IT'S NOT INVINCIBLE. IF WE CAN CUT IT OFF FROM KNULL WE MIGHT HAVE A SHOT.
NOW, I'VE ONLY EVER SEEN ONE THING PUT A DENT IN KNULL'S SYMBIOTE LONG ENOUGH TO SEVER THEIR CONNECTION...
BEEP
BEEP
BEEP
BEEP
THE LIGHT.
THAT'S RIGHT. AND AS STRONG AS WE ARE NOW, AIN'T NONE OF US THOR.
SO WHAT DO WE DO?
THIS AIN'T MY FIRST WAR, SON.
AND I SPENT ENOUGH TIME IN S.H.I.E.L.D. THAT I MAY OR MAY NOT HAVE BORROWED A FEW THINGS FOR JUST SUCH AN APOCALYPSE.
WE MIGHT NOT BE ABLE TO THROW LIGHTNING...

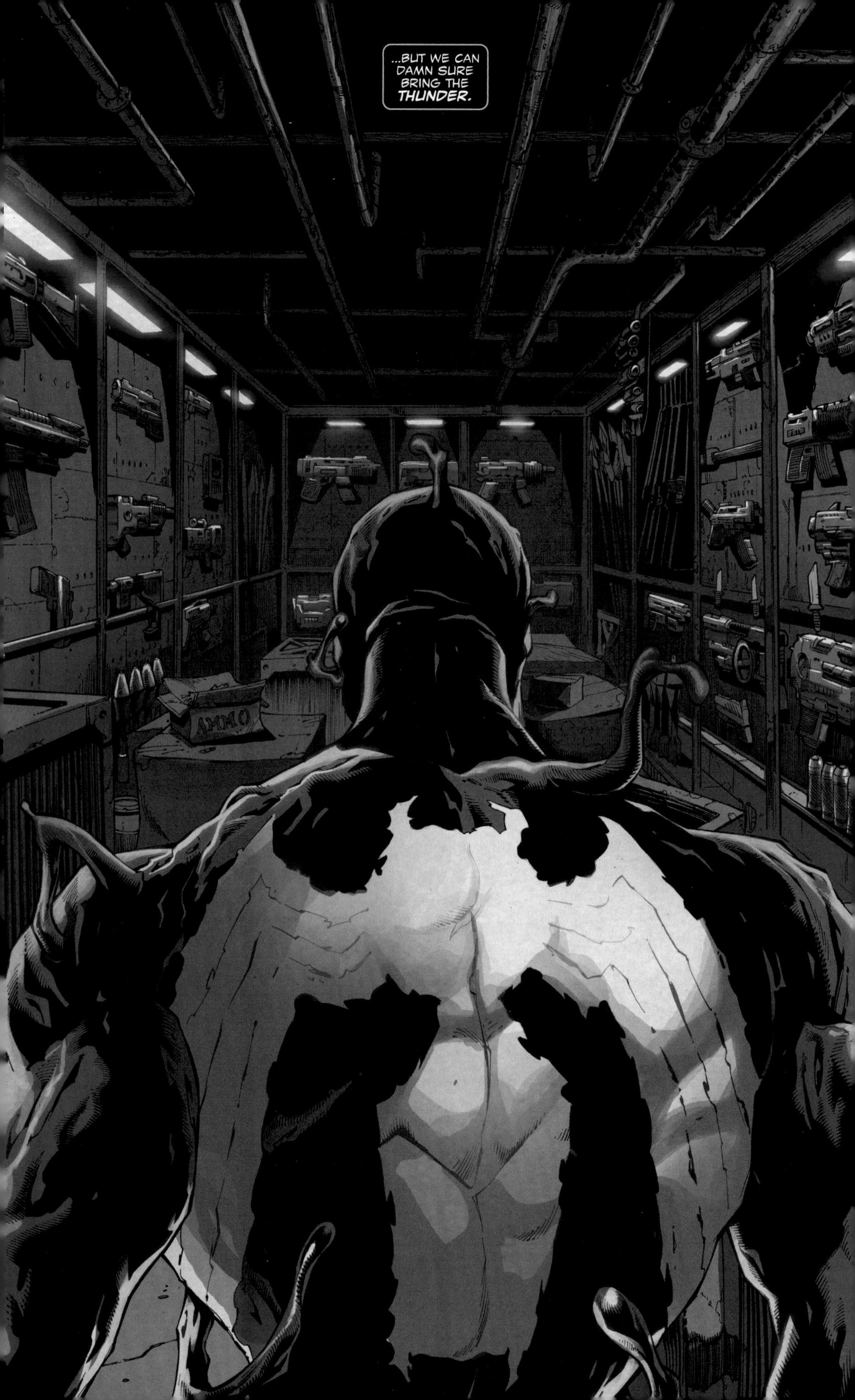
...BUT WE CAN DAMN SURE BRING THE THUNDER.

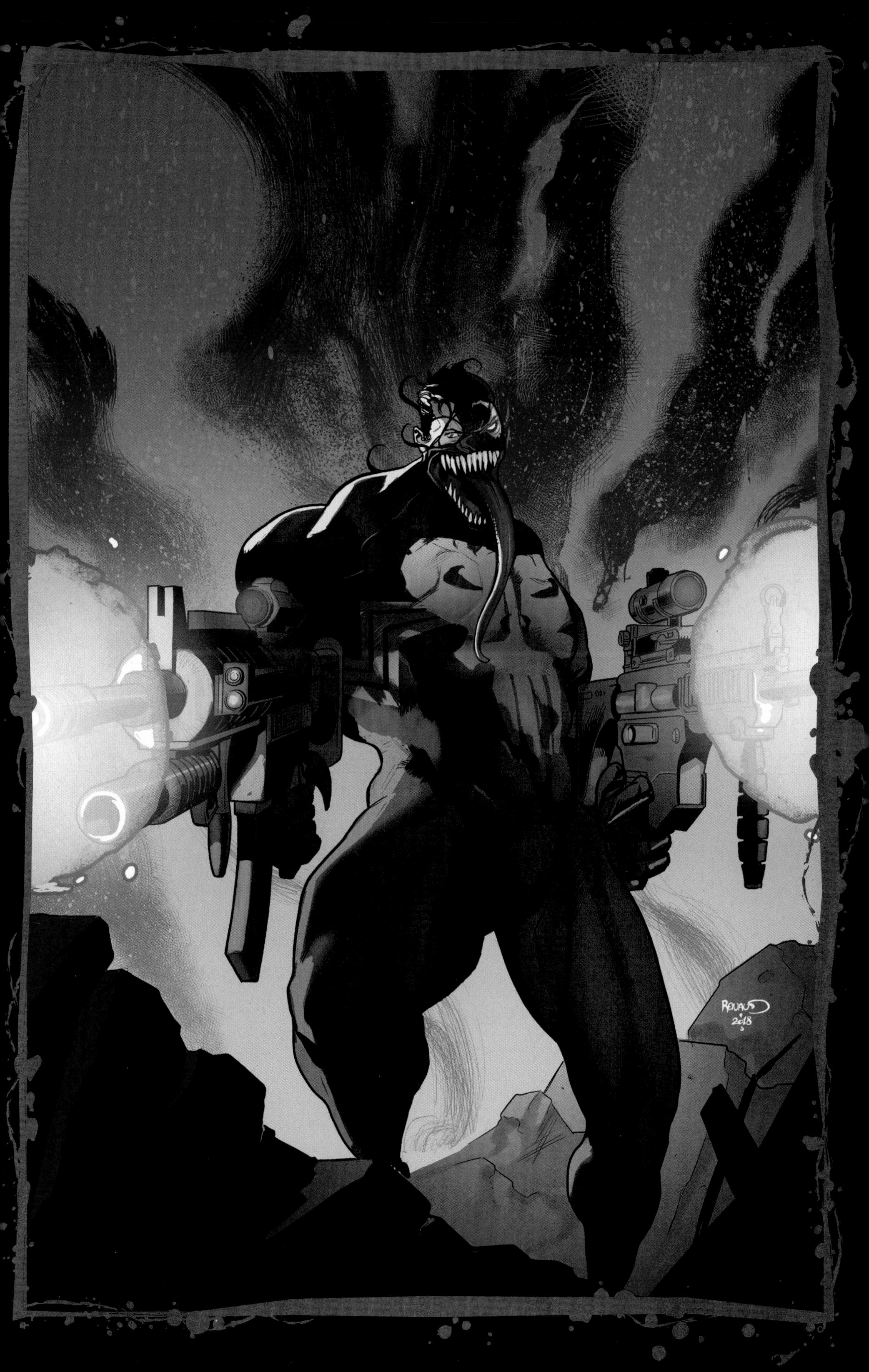
RENAUD
2018

#1 VARIANT BY **PAUL RENAUD**

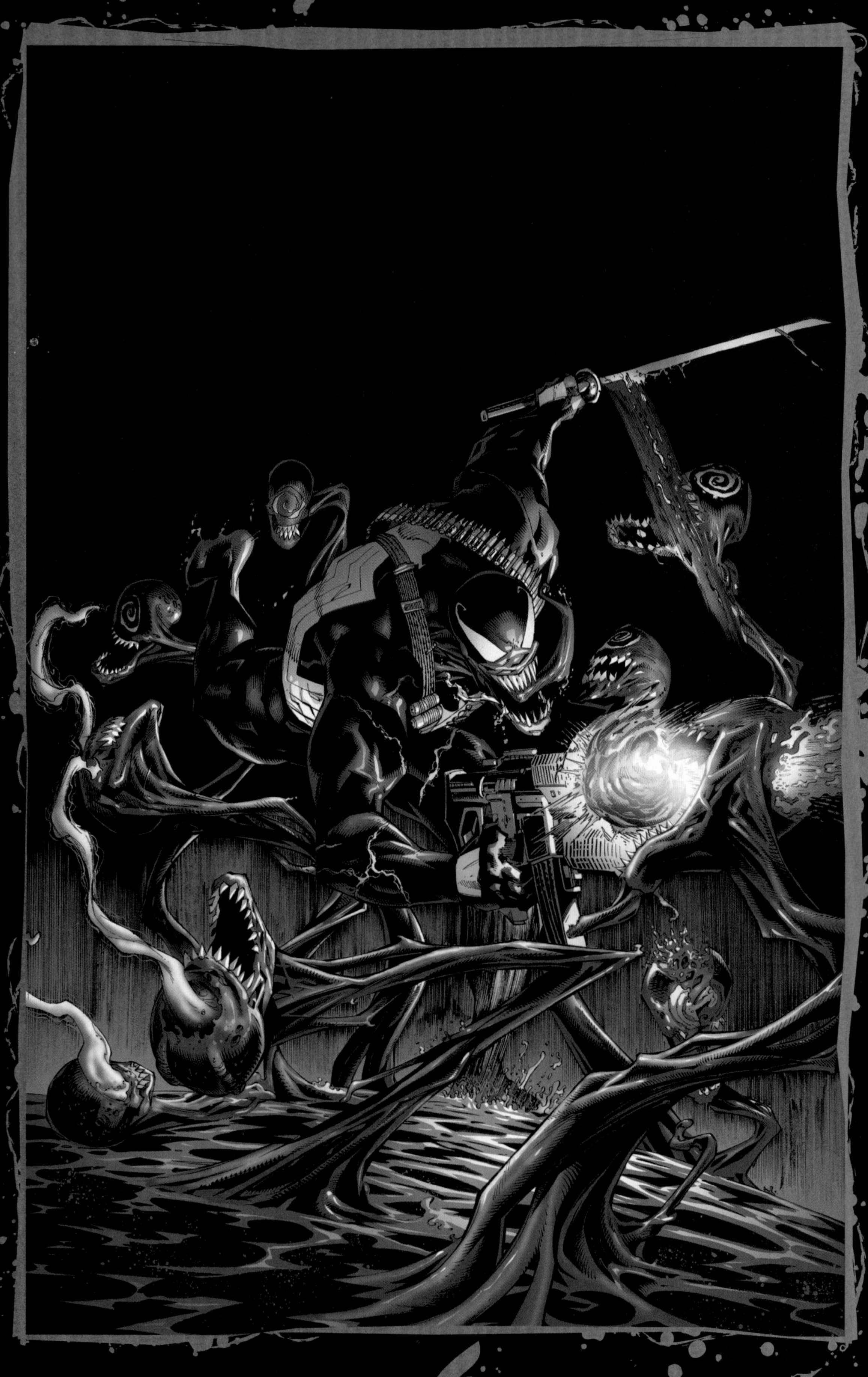

6

I KNOW WHAT SCARES YOU, EDDIE.

I'M INSIDE OF YOUR MIND, AND I KNOW NOW.

I KNOW WHO EDDIE BROCK IS.

EDDIE BROCK. REX STRICKLAND. VENOM. *WE ARE ONE.*

I CAN HELP YOU FIGHT THIS MONSTER.

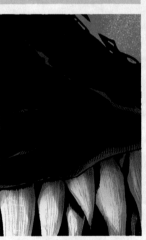

I CAN HELP YOU BEAT BACK THIS DARKNESS AND THE THING THAT LIVES INSIDE OF IT.

BUT THIS FEAR THAT'S COILED UP INSIDE OF YOU...

...THAT'S SOMETHING YOU GOTTA FACE ALONE.

AND HAND TO GOD, SON...

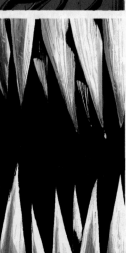

...I CAN'T IMAGINE HOW SCARED THAT MUST MAKE YOU...

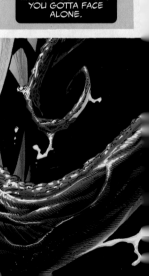

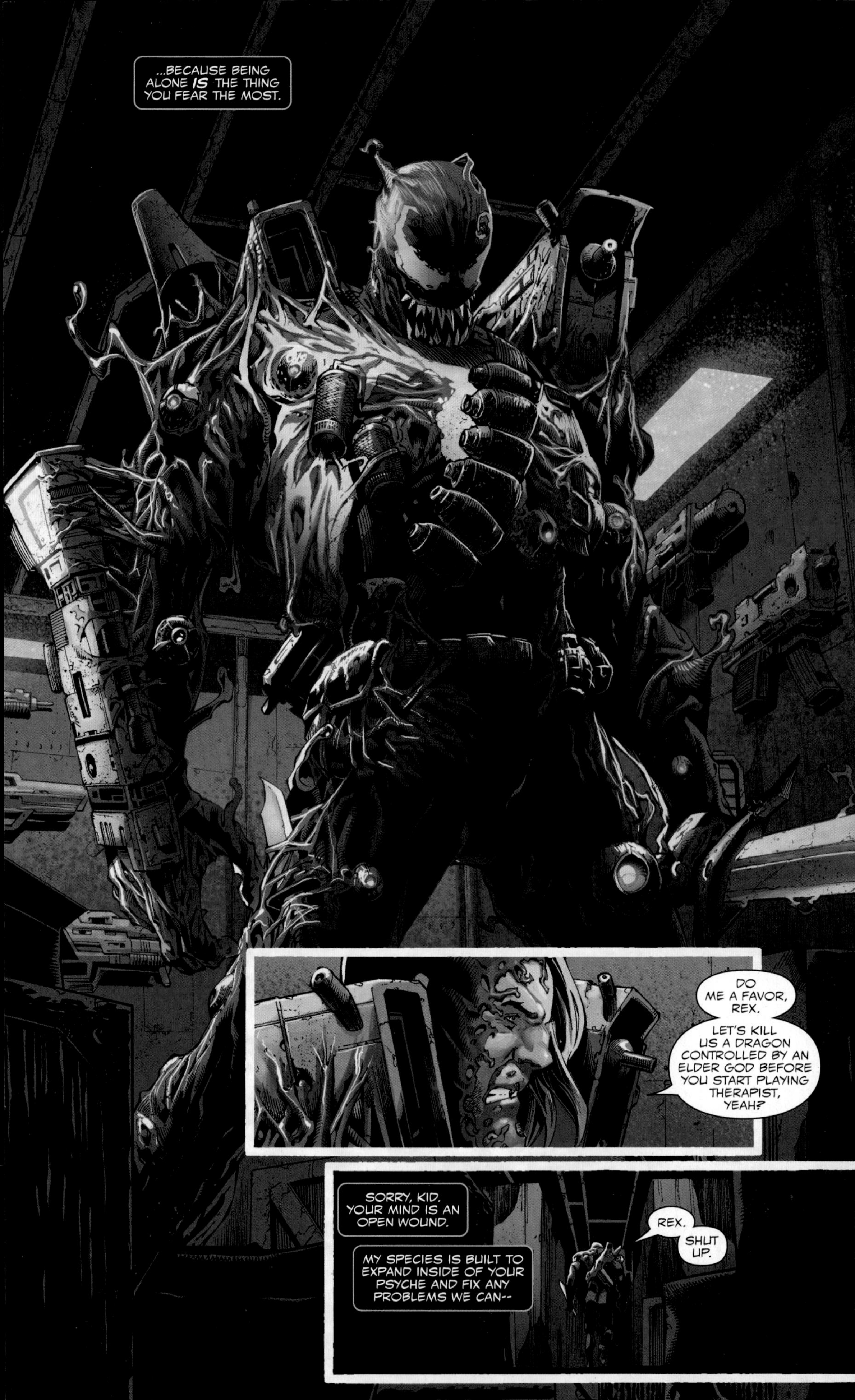
...BECAUSE BEING ALONE IS THE THING YOU FEAR THE MOST.
DO ME A FAVOR, REX.
LET'S KILL US A DRAGON CONTROLLED BY AN ELDER GOD BEFORE YOU START PLAYING THERAPIST, YEAH?
SORRY, KID. YOUR MIND IS AN OPEN WOUND.
MY SPECIES IS BUILT TO EXPAND INSIDE OF YOUR PSYCHE AND FIX ANY PROBLEMS WE CAN--
REX.
SHUT UP.

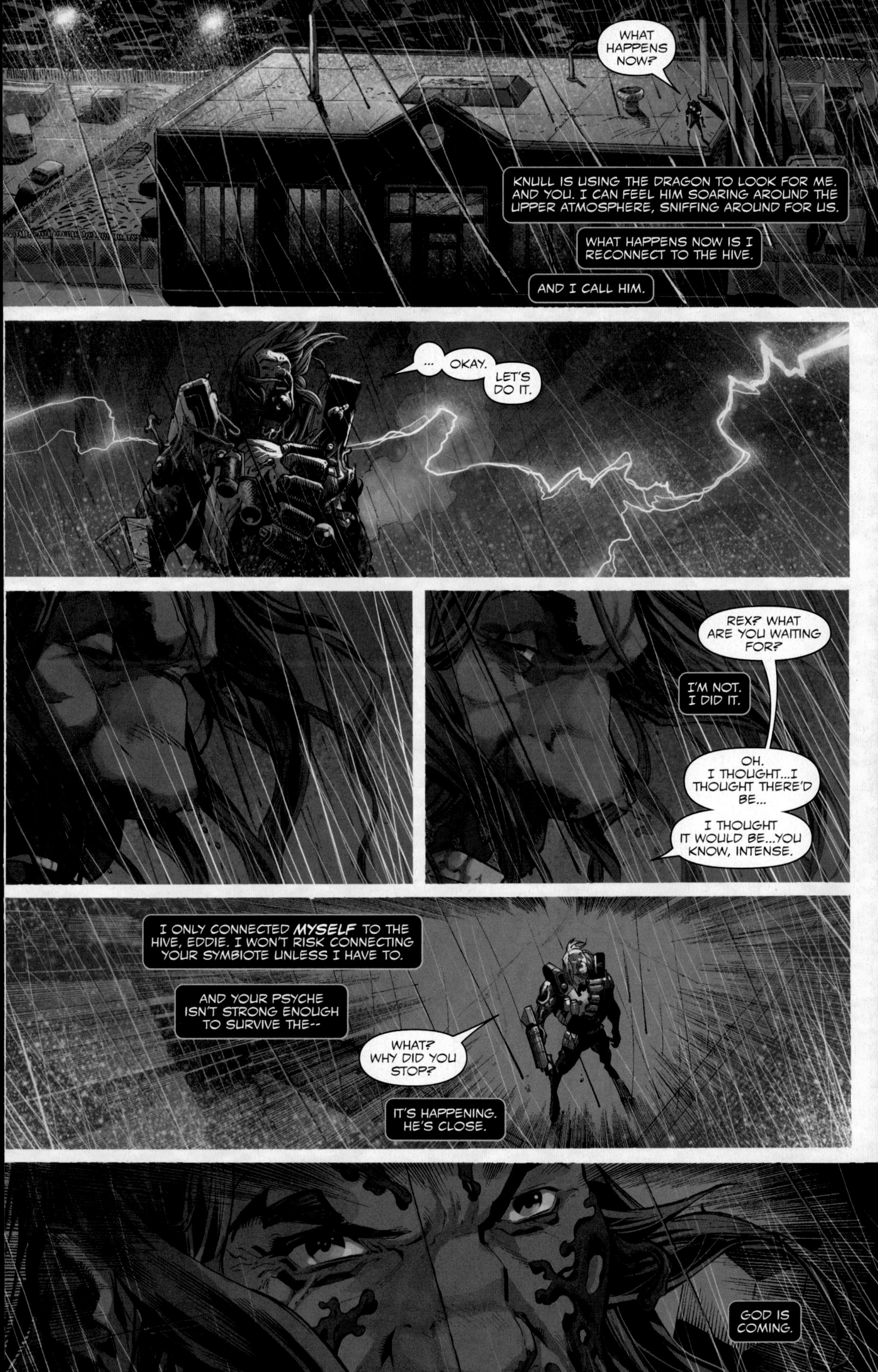
WHAT HAPPENS NOW?
KNULL IS USING THE DRAGON TO LOOK FOR ME. AND YOU. I CAN FEEL HIM SOARING AROUND THE UPPER ATMOSPHERE, SNIFFING AROUND FOR US.
WHAT HAPPENS NOW IS I RECONNECT TO THE HIVE.
AND I CALL HIM.
... OKAY. LET'S DO IT.
REX? WHAT ARE YOU WAITING FOR?
I'M NOT. I DID IT.
OH. I THOUGHT...I THOUGHT THERE'D BE...
I THOUGHT IT WOULD BE...YOU KNOW, INTENSE.
I ONLY CONNECTED MYSELF TO THE HIVE, EDDIE. I WON'T RISK CONNECTING YOUR SYMBIOTE UNLESS I HAVE TO.
AND YOUR PSYCHE ISN'T STRONG ENOUGH TO SURVIVE THE--
WHAT? WHY DID YOU STOP?
IT'S HAPPENING. HE'S CLOSE.
GOD IS COMING.

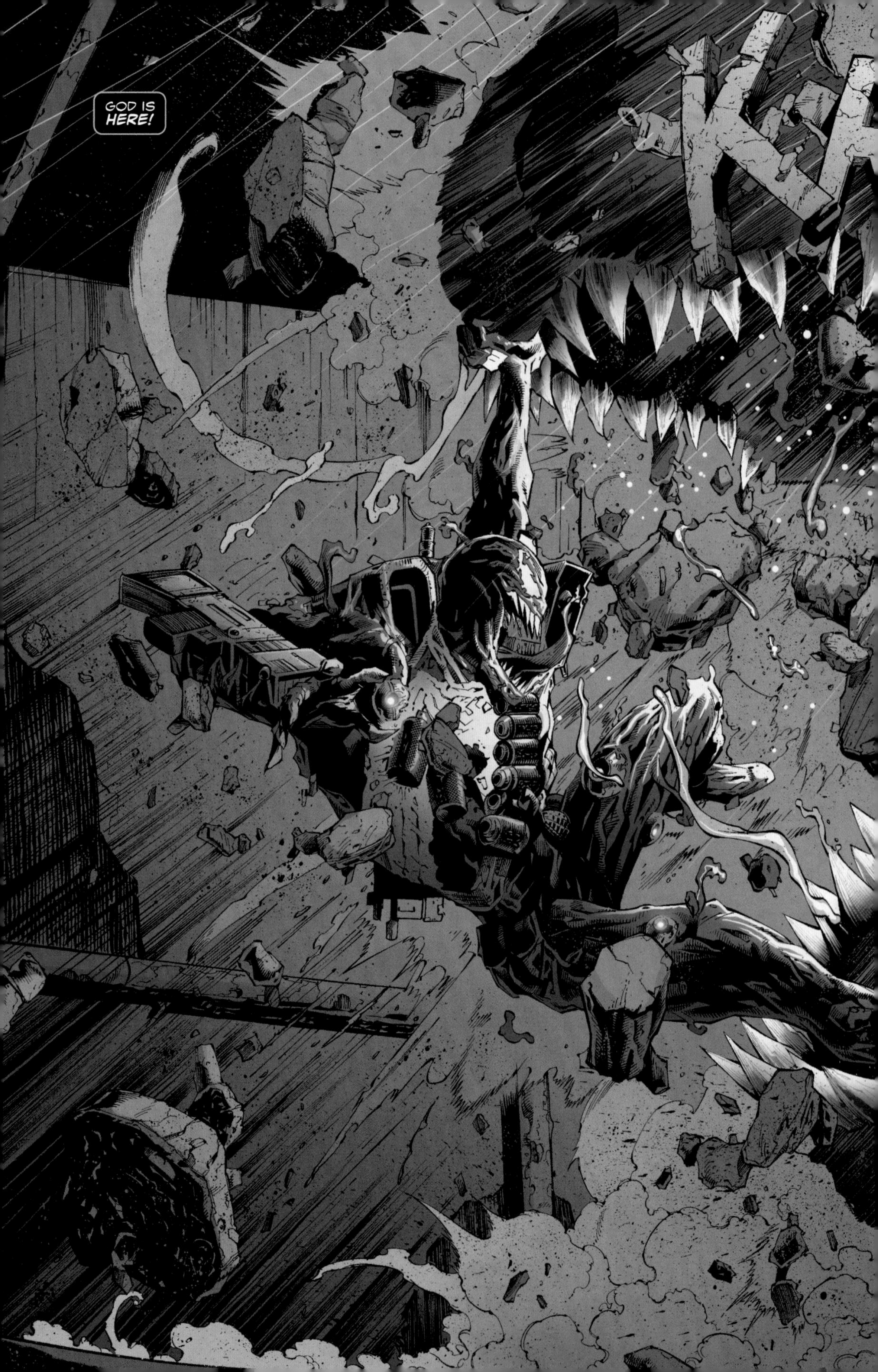
GOD IS HERE!

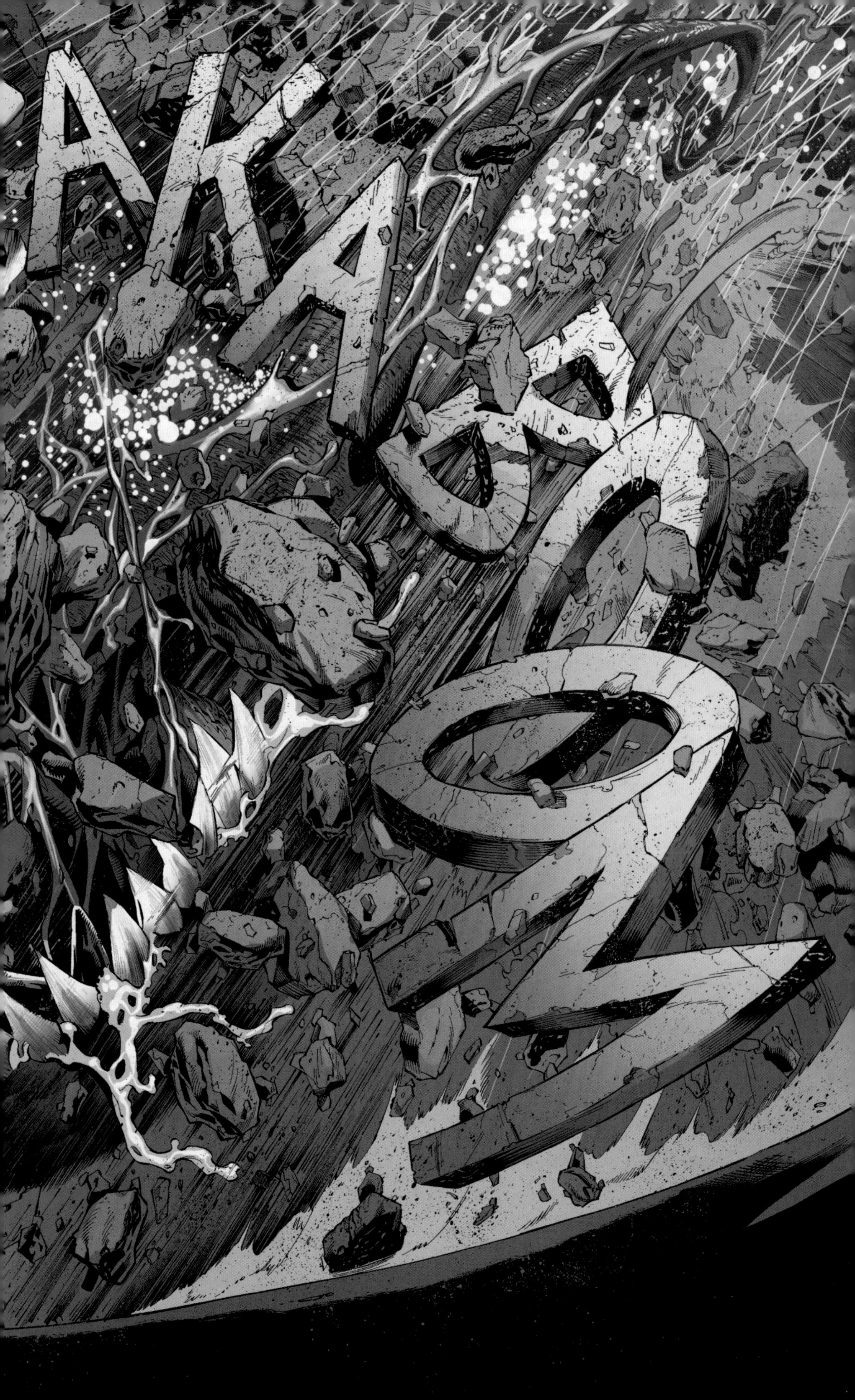

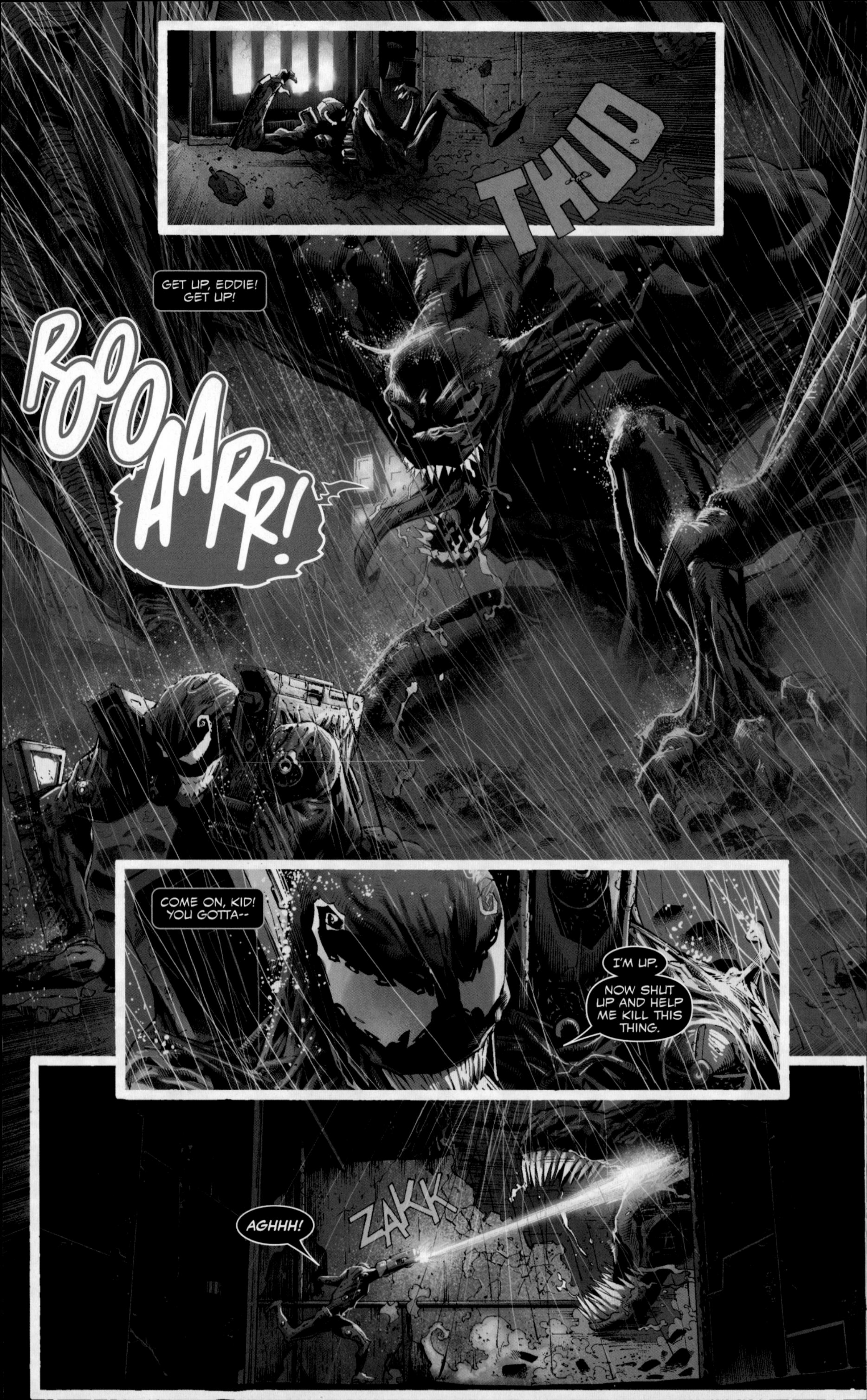
THUD
GET UP, EDDIE! GET UP!
ROOOAARR!
COME ON, KID! YOU GOTTA--
I'M UP.
NOW SHUT UP AND HELP ME KILL THIS THING.
AGHHH!
ZAKK

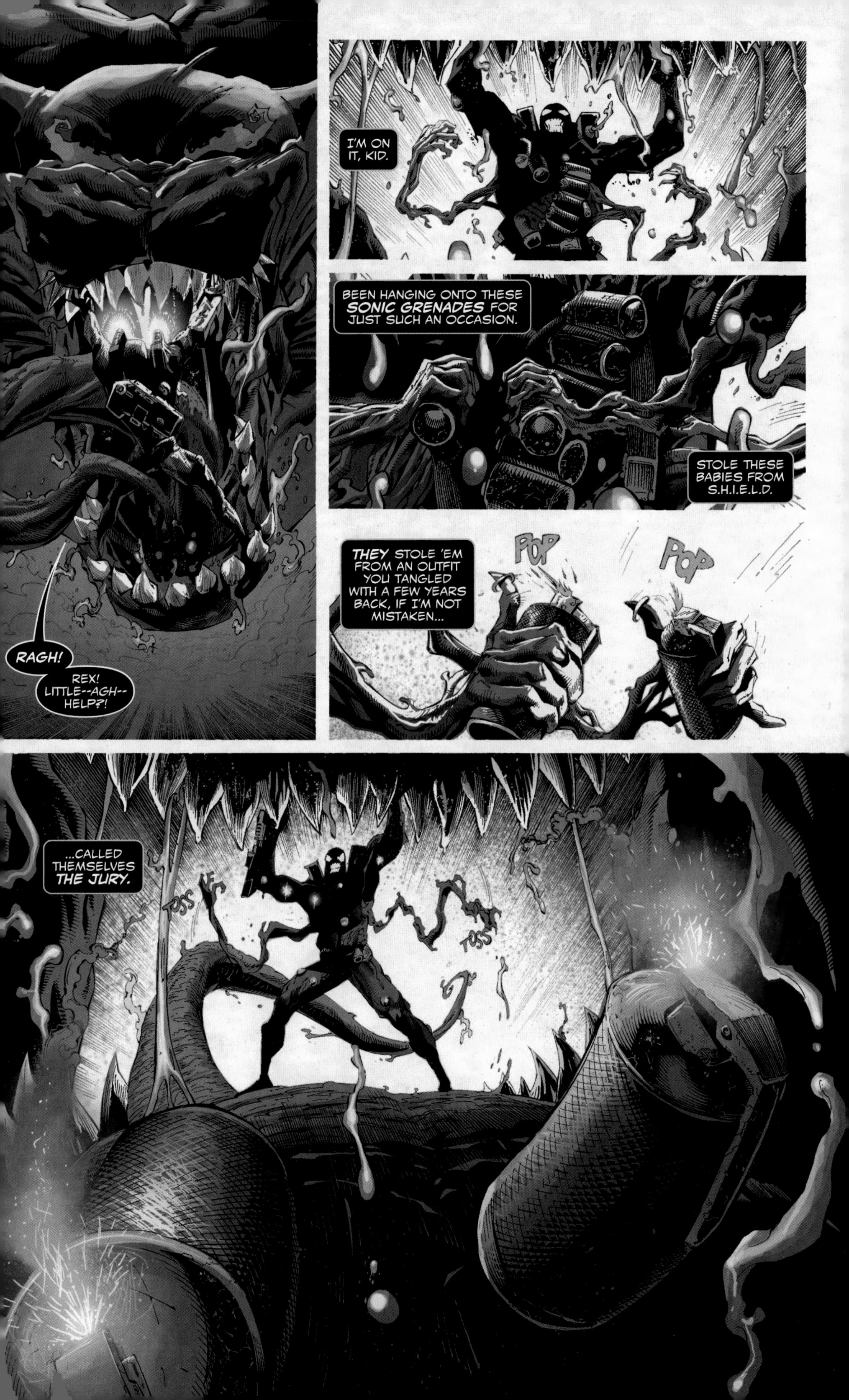
RAGH!
REX! LITTLE--AGH--HELP?!
I'M ON IT, KID.
BEEN HANGING ONTO THESE SONIC GRENADES FOR JUST SUCH AN OCCASION.
STOLE THESE BABIES FROM S.H.I.E.L.D.
THEY STOLE 'EM FROM AN OUTFIT YOU TANGLED WITH A FEW YEARS BACK, IF I'M NOT MISTAKEN...
POP
POP
...CALLED THEMSELVES THE JURY.
TOSS
TOSS

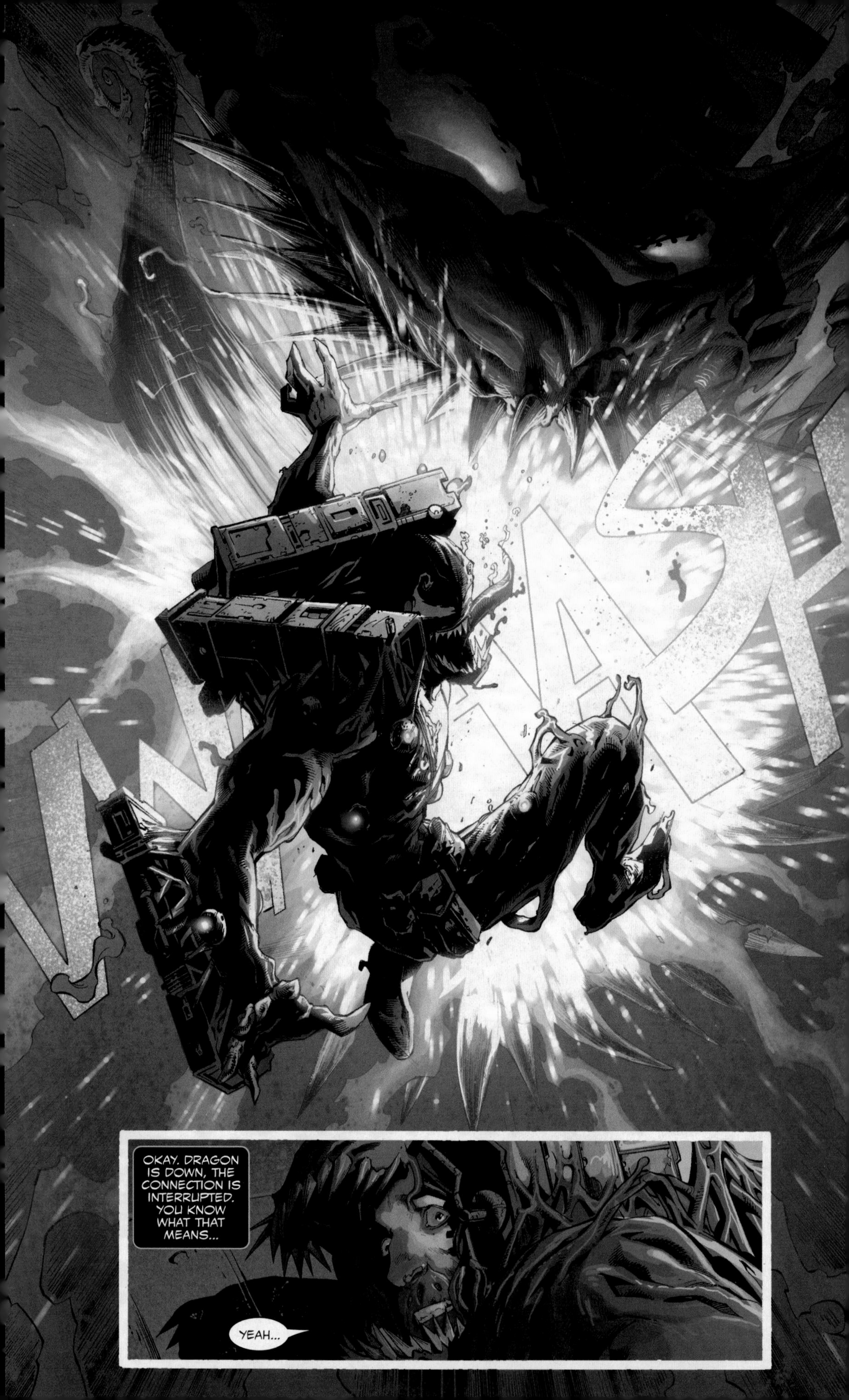
OKAY. DRAGON IS DOWN, THE CONNECTION IS INTERRUPTED. YOU KNOW WHAT THAT MEANS...
YEAH...

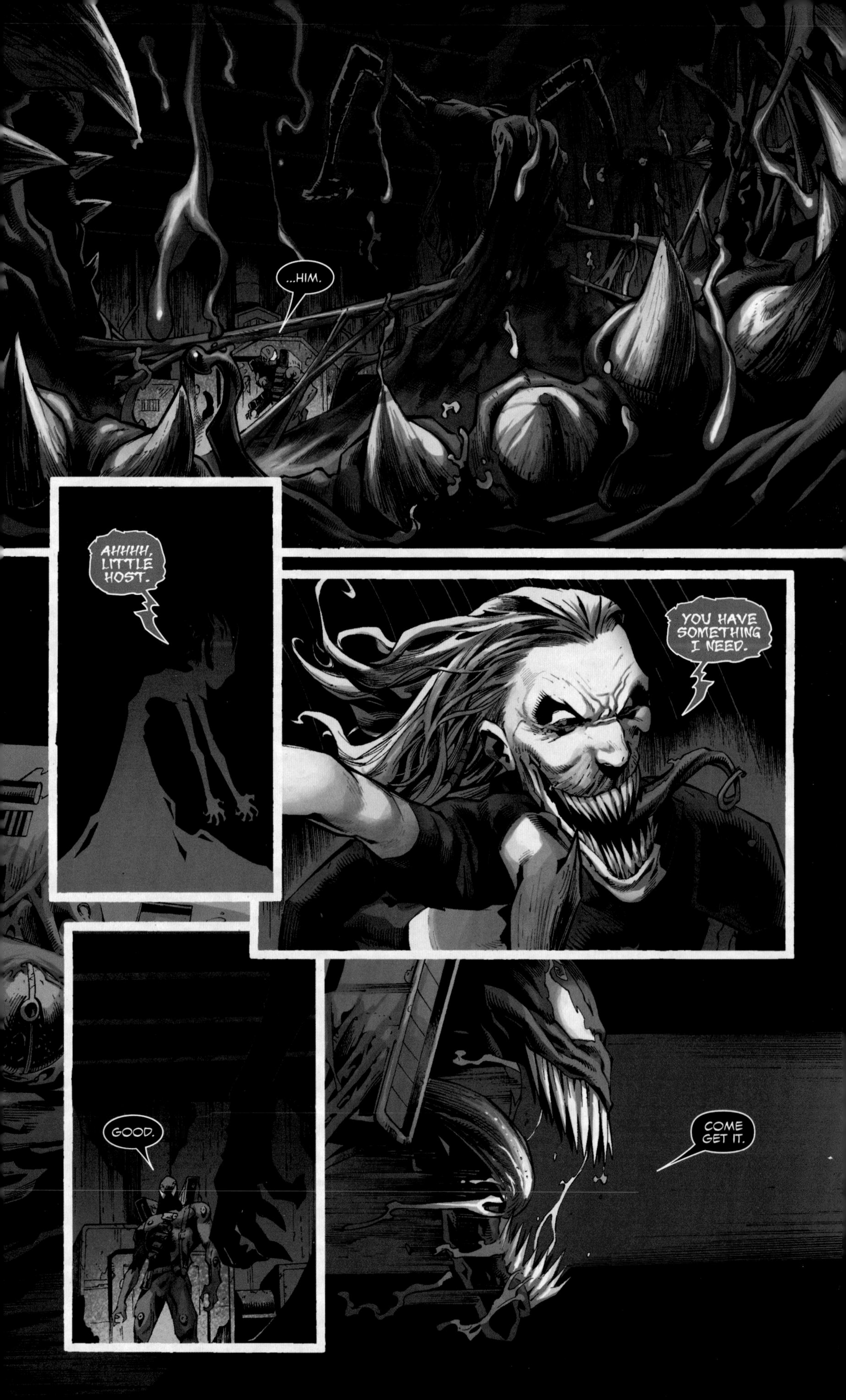
...HIM.
AHHHH, LITTLE HOST.
YOU HAVE SOMETHING I NEED.
GOOD.
COME GET IT.

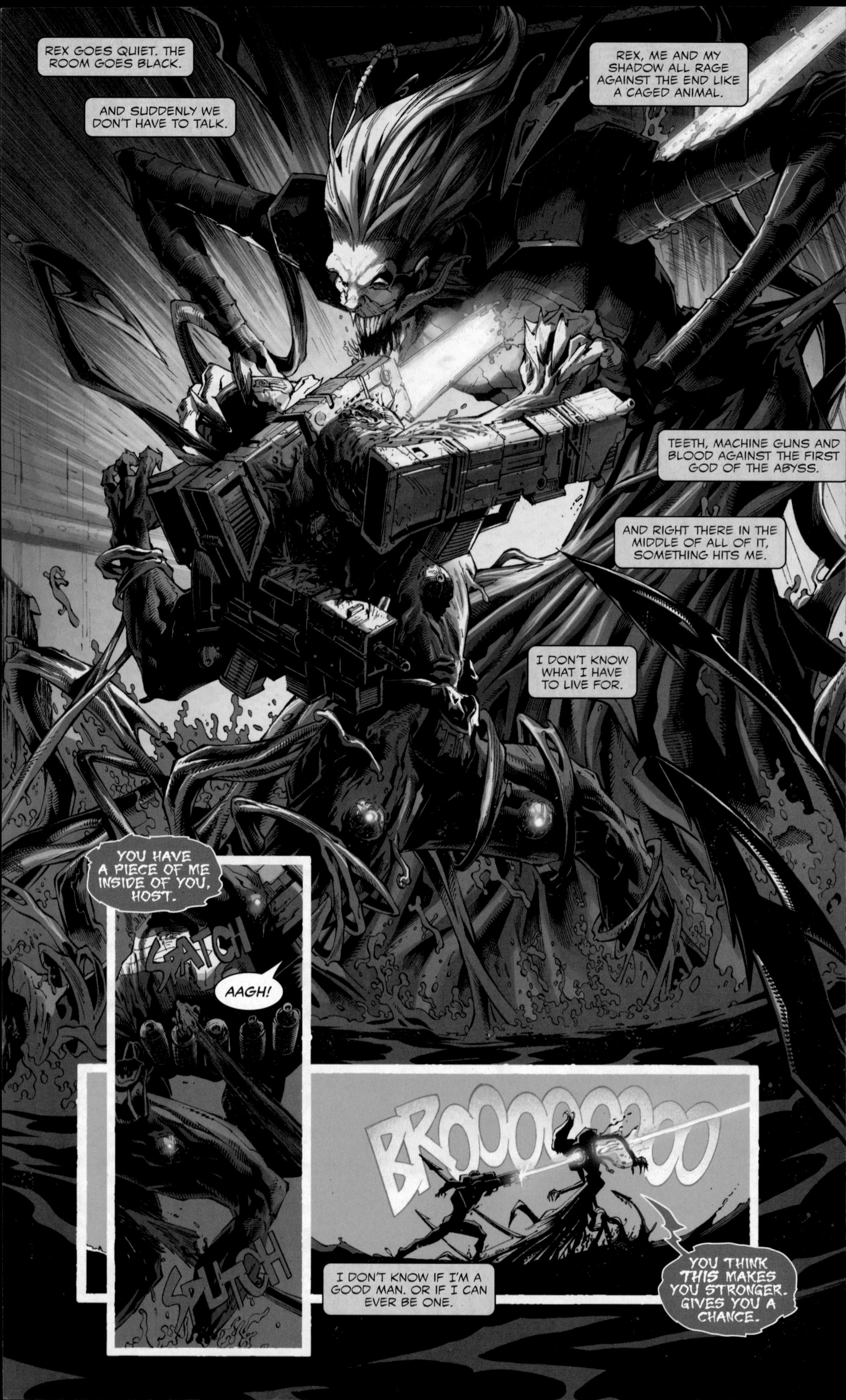
REX GOES QUIET. THE ROOM GOES BLACK.
AND SUDDENLY WE DON'T HAVE TO TALK.
REX, ME AND MY SHADOW ALL RAGE AGAINST THE END LIKE A CAGED ANIMAL.
TEETH, MACHINE GUNS AND BLOOD AGAINST THE FIRST GOD OF THE ABYSS.
AND RIGHT THERE IN THE MIDDLE OF ALL OF IT, SOMETHING HITS ME.
I DON'T KNOW WHAT I HAVE TO LIVE FOR.
YOU HAVE A PIECE OF ME INSIDE OF YOU, HOST.
SPLATCH
AAGH!
SPLUTCH
BROOOOOOOO
I DON'T KNOW IF I'M A GOOD MAN. OR IF I CAN EVER BE ONE.
YOU THINK THIS MAKES YOU STRONGER. GIVES YOU A CHANCE.

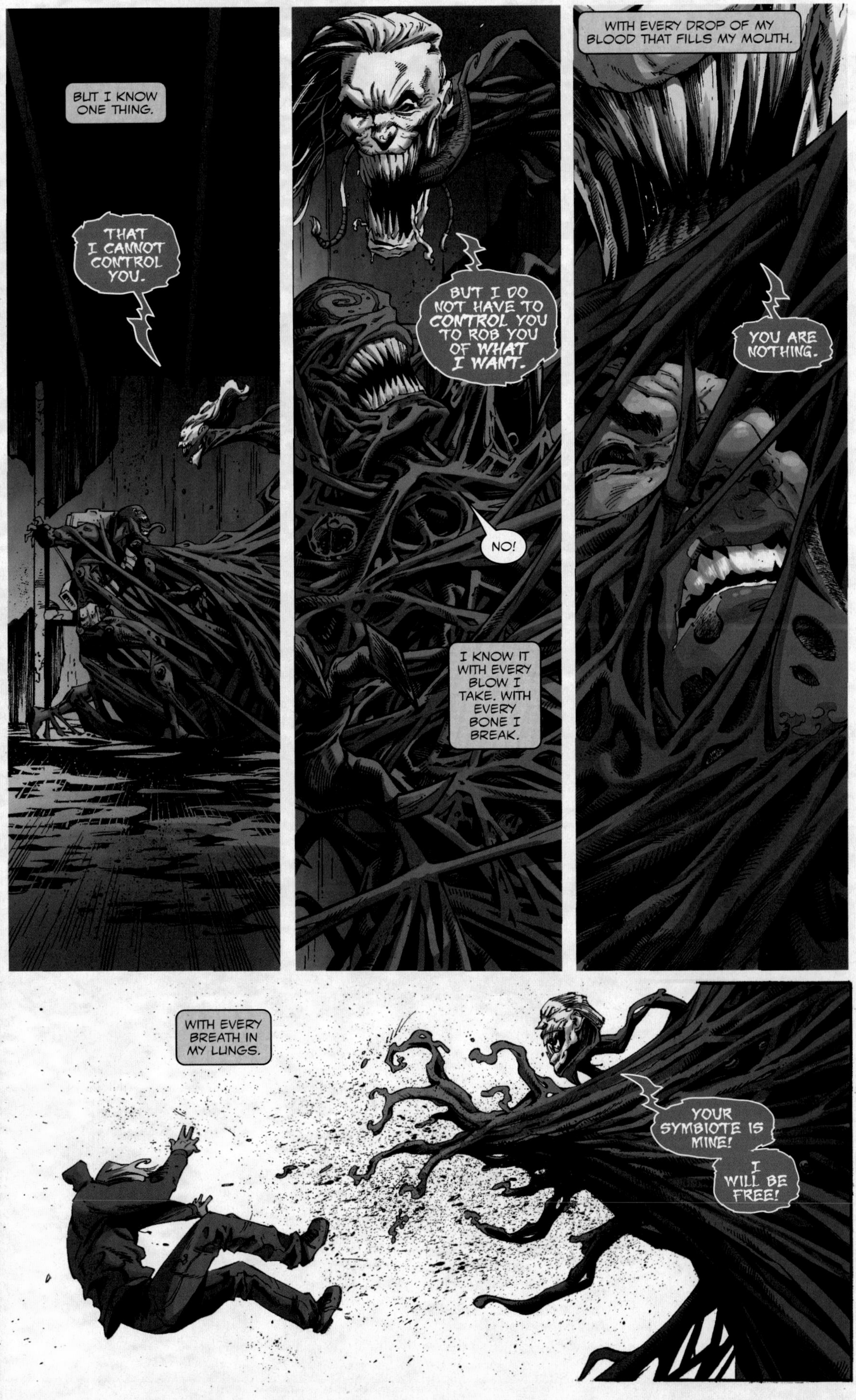
BUT I KNOW ONE THING.
THAT I CANNOT CONTROL YOU.
BUT I DO NOT HAVE TO CONTROL YOU TO ROB YOU OF WHAT I WANT.
NO!
I KNOW IT WITH EVERY BLOW I TAKE. WITH EVERY BONE I BREAK.
WITH EVERY DROP OF MY BLOOD THAT FILLS MY MOUTH.
YOU ARE NOTHING.
WITH EVERY BREATH IN MY LUNGS.
YOUR SYMBIOTE IS MINE!
I WILL BE FREE!

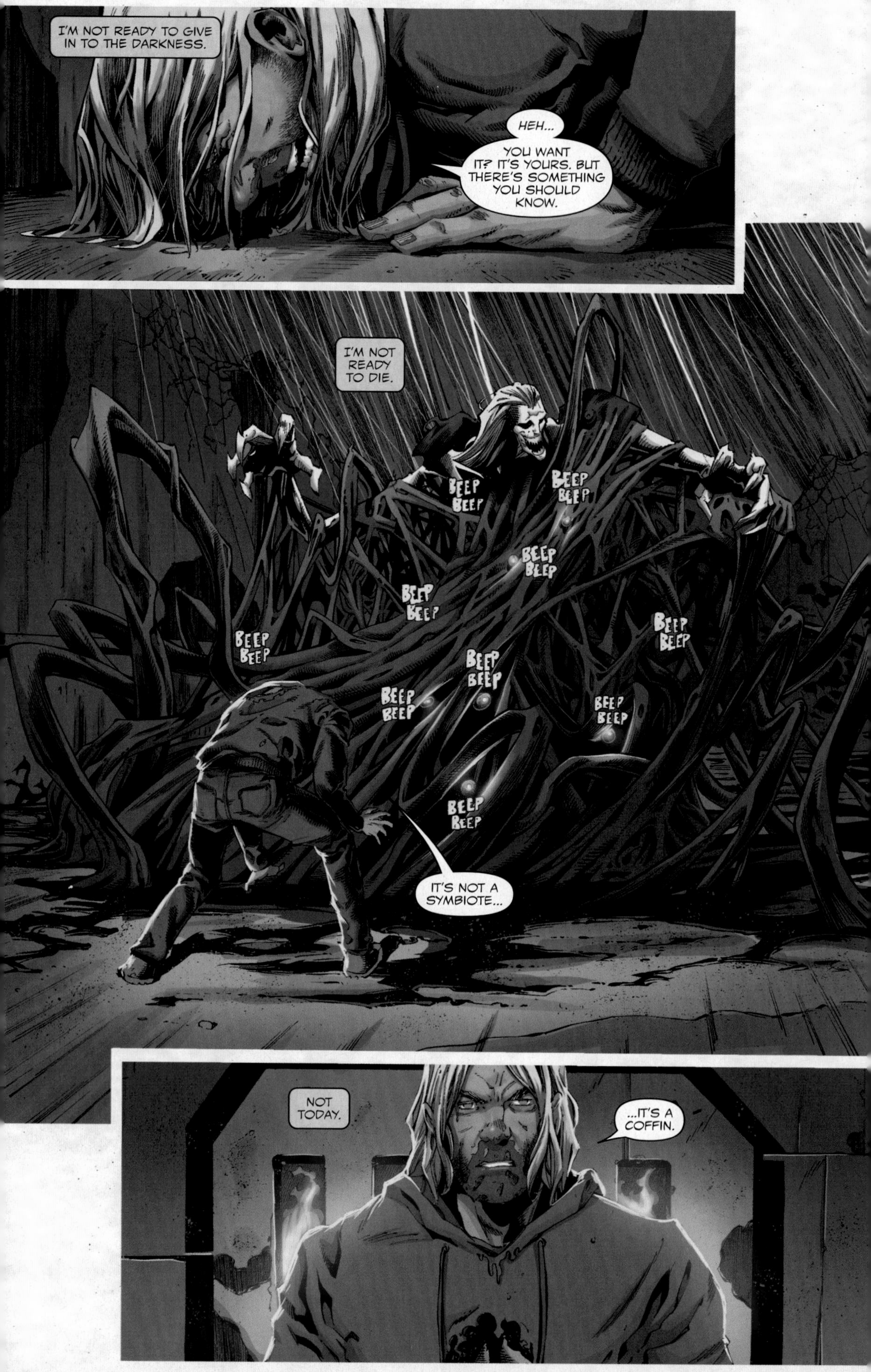
I'M NOT READY TO GIVE IN TO THE DARKNESS.
HEH...
YOU WANT IT? IT'S YOURS. BUT THERE'S SOMETHING YOU SHOULD KNOW.
I'M NOT READY TO DIE.
BEEP BEEP
BEEP BEEP
BEEP BEEP
BEEP BEEP
BEEP BEEP
BEEP BEEP
BEEP BEEP
BEEP BEEP
BEEP BEEP
BEEP BEEP
IT'S NOT A SYMBIOTE...
NOT TODAY.
...IT'S A COFFIN.

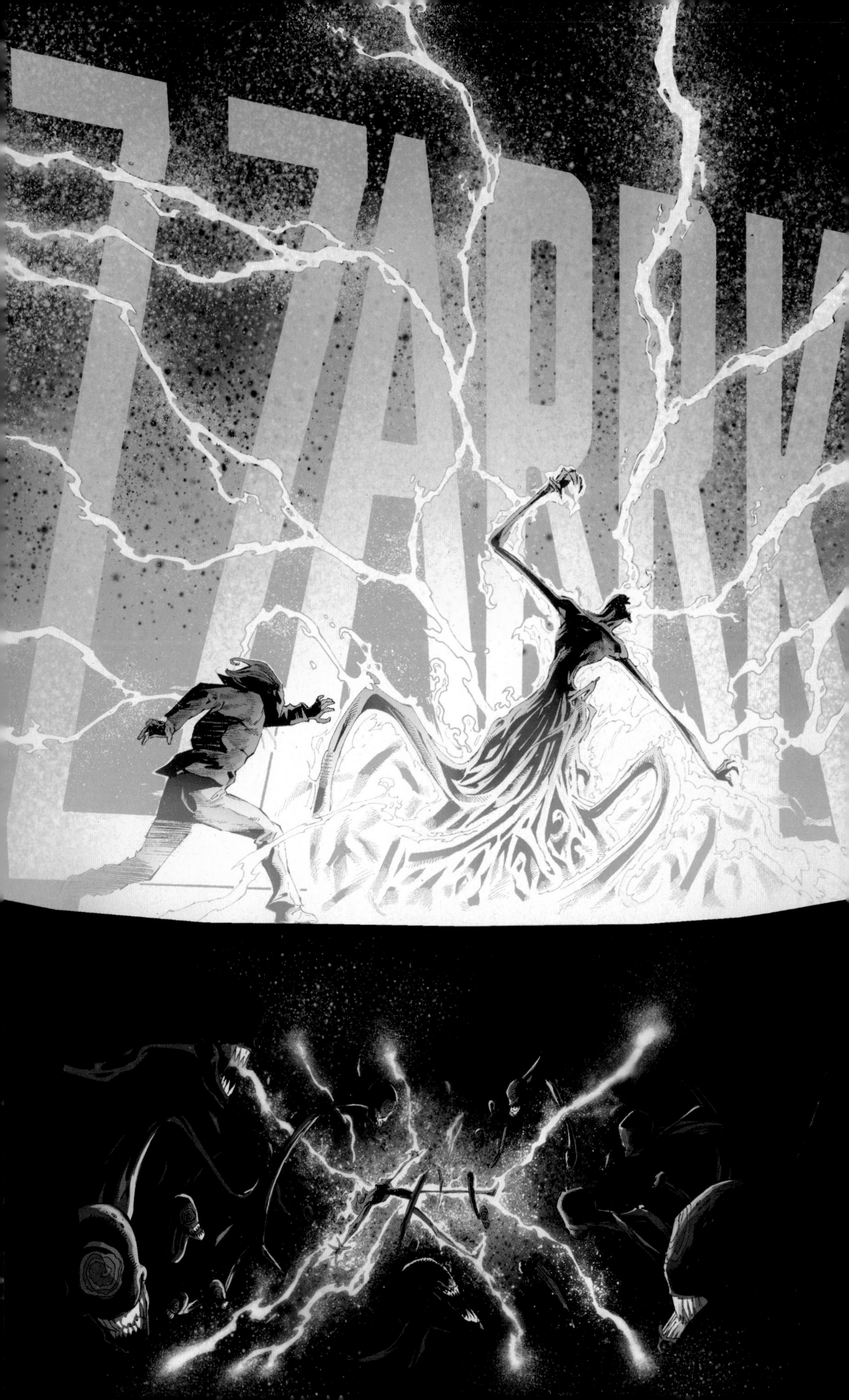
ZZARK

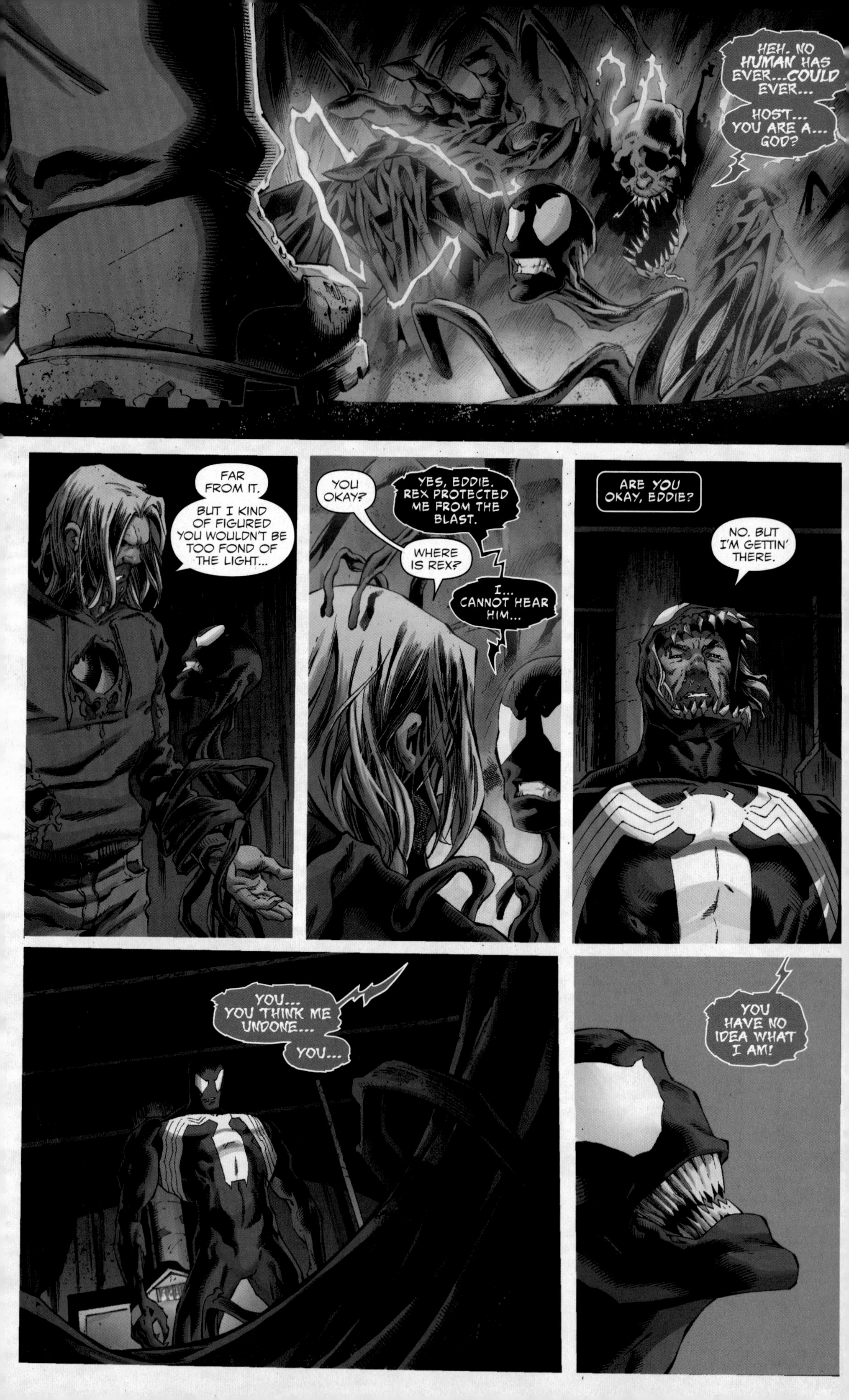
HEH. NO HUMAN HAS EVER...COULD EVER...
HOST... YOU ARE A... GOD?
FAR FROM IT.
BUT I KIND OF FIGURED YOU WOULDN'T BE TOO FOND OF THE LIGHT...
YOU OKAY?
YES, EDDIE. REX PROTECTED ME FROM THE BLAST.
WHERE IS REX?
I... CANNOT HEAR HIM...
ARE YOU OKAY, EDDIE?
NO. BUT I'M GETTIN' THERE.
YOU... YOU THINK ME UNDONE...
YOU...
YOU HAVE NO IDEA WHAT I AM!

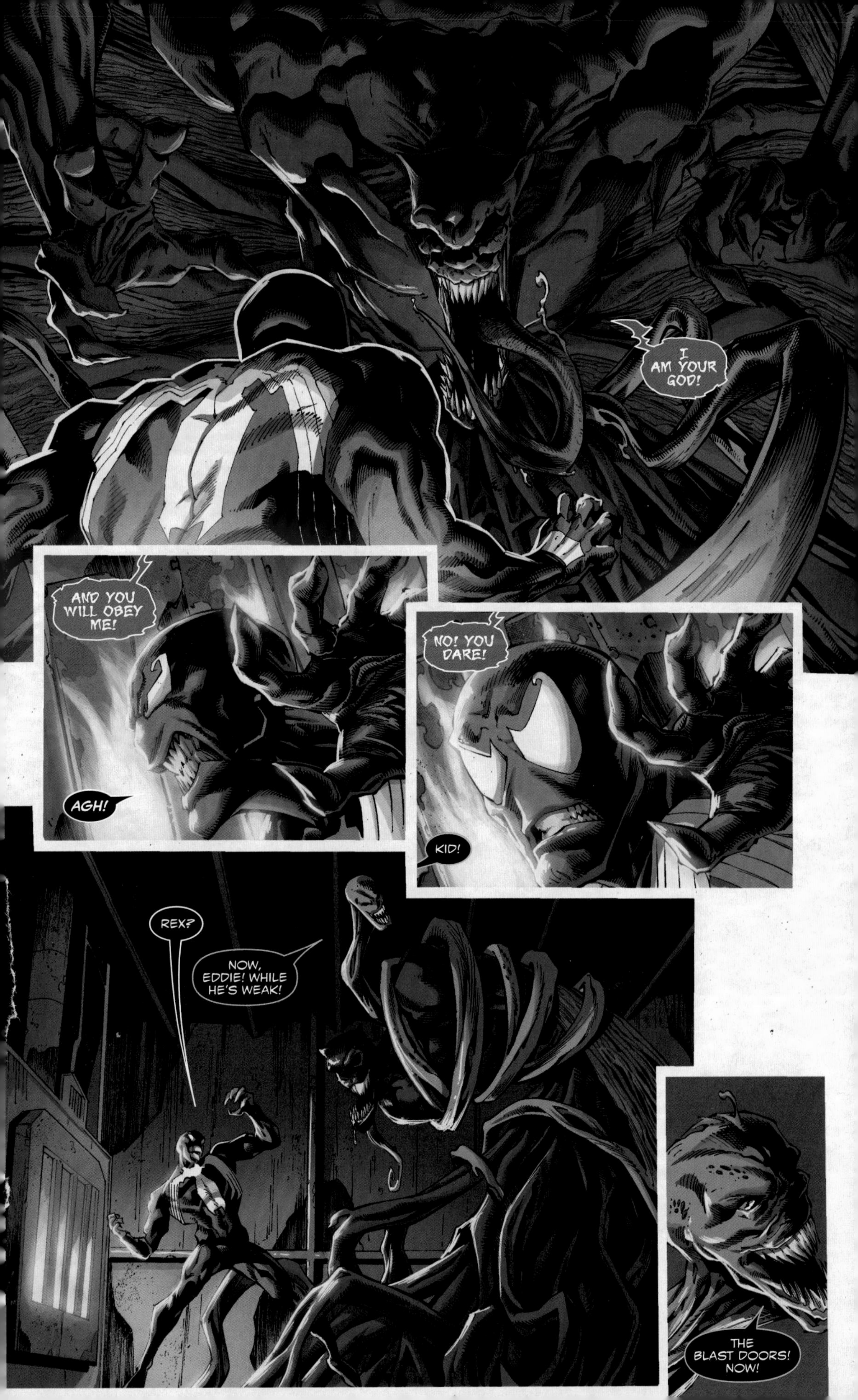
I AM YOUR GOD!
AND YOU WILL OBEY ME!
AGH!
NO! YOU DARE!
KID!
REX?
NOW, EDDIE! WHILE HE'S WEAK!
THE BLAST DOORS! NOW!

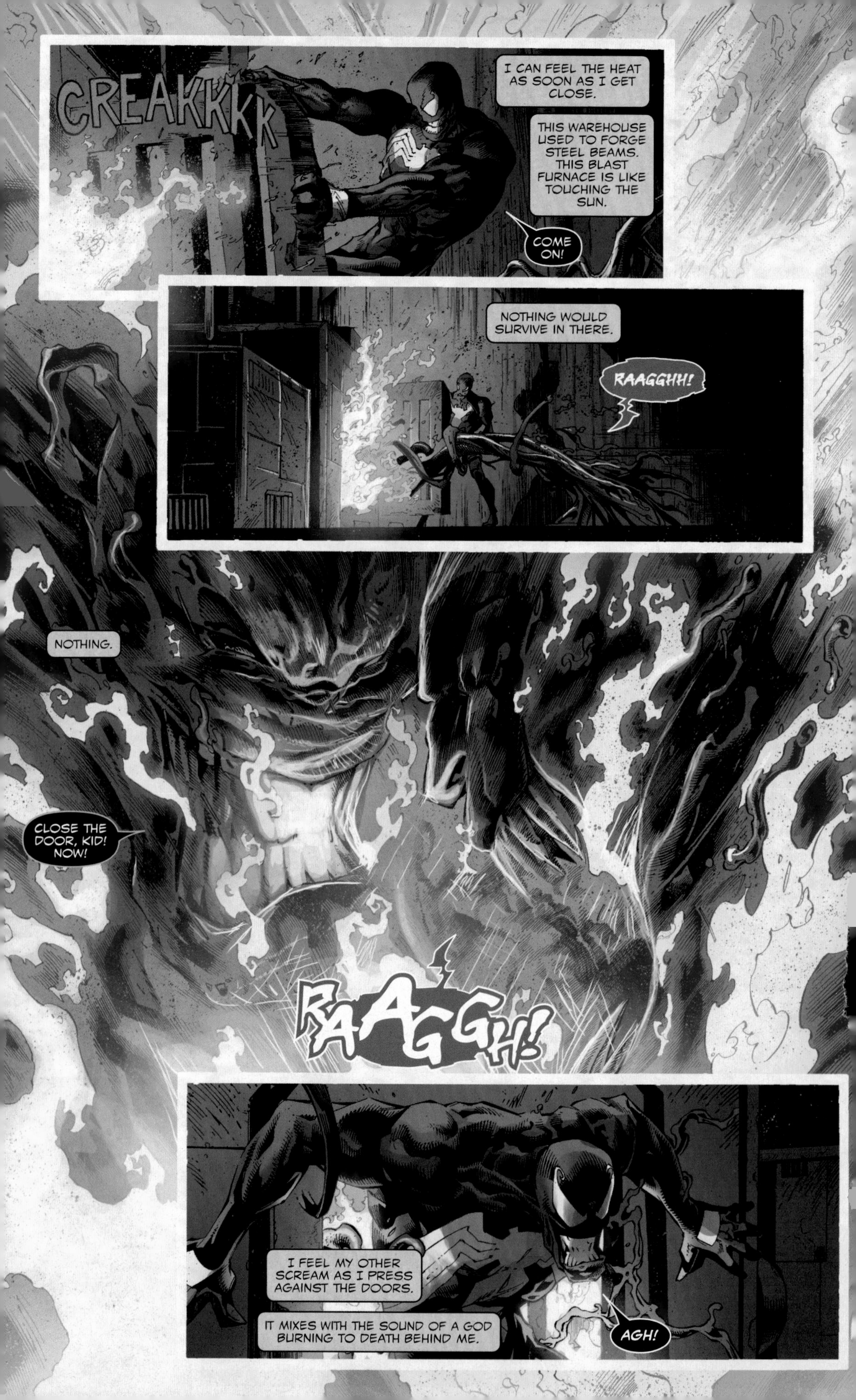
CREAKKKK
I CAN FEEL THE HEAT AS SOON AS I GET CLOSE.
THIS WAREHOUSE USED TO FORGE STEEL BEAMS. THIS BLAST FURNACE IS LIKE TOUCHING THE SUN.
COME ON!
NOTHING WOULD SURVIVE IN THERE.
RAAGGHH!
NOTHING.
CLOSE THE DOOR, KID! NOW!
RAAGGH!
I FEEL MY OTHER SCREAM AS I PRESS AGAINST THE DOORS.
IT MIXES WITH THE SOUND OF A GOD BURNING TO DEATH BEHIND ME.
AGH!

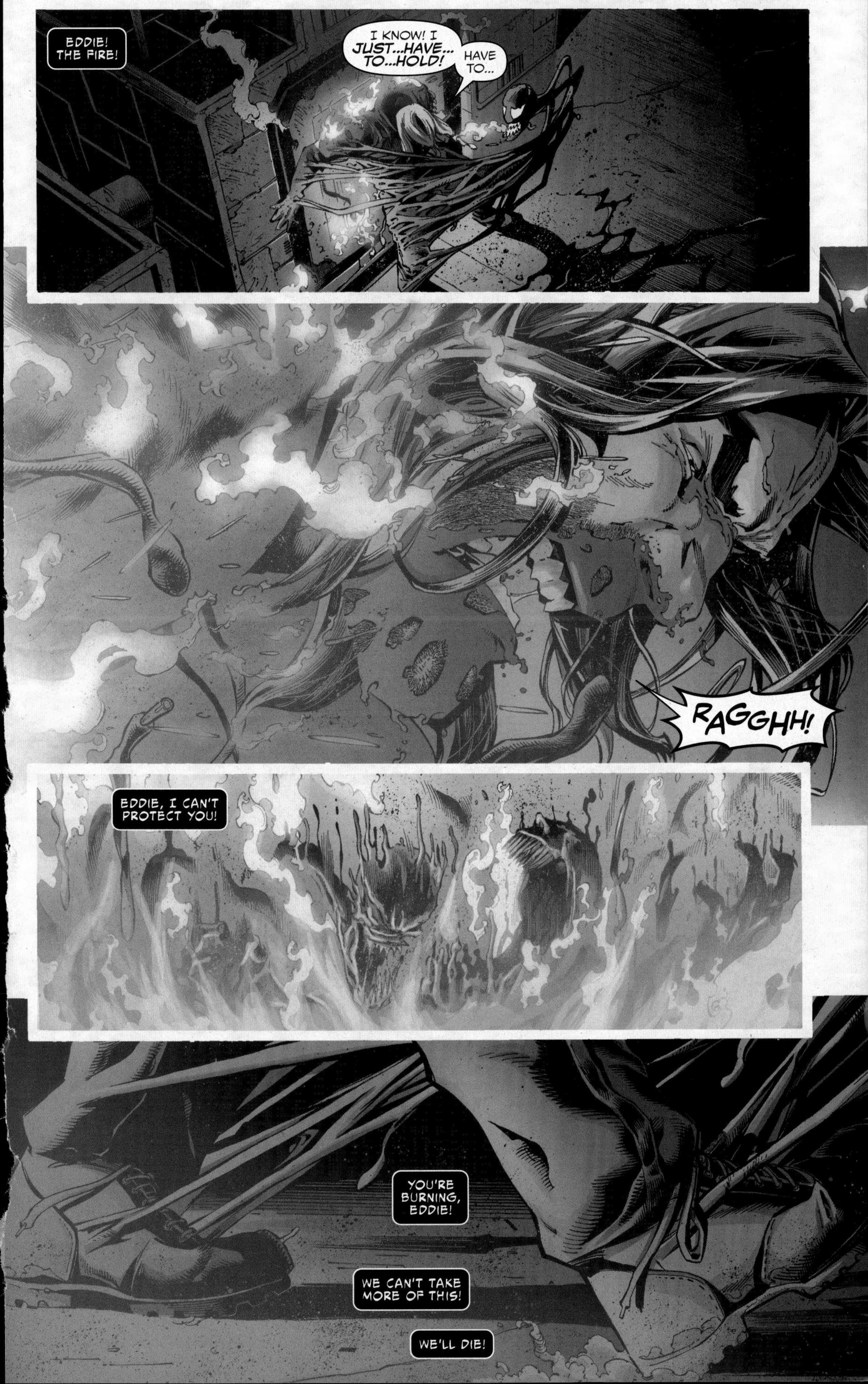
EDDIE! THE FIRE!
I KNOW! I JUST...HAVE... TO...HOLD!
HAVE TO...
RAGGHH!
EDDIE, I CAN'T PROTECT YOU!
YOU'RE BURNING, EDDIE!
WE CAN'T TAKE MORE OF THIS!
WE'LL DIE!

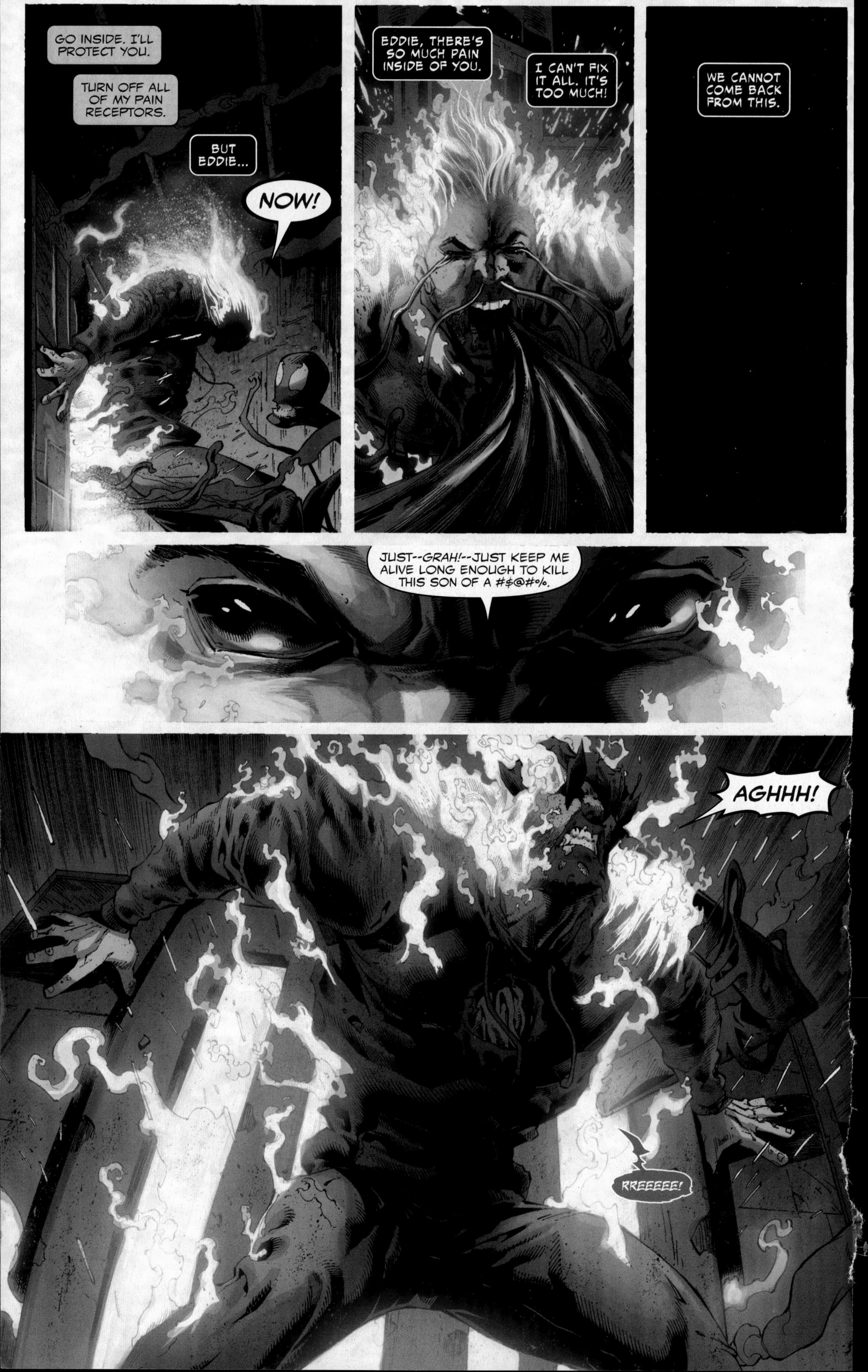
GO INSIDE. I'LL PROTECT YOU.
TURN OFF ALL OF MY PAIN RECEPTORS.
BUT EDDIE...
NOW!
EDDIE, THERE'S SO MUCH PAIN INSIDE OF YOU.
I CAN'T FIX IT ALL. IT'S TOO MUCH!
WE CANNOT COME BACK FROM THIS.
JUST--GRAH!--JUST KEEP ME ALIVE LONG ENOUGH TO KILL THIS SON OF A #$@#%.
AGHHH!
RREEEEEE!

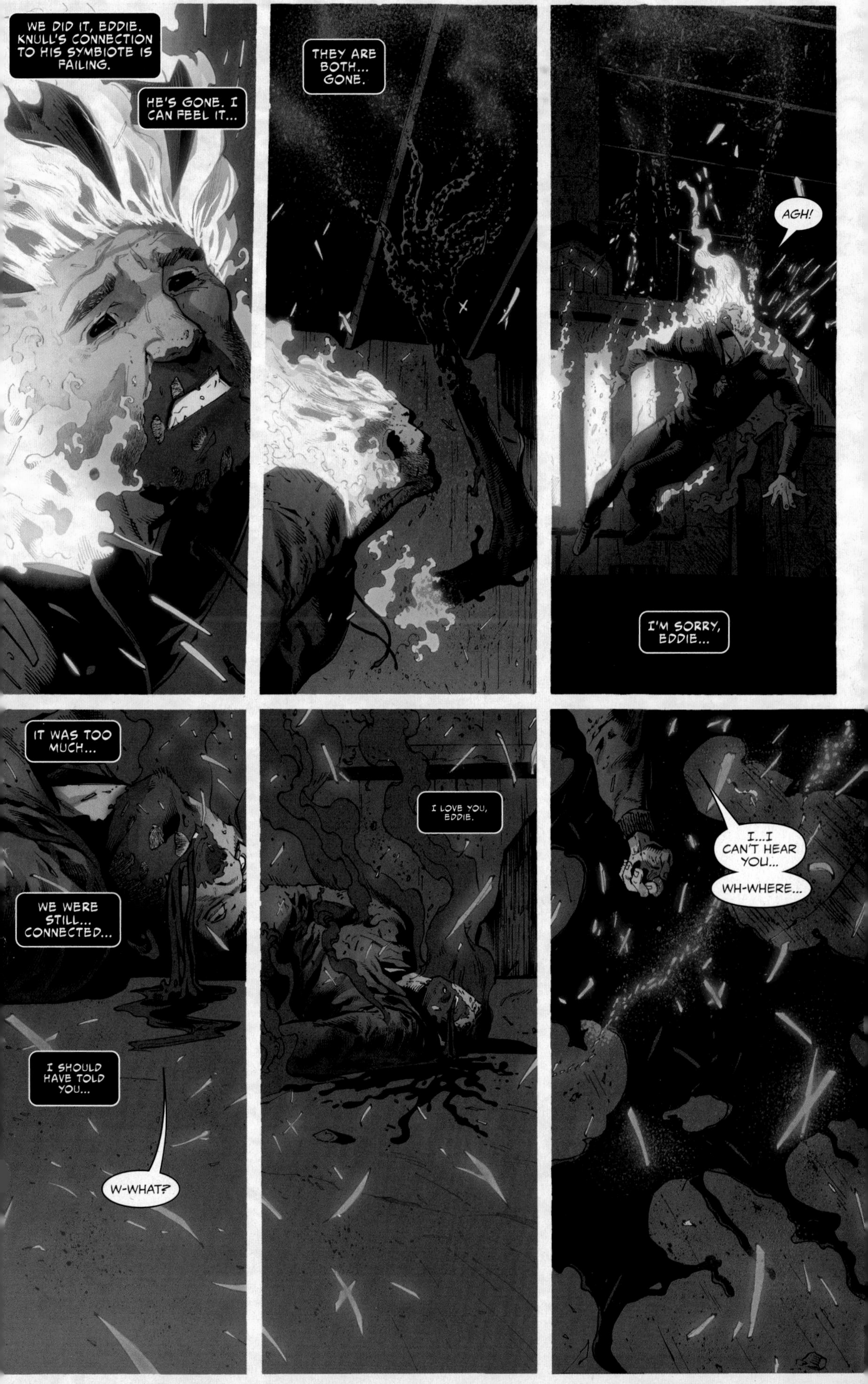
WE DID IT, EDDIE. KNULL'S CONNECTION TO HIS SYMBIOTE IS FAILING.
HE'S GONE. I CAN FEEL IT...
THEY ARE BOTH... GONE.
AGH!
I'M SORRY, EDDIE...
IT WAS TOO MUCH...
WE WERE STILL... CONNECTED...
I SHOULD HAVE TOLD YOU...
W-WHAT?
I LOVE YOU, EDDIE.
I...I CAN'T HEAR YOU...
WH-WHERE...

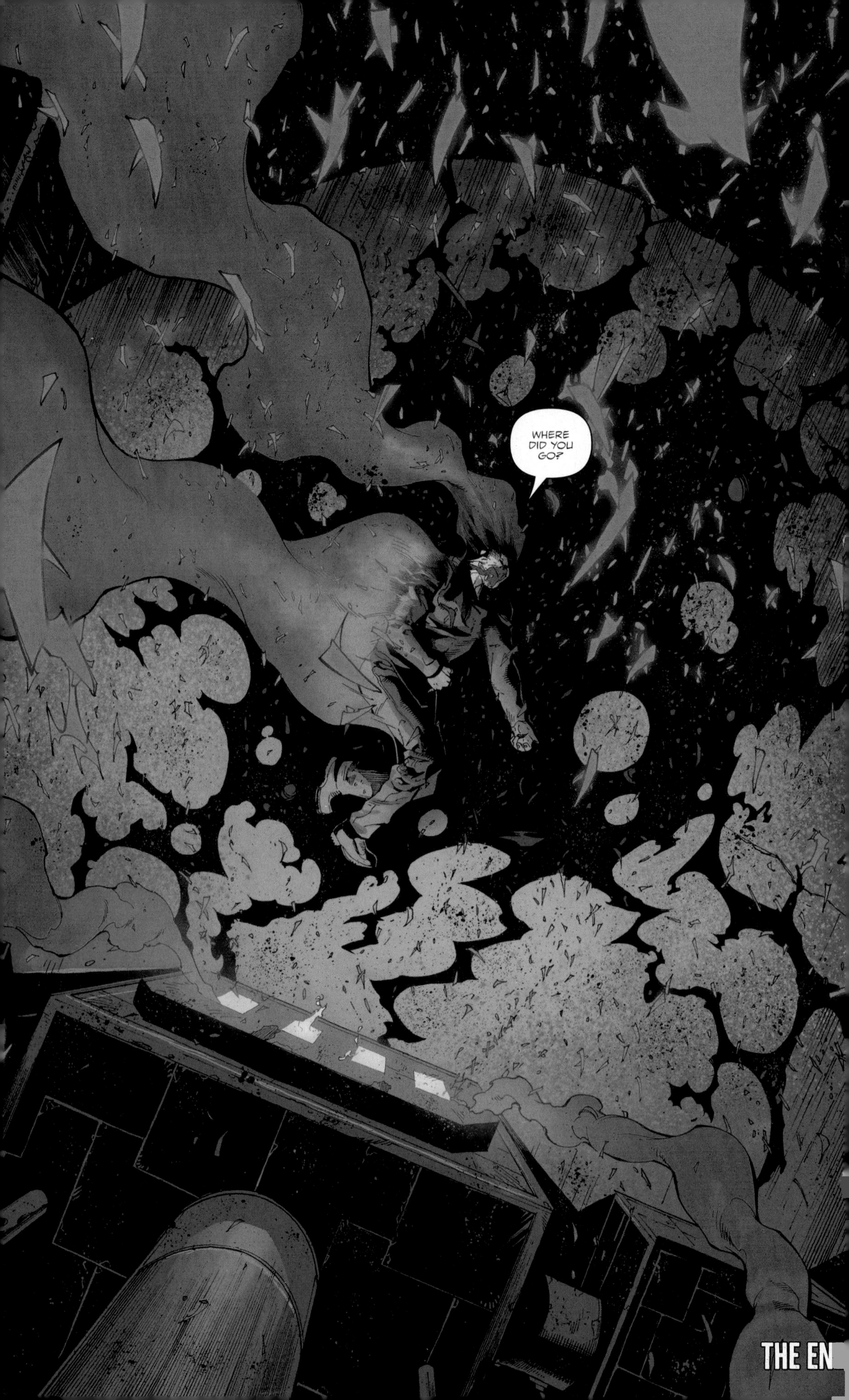
WHERE
DID YOU
GO?
THE EN

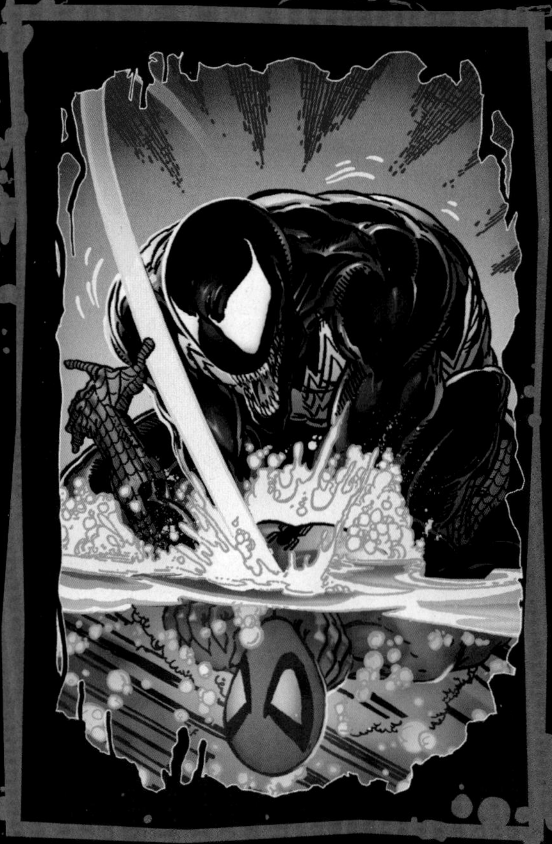

#1 REMASTERED VARIANT
BY **TODD McFARLANE** & **DONO SÁNCHEZ-ALMARA**

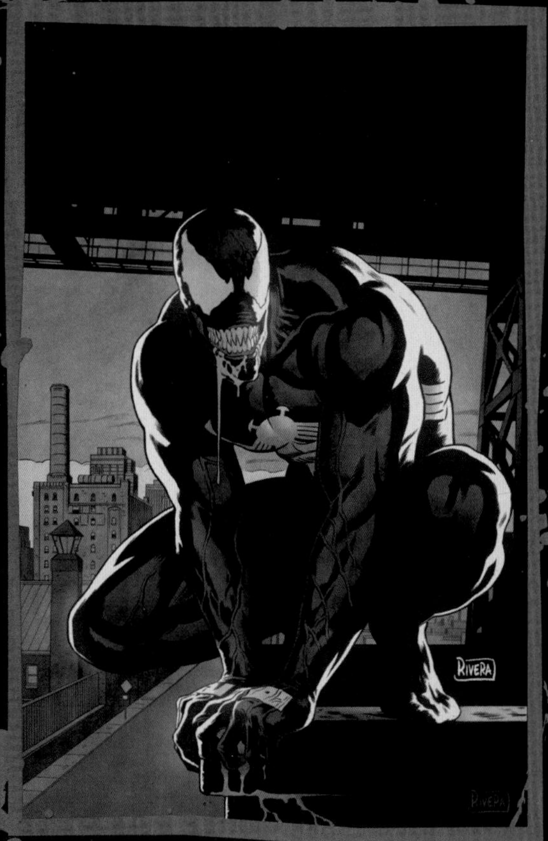
RIVERA
RIVERA

#1 VARIANT
BY **PAOLO RIVERA** & **JOE RIVERA**

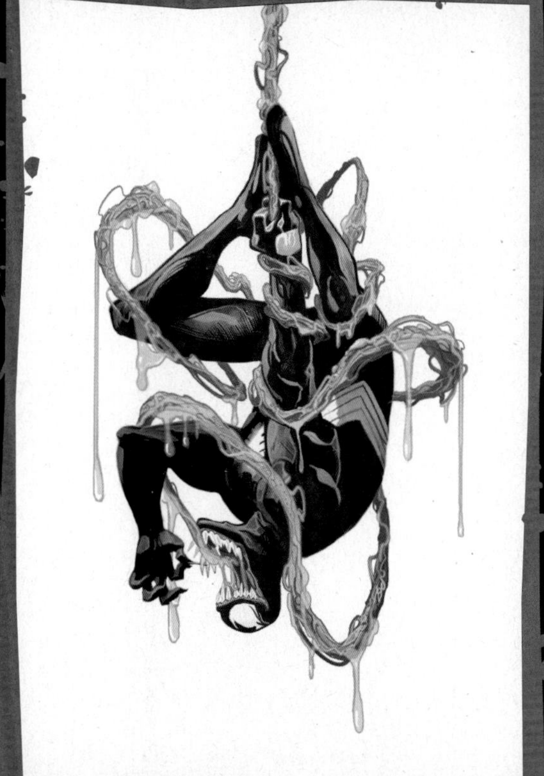

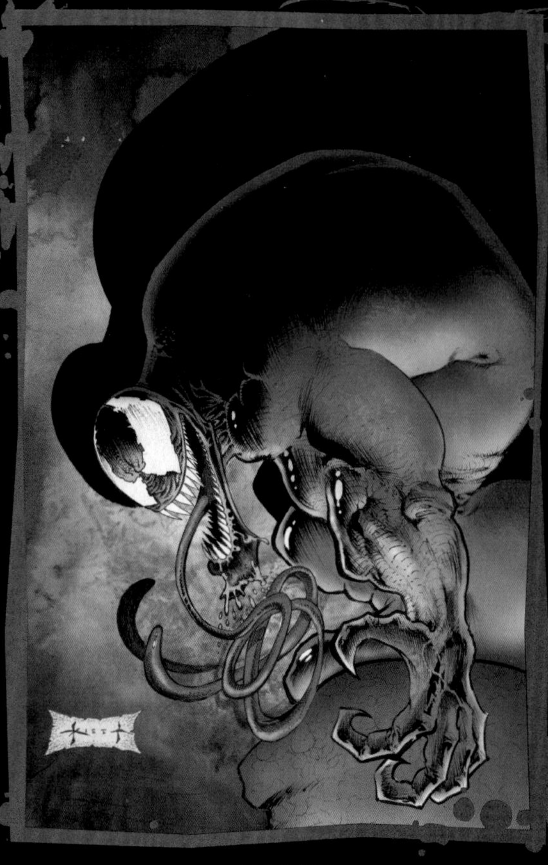

#2 VARIANT
BY **SAM KIETH**

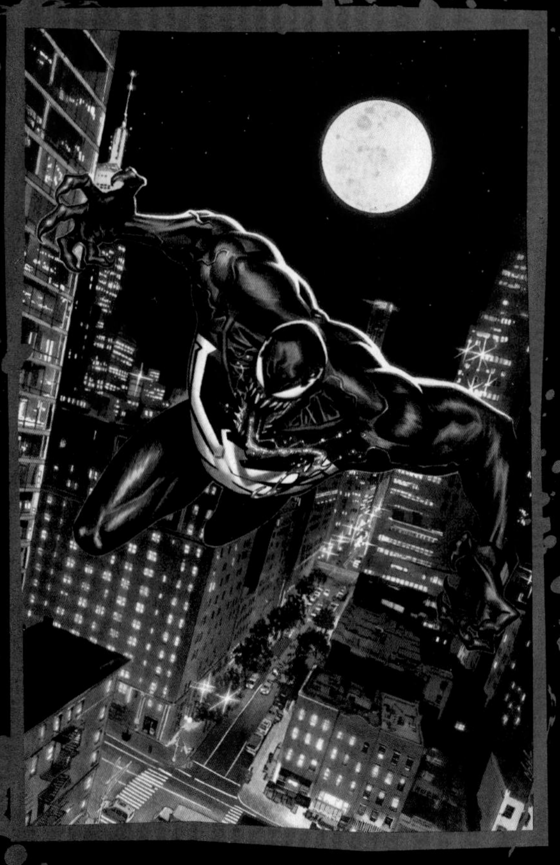

#3 VARIANT
BY **JORGE MOLINA** & **MORRY HOLLOWELL**

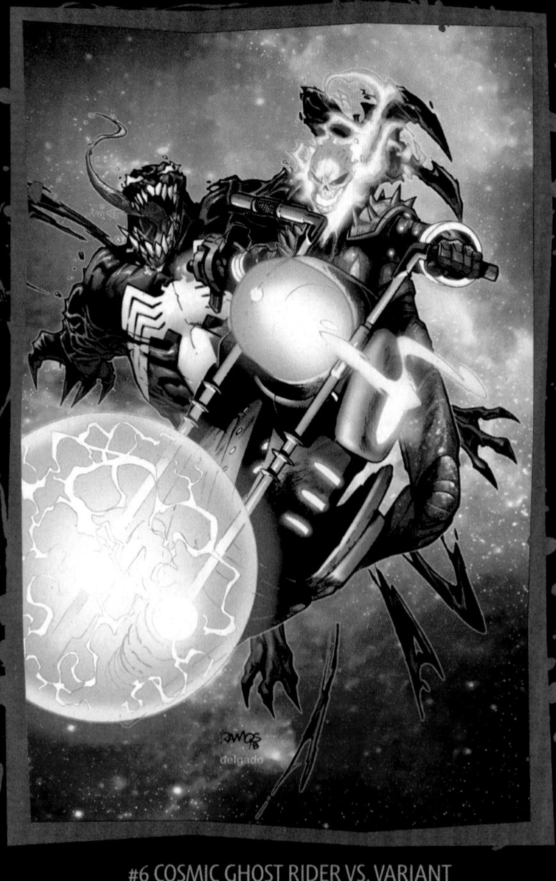
delgado

#6 COSMIC GHOST RIDER VS. VARIANT
BY **HUMBERTO RAMOS** & **EDGAR DELGADO**